I0900942

IMAGES
of America

AFRICAN AMERICANS IN CORPUS CHRISTI

On the Cover: The James Crawford Band marches down Water Street in celebration of Juneteenth in the 1940s.

IMAGES
of America

AFRICAN AMERICANS IN CORPUS CHRISTI

Bruce A. Glasrud, Mary Jo O'Rear, Gloria Randle Scott,
Cecilia Gutierrez Venable, and Henry J. Williams

ARCADIA
PUBLISHING

ISBN 978-0-7385-8528-4

Published by Arcadia Publishing
Charleston, South Carolina

Printed in the United States of America

Library of Congress Control Number: 2011937411

For all general information, please contact Arcadia Publishing:
Telephone 843-853-2070
Fax 843-853-0044
E-mail sales@arcadiapublishing.com
For customer service and orders:
Toll-Free 1-888-313-2665

Visit us on the Internet at www.arcadiapublishing.com

Dedicated to the African American community in Corpus Christi

Contents

Acknowledgments

Every editor acquires obligations and receives support; we are not exceptions. We received considerable help in preparing and publishing this book. As a result, our obligations are numerous. We wish to thank a number of people for their assistance. The staff at the Corpus Christi Public Library—particularly Gerlinda Riojas, Rosemary Loa, and Veronica Martinez—provided substantial help, so, too, did Dr. Thomas Kreneck and Grace Charles at Texas A&M University-Corpus Christi (TAMU-CC) Special Collections. Special thanks go to Terry Mills, current president of the local NAACP; Jewel Wilson, vice president; and Ruth Ross, who opened their materials to us and actively garnered various pictures for our use. Thanks also are extended to Dr. Geraldine Johnson, chairman of the board for the Black Chamber of Commerce, who made the trek to TAMU-CC to bring pictures and information. The *Corpus Christi Caller-Times* and Allison Ehrlich not only helped Cecilia Venable locate materials, but also allowed her to set up at a desk and peruse their photographs and articles, which proved vital for this book. Thanks, Allison. Members of the Catholic Diocese of Corpus Christi, the Reverend Joseph A. Lopez, JCL, and Cy Richards gave time and help as did Solomon M. Coles School principal Monica Bayarena. The Rising Star Baptist Church aided our search for photographs; thanks, Robert Russell. Shirley Doris Rhodes enabled us to locate photographs about Tony Lott and Bernice Crecy. We also give special thanks to Msgr. Michael Howell and Geraldine McGloin for their extensive research on African Americans in Corpus Christi. Jesenia Guerra at the Corpus Christi Museum of Science and History diligently worked on our behalf. Thanks go to Sandra Black, executive assistant at the Corpus Christi Fire Department, who put us in touch with Deborah Johnson, the first black female firefighter, and several others. Lauren Hummer, our acquisitions editor at Arcadia, provided initial acceptance and encouragement for our proposal, moved our idea to a manuscript, and then to a book. Thanks, Lauren. Arcadia publisher Kristie Kelly also provided encouragement and support. Overall, we acknowledge the fact that many people in Corpus Christi gave help and assistance to this project. Thanks, Corpus Christi. We apologize for any oversights.

INTRODUCTION

Corpus Christi, a uniquely original South Texas seaport, perches on the southern bend of the Texas Gulf Coast. Bracketed by a river and two bays on the west and a long lagoon on the east, the city faces a chain of barrier islands between it and the Gulf of Mexico. A mecca for tourists most times of the year, Corpus Christi also harbors a major international port, a naval air station, a thriving oil-and-gas industry, a significant ranching presence, and the base for a worldwide agricultural operation. With a total population near 300,000, Corpus Christi ranks eighth in size among Texas cities. Its residents are a multiethnic mixture, with Mexican Americans, whites, blacks, and Asians the largest groups. However, blacks and Asians each comprise less than five percent of the total city population.

Originally, African Americans in Corpus Christi came to the Texas coast with Spanish explorers; some arrived later as slaves. These included Samuel Moore and his wife, Malvina, as well as Maria Cox and her daughter Sally. They, with others, formed their own community on the city's Bluff after emancipation. There, they welcomed newcomers who migrated to South Texas for a better life than that in their home states. In 1877, Solomon Melvin Coles, one such former slave, arrived in Corpus Christi, where he remained for 20 years, becoming an influential religious and educational leader. As the first African American to officially enroll in the Yale Divinity School in 1872, Coles realized a dream seldom available to his contemporary black Americans. A few photographs exist of Coles, and there are other stories about and images of exceptional black Americans in Corpus Christi, their community lives, their interests, and their achievements.

Those African Americans contributed to black community development. Matt Thomas, a bellboy, worked from the late 1920s into the 1950s at hotels in Corpus Christi; in his book *Hopping on the Border: The Life Story of a Bellboy*, Thomas emphasized using his skills and knowledge to accomplish his goals. He was not alone. Local musician James Mifflin Mays performed in the Nueces Hotel, the city's finest inn, for a number of years. Henry Larkin established a barbershop in the area, and Tom Brashear's billiards drew many a railway man and porter after hours. The upper hill of Corpus Christi became a haven for military men, roundhouse workers, preachers, store owners, and housekeepers who spent their working days in the downtown white world.

In 1879, two years after Coles's arrival in Corpus Christi, African Americans in Nueces County (Corpus Christi) established Roberts Rifles, an all-black militia unit, with Evan M. Mark selected as captain. The company changed its name in 1892 to the Bluff City Guards, and Mark remained as captain. Corpus Christi's black community, though small, developed with both positive and negative experiences, partially because, as Rue Wood argues, "the development of the black community between the end of the War and the turn of the century contains elements of both a western and a southern urban experience."

The availability of education was essential to the pursuit of black opportunity, as Solomon Melvin Coles discovered when he arrived in Corpus Christi. But it did not stop with his establishment of the city's first public school for his people. Individuals and churches set up their own, ranging from day care to elementary. Prominent among them was the parochial school run by the nuns at Holy Cross parish. The educational need continued to be pursued through the 20th century. With the desegregation of schools in the late 1950s and 1960s, education for African Americans changed as blacks began attending formerly all-white colleges; Del Mar College in Corpus Christi admitted blacks even before the *Brown v. Board of Education* decision in May 1954.

Music for listening and dancing provided a means for relaxing and enjoyment in the South Texas black community going all the way back to the early 20th century. But venues were limited until mid-century. Constructed in 1950, the Galvan Ballroom became a popular site for public and private dances and other social events for Mexicans, blacks, and whites in Corpus Christi. Although the ballroom was home to the Galvan Orchestra, it also hosted a broad array of local and nationally prominent musicians and bands, including Duke Ellington. Just as vital was religious activity. From the establishment of the Congregational church in the 1870s—actually integrated for a time—to the St. John Baptist Church today, Christian fellowship has been basic to many Corpus Christi African Americans.

The African American experience in Corpus Christi is rich and varied. The city bred and attracted astute, hardworking, and courageous individuals who left an imprint on the area, especially in avoiding much of the bloody history of other urban areas. Their status has changed over the years, thanks in part to education, the growth of the city, civil rights laws and activities, and the right to vote. Black individuals in Corpus Christi have weathered the trials of white supremacy, though problems still exist from time to time. Some assumed national recognition. Dr. Gloria Randle Scott, coauthor of this book, became the first black president of Girl Scouts of America and later assumed the presidency of Bennett College in Greensboro, North Carolina. During the lengthy journey from slavery, segregation, and second-class treatment to freedom, integration, and equality, Corpus Christi blacks have persevered.

Our objective with this work is to use photographs and captions to depict the synergy of this oft-overlooked group of Corpus Christi residents. There are two intertwined approaches—historic and thematic. The book is divided into six chapters, with each chapter covering a particular time frame. We begin in the 1850s and continue to the present. This was a cumulative effort from five authors; each brought a variety of skills, backgrounds, and diversity to this project.

One

Creating Community 1852–1925

Likely, the first black to reach what is today Corpus Christi was Estevan, an African slave shipwrecked with Cabeza de Vaca in 1528. A few other black slaves arrived later with white settlers. Even in 1850, only a few slaves (47) lived in Nueces County; one free woman, Jane Bias, resided in the town. Corpus Christi incorporated in 1852, and by 1860, some 55 or 56 slaves lived there; the number of slaves in the county increased to 216. After the Civil War, some blacks remained as freemen and free women and were joined by a few soldiers of the US Army's all-black 25th Infantry. They established a Congregational church but struggled for educational opportunities until the arrival in 1877 of Solomon Melvin Coles, a Yale-educated ordained minister committed to expanding educational opportunities. Coles became principal of the Public Free School for Colored. The black population remained a small part of the community in 1880, with only 629 blacks in the county and 400 in the city.

By 1910, there were 742 blacks residing in Nueces County and 436 in the city. Segregation, or Jim Crow, prevailed; black families were pressed into a small area of Corpus Christi, thereby creating a need for services in their community. Black businesses emerged, including Henry Larkin's barbershop; Tom Blackshear's billiards; and Etkin Johnson's restaurant. These and others received patronage from blacks not allowed in white establishments and added to the sense of community established within the black enclave.

Warlike conditions with Mexico in the mid-teens, US involvement in World War I, and the hurricane of 1919 affected blacks. By 1920, only 456 blacks resided in the city and 792 in Nueces County. Rapid population growth occurred in the 1920s with employment opportunities for Afro-Texans that included working on the port, repairing and cleaning up the city, and laboring in the rail yards. At the same time, however, the white primary effectively disfranchised African Americans in Corpus Christi. Educational concerns continued because black children only attended through the eighth grade. In 1925, a community-wide effort provided better educational opportunities by building the Solomon M. Coles School.

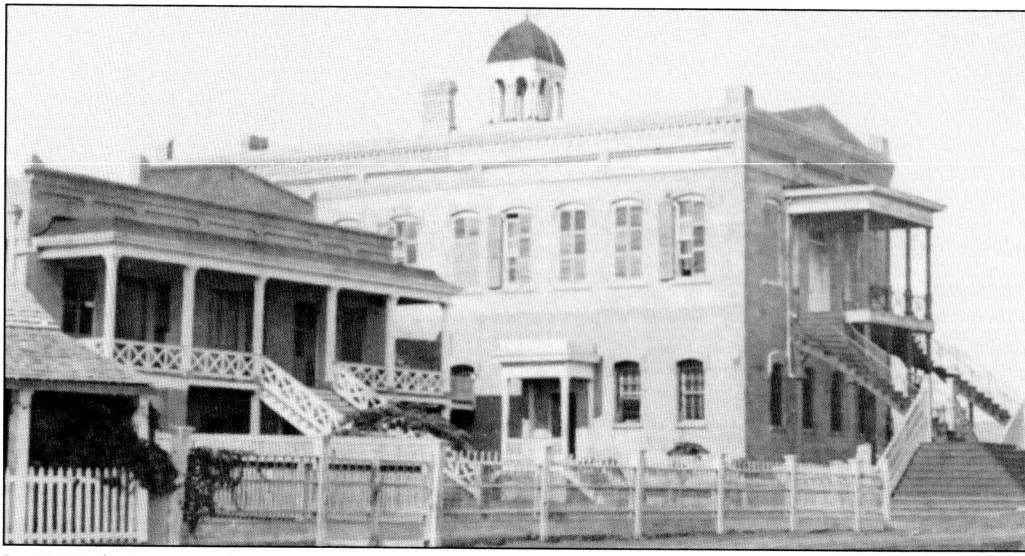

In 1866, the Reverend Aaron Rowe (white), chaplain of the 122nd US Infantry, and Corpus Christi resident Esquire Leonard (black) formed the Freedom Congregational Church. Their first meeting was held in the Nueces County Courthouse (at left). This structure, designed by Felix A. Blucher in 1853, held services every Sunday morning and Sunday school every afternoon for the next five years until the permanent church was completed. (Courtesy of the *Corpus Christi Caller-Times.*)

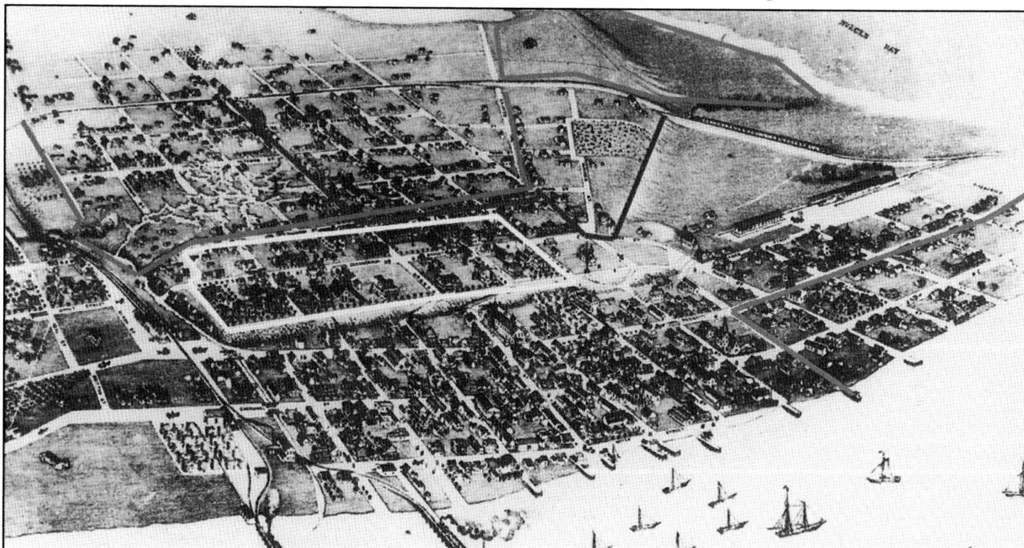

By 1887, Corpus Christi was a city defined by geography and custom. African Americans' location in Corpus Christi extended from the western part of the Bluff, a 40-foot escarpment overlooking the shore, to the northern reaches of town. This area became known as the "Northside." African Americans shared the Bluff with Mexican Americans. Irish Americans lived on the beach, while wealthy Anglos resided along the front of the Bluff facing the bay. (Courtesy of Corpus Christi Public Libraries.)

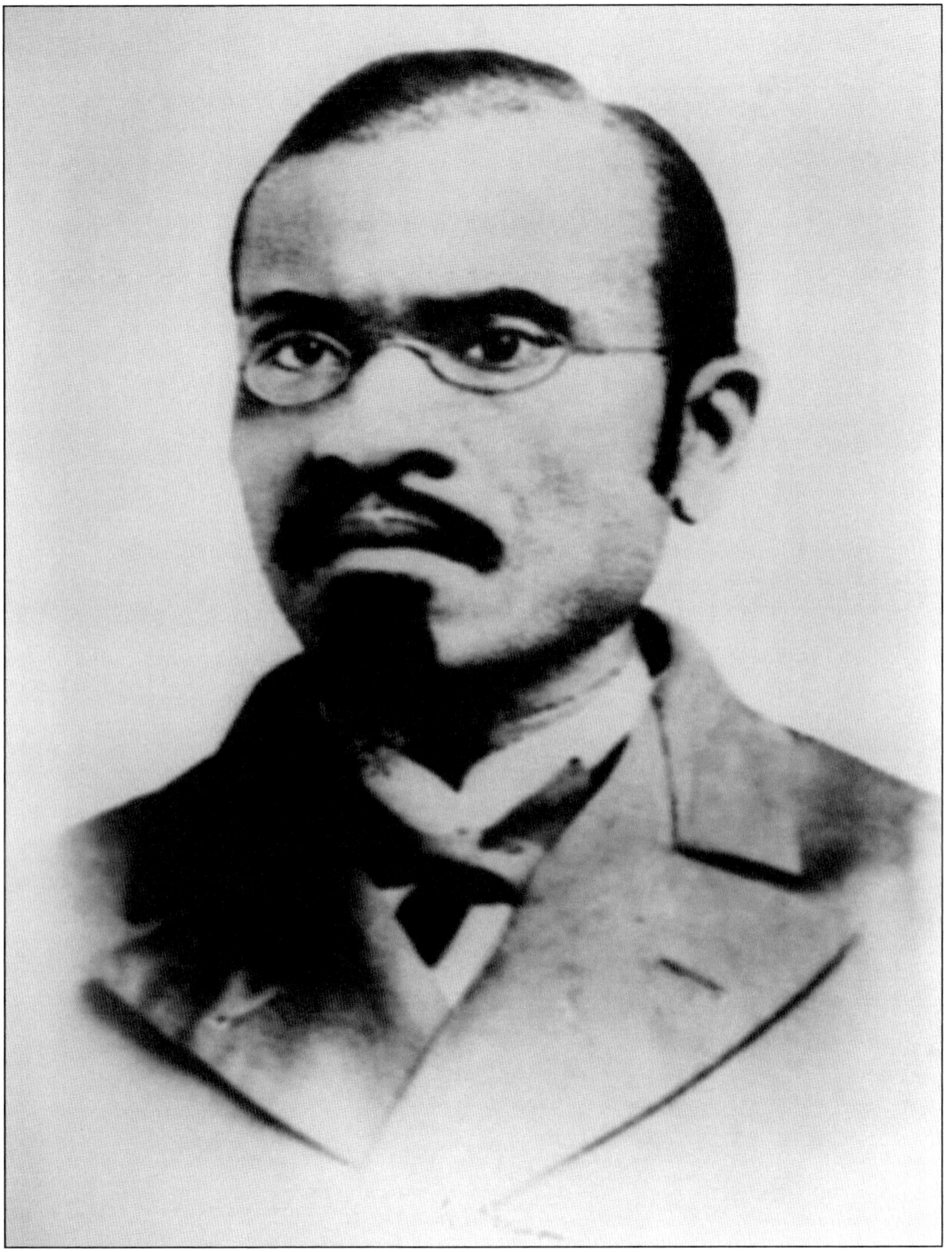

Solomon Melvin Coles arrived in Corpus Christi in 1877 as minister of the Freedom Congregational Church. Coles was born a Virginia slave in 1844 and attended Guilford Institute, Lincoln University, and Yale Divinity School before settling in this coastal region. Because blacks had few educational opportunities in this city, he began teaching and the following year established the Public Free School for Colored, to which he devoted his efforts for the next 17 years. (Courtesy of Solomon M. Coles School.)

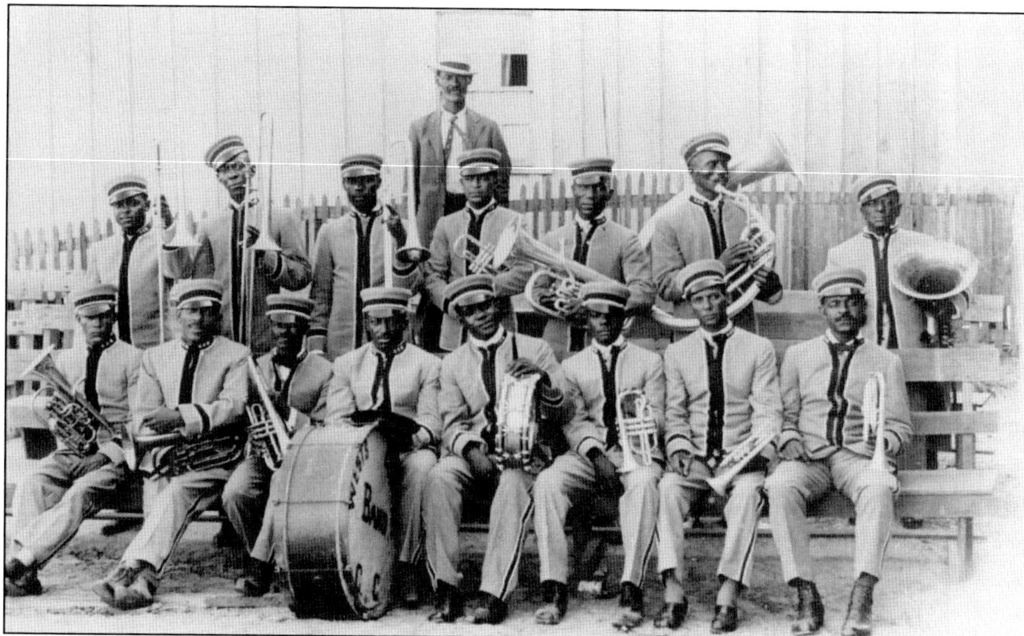

The Pick Wick Band, one of the first black bands in Corpus Christi, played for dances, rallies, parties, and parades. Among those pictured, in no particular order, are Dave Smith, Tom Garcia, Arthur Johnson, Mifflin Mays, Sidney Wilson, Sam West, Buddy Steen, Ed Grant, Frank Ward, Ed Williams, and Aaron Pruitt. (Courtesy of the Corpus Christi Museum of Science and History, Alclair Pleasant Collection.)

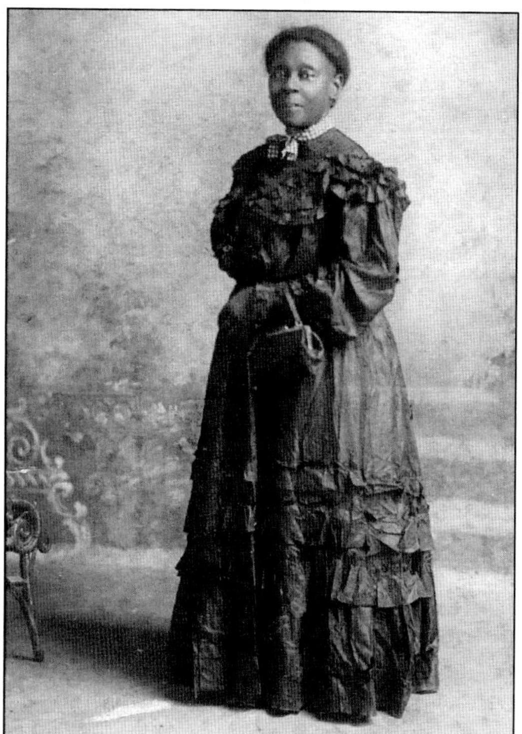

Among the earliest to settle in the Northside after emancipation, Sallie Cox Garcia and her mother, Mariah Merriweather Cox, cleared land on the Bluff "where no white man would go." Their home stood at Buffalo and Tancahua Streets. Several years later, Sallie married Florentino Garcia and raised eight children. (Courtesy of the Corpus Christi Museum of Science and History, Alclair Pleasant Collection.)

Florentino Garcia, a ranch hand on the Shaffer Ranch, met and fell in love with Sallie Cox when she worked there as a cook. The two were married in Corpus Christi by the Reverend Strong and, along with their children, managed properties in the Northside and on the beach. (Courtesy of the Corpus Christi Museum of Science and History, Alclair Pleasant Collection.)

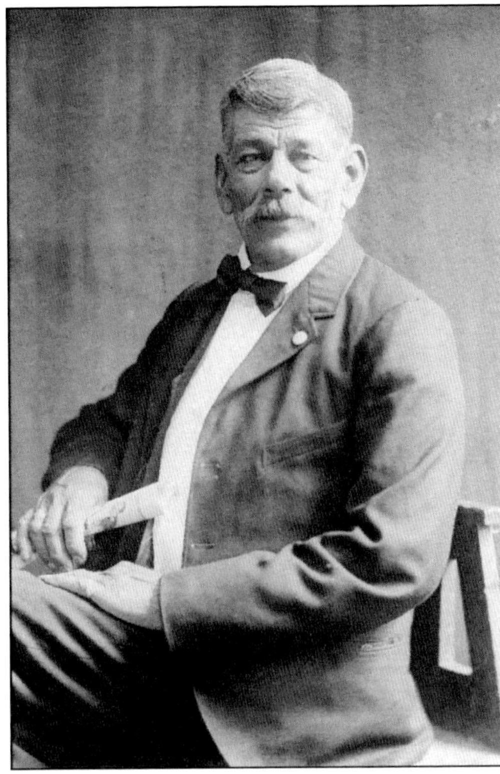

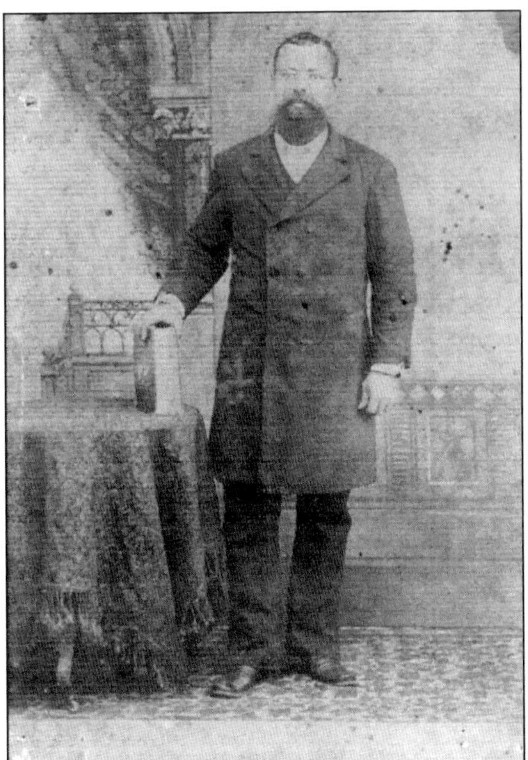

Rev. Moses H. Sinclair (St. Clair) was born in 1848 in Louisiana and moved to Texas where he met and married Winina Sinclair. In his youth, he worked as a carpenter and later found his calling as a minister. Moses traveled through South Texas preaching to various groups and eventually became a minister at the Freedom Congregational Church after its completion in 1871. (Courtesy of Corpus Christi Public Libraries.)

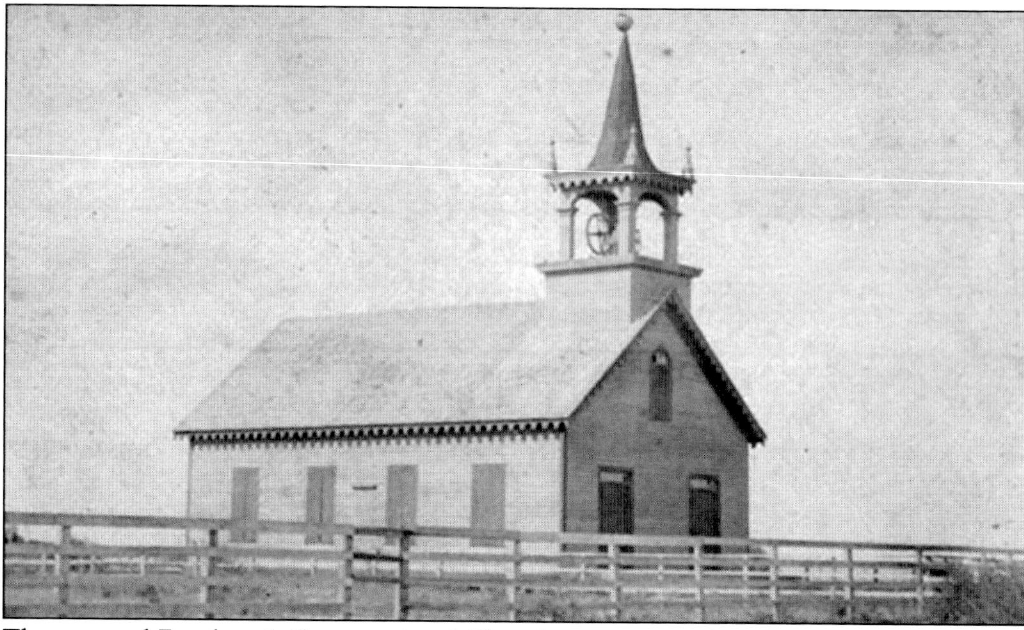

The renamed Freedman's Congregational Church was organized in the 1853 Nueces County Courthouse. Its first meeting, held in 1866 under the direction of Rev. Aaron Rowe, formed a multicultural church. The congregation soon built a schoolhouse, and by 1871 the foundation was laid for a permanent structure. Upon completion, a 1,300-pound bell hung in the steeple and, with city council permission, rang three times a day sounding the hour. (Courtesy of Corpus Christi Public Libraries.)

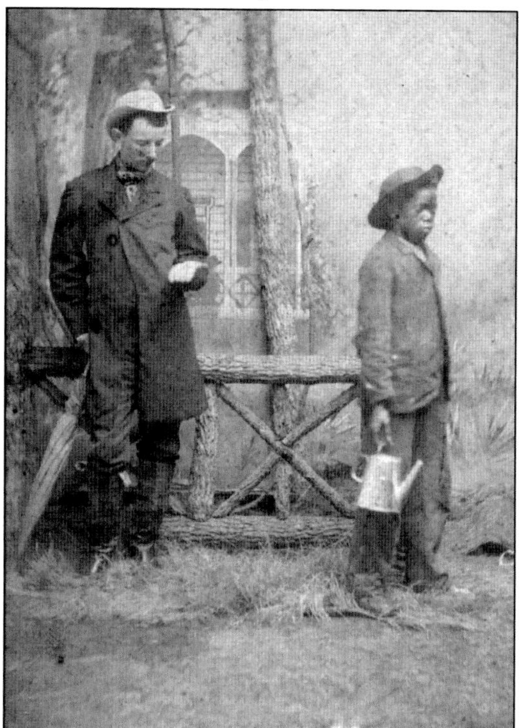

This boy pictured with Alex Meuly (left) probably worked around the family residence. Around 1880, the Meuly family employed several people to maintain their land and house. (Courtesy of Texas A&M University-Corpus Christi, Meuly Daimwood Collection.)

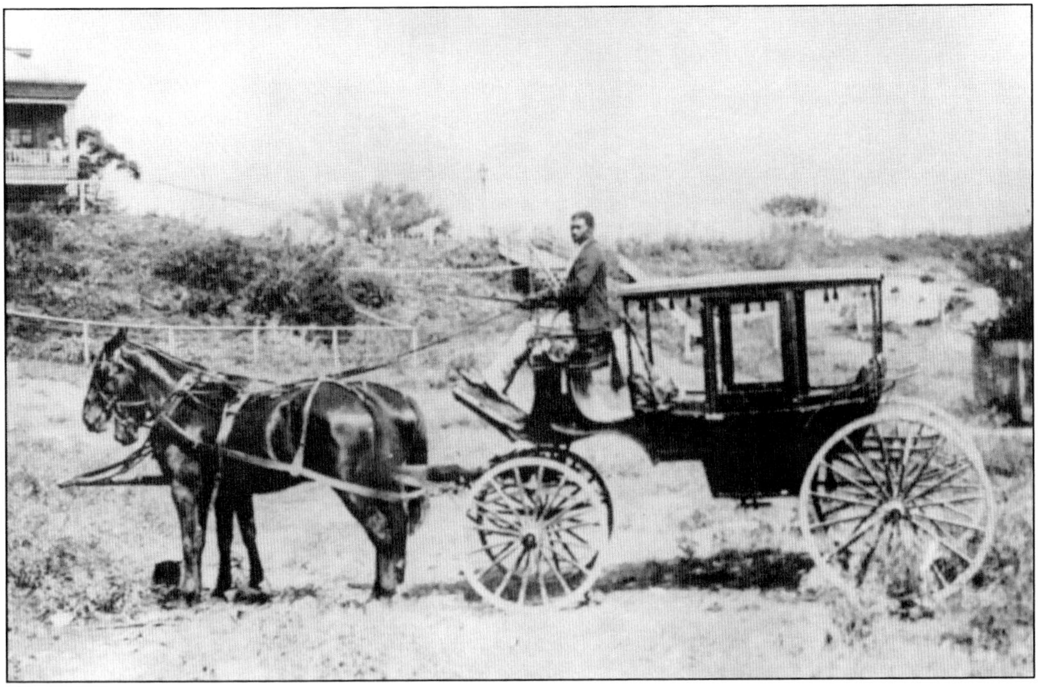

Hack drivers provided a much-needed service for city residents, and several wealthy families owned their own carriages. Some businesses also employed hacks to haul goods to their customers, and the city used them to take prisoners to jail. (Courtesy of Corpus Christi Public Libraries.)

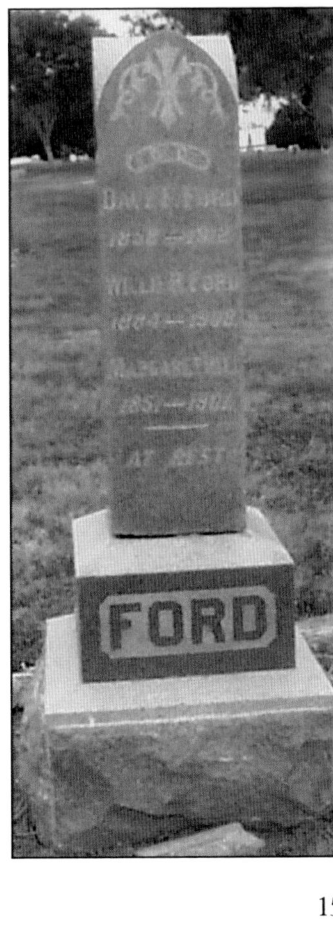

This tombstone marks the resting place of the Ford family. David Francis Ford was a hack driver for Benyon's livery stable. This monument and several others mark the graves of many Corpus Christi African Americans in Old Bayview Cemetery. This burial ground, one of the oldest cemeteries west of the Mississippi River, contains several buffalo soldiers and many early residents of the city. (Courtesy of Corpus Christi Public Libraries, Rosa G. Gonzales.)

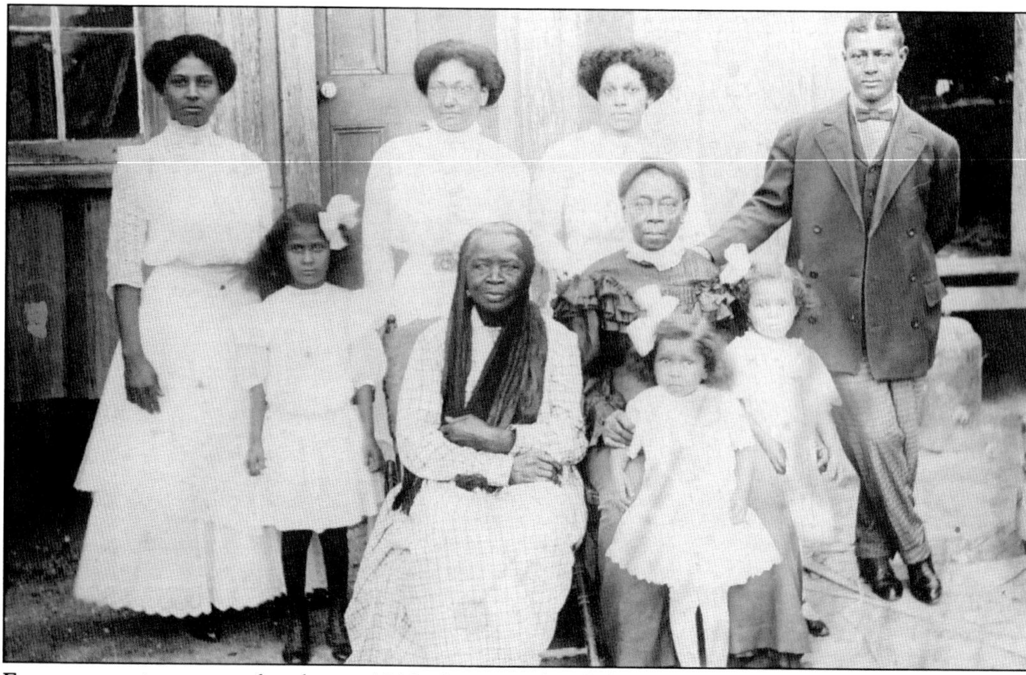

Four generations pose for this c. 1910 photograph of the Cox-Garcia family. They are, from left to right, (first row) unidentified, matriarch Mariah Merriweather Cox, her daughter Sallie Cox Garcia, and great-granddaughters Alclair and Anita Mays; (second row) two unidentified, granddaughter Annie Garcia Mays, and her husband James Mifflin Mays. (Courtesy of the Corpus Christi Museum of Science and History, Alclair Pleasant Collection.)

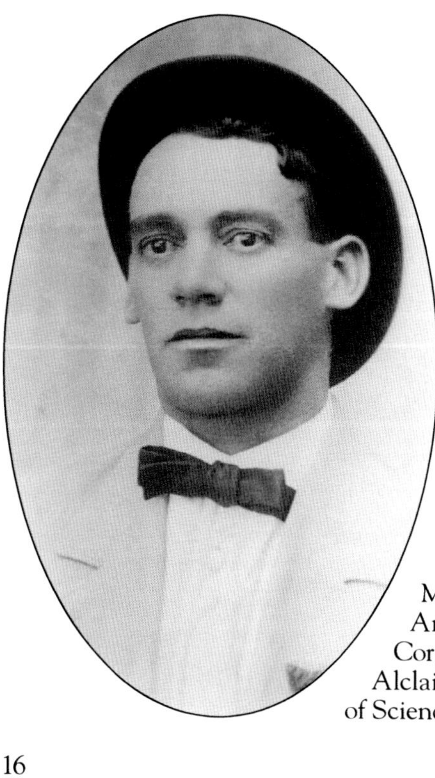

Musician James Mifflin Mays built a home for his bride, Annie Garcia, in Irish Town on the northern section of Corpus Christi's beach. There, Annie gave birth to daughters Alclair and Anita. (Courtesy of the Corpus Christi Museum of Science and History, Alclair Pleasant Collection.)

Babies transcend all boundaries. Here, Annie Garcia Mays Bohman holds Luella Eischelman, the granddaughter of W.W. Jones, Bohman's employer. (Courtesy of the Corpus Christi Museum of Science and History, Alclair Pleasant Collection.)

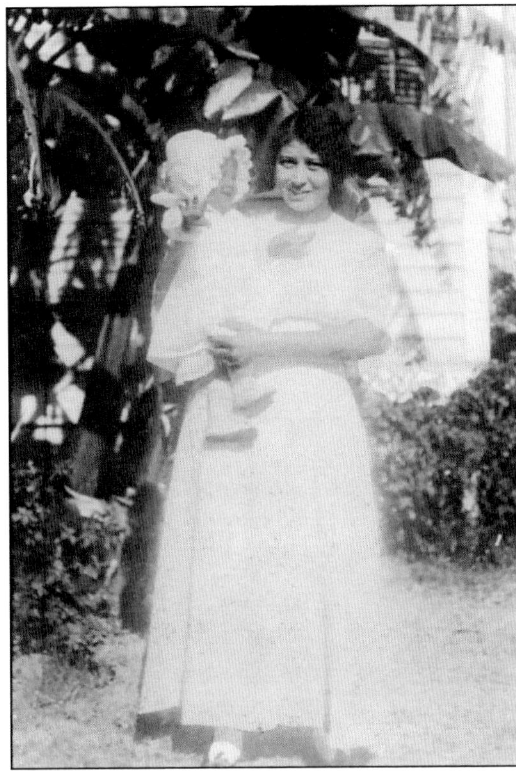

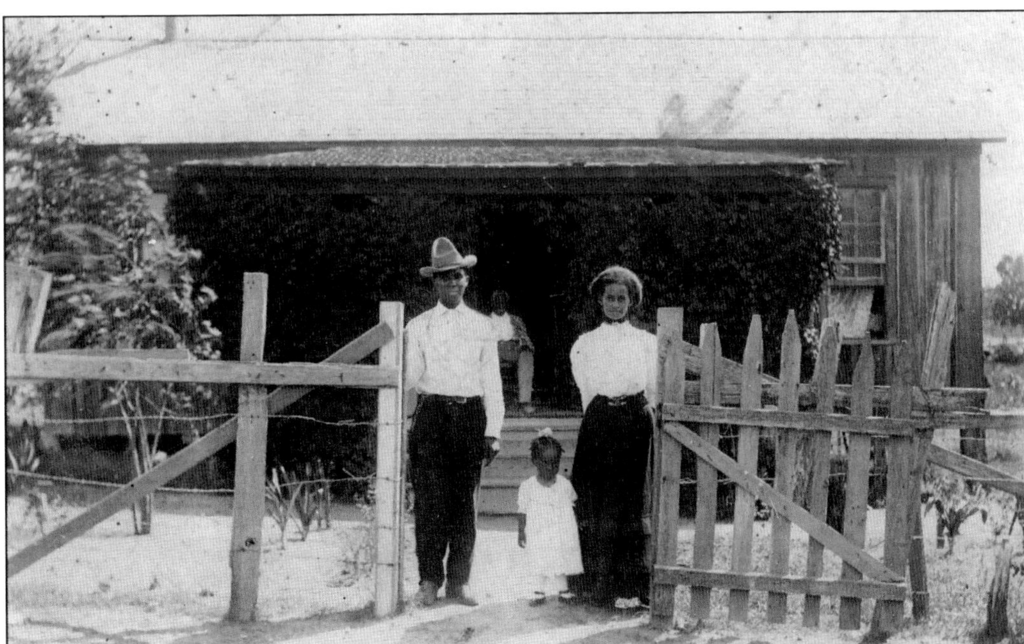

The McCullough family stands in front of their home in the early 1900s. Celowell McCullough worked as a brakeman for the Missouri Pacific Railroad (MoPac) and later worked at Bethune Day Nursery. His wife was a seamstress and dressmaker and later also taught school at Bethune Day Nursery. (Courtesy of Murphy Givens.)

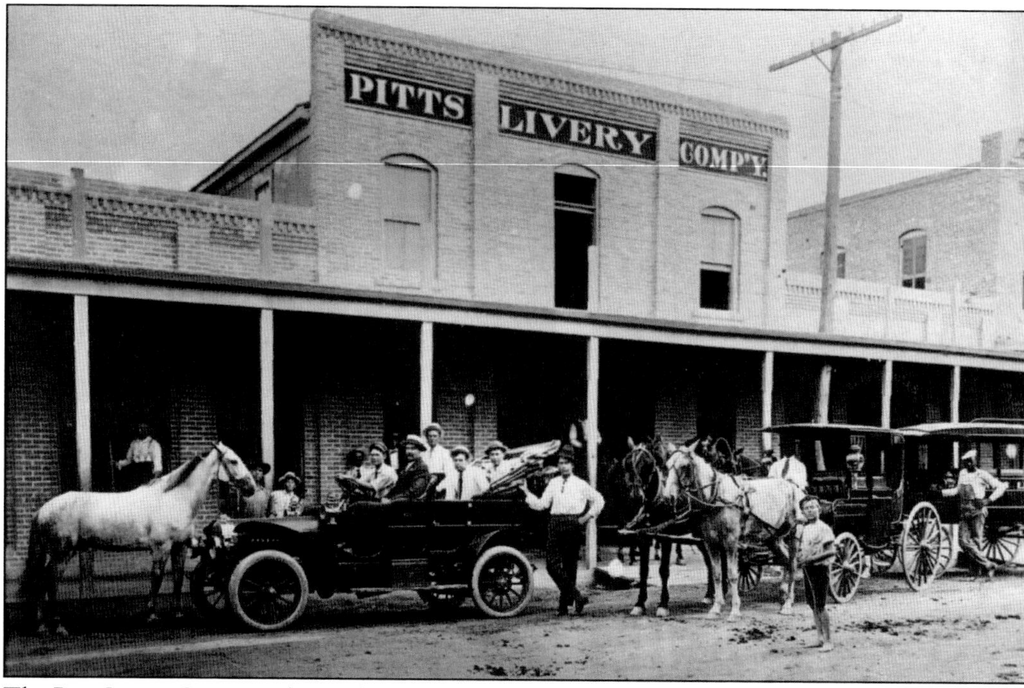

The Pitts Livery Company located at 310 Mesquite Street employed several African Americans at its livery and boarding stable. By 1905, the business evolved and expanded to include an automobile sales and service company. (Courtesy of Corpus Christi Public Libraries.)

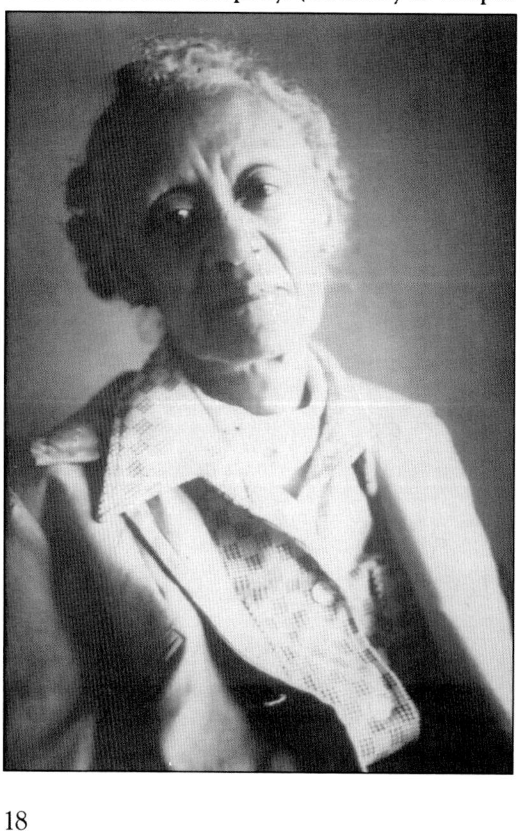

Mary Belle Littles Martin, born to emancipated slave Hattie Moore Littles in Corpus Christi, attended Incarnate Word Academy, where she learned piano. Martin told several people she studied piano in the shadows of the evening where she would not be noticed. Littles married Abraham Martin and had several children. She was a member of Holy Cross Church and gave the gift of music to many neighborhood children. (Courtesy of the Corpus Christi NAACP.)

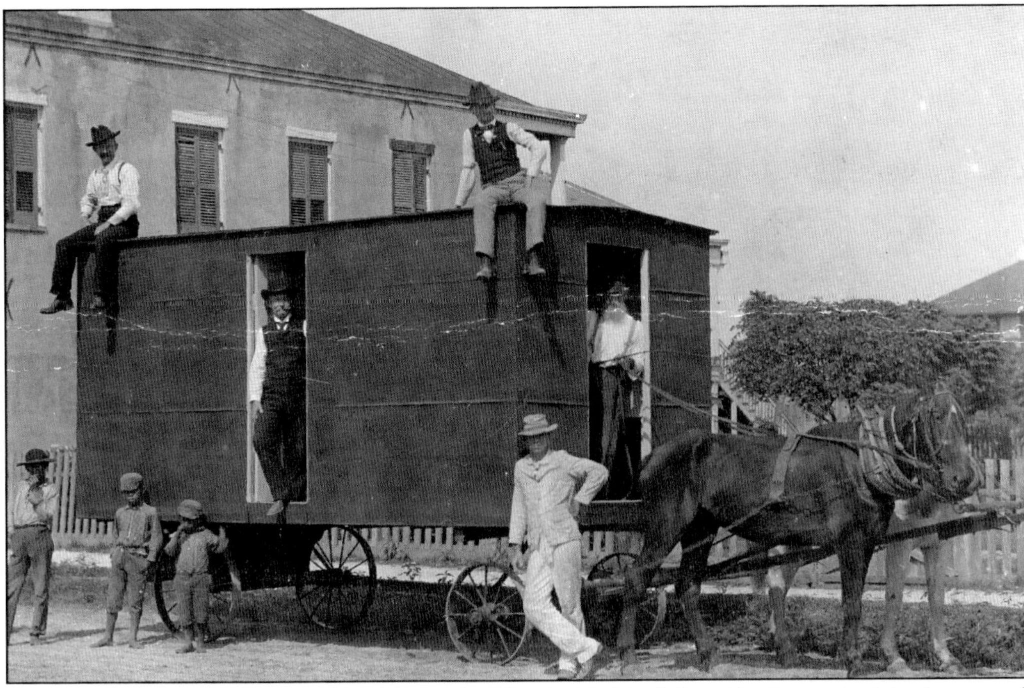

Several children are fascinated by Alexander Humboldt Meuly's trailer house in this photograph from about 1910. Meuly pulled this trailer to different areas in search of oil and gold. (Courtesy of Texas A&M University-Corpus Christi, Meuly Daimwood Collection.)

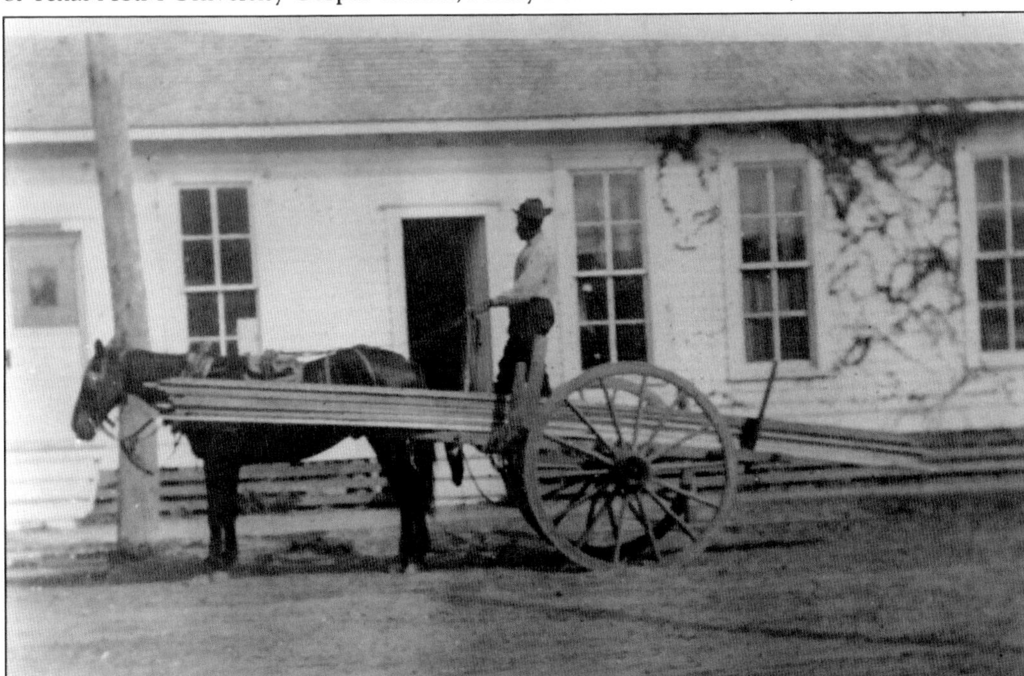

The man in this photograph from around 1908 probably worked for the E.D. Sidbury lumber company located at 222 Chaparral Street. The company supplied interior and exterior wood building supplies and specialized in pine and cypress. (Courtesy of Corpus Christi Public Libraries.)

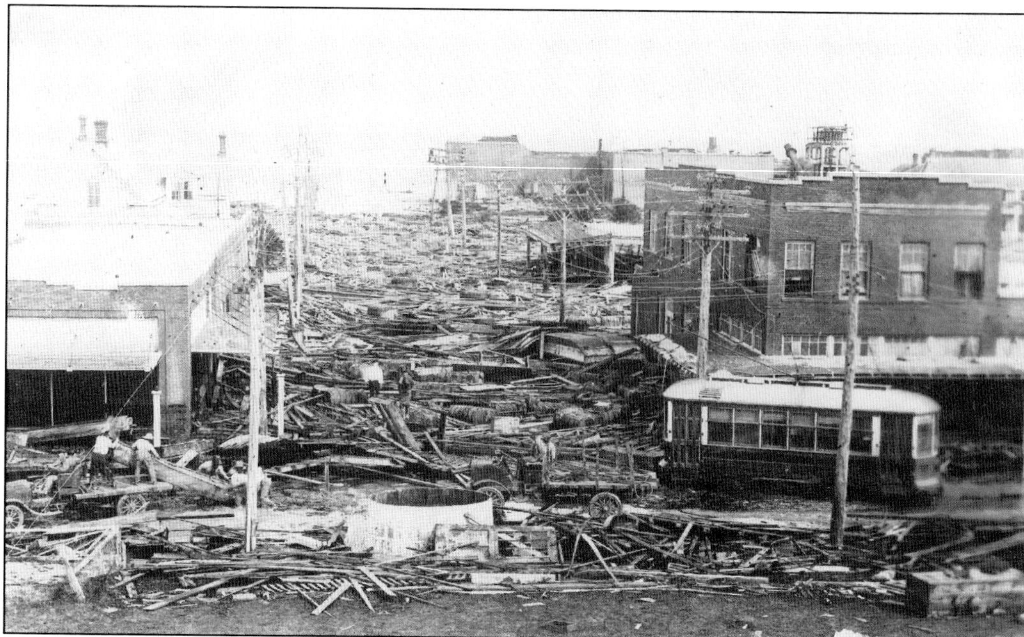

The devastation of the 1919 hurricane drew many black workers to Corpus Christi. The city hired several crews to salvage and rebuild what was left of the city by the sea (Courtesy of Texas A&M University-Corpus Christi, Kilgore Collection.)

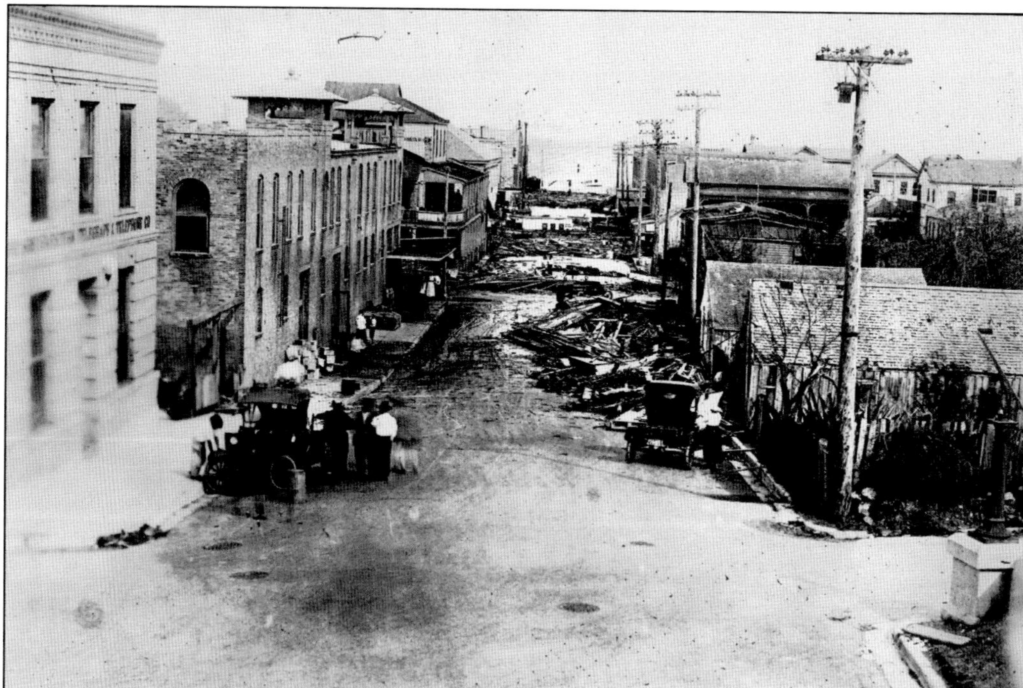

Lawrence Street is littered with debris from the 1919 storm. This hurricane claimed an untold number of people. Rose Hill Cemetery commemorated the unknown loss with a large stone monument. (Courtesy of Texas A&M University-Corpus Christi, Kilgore Collection.)

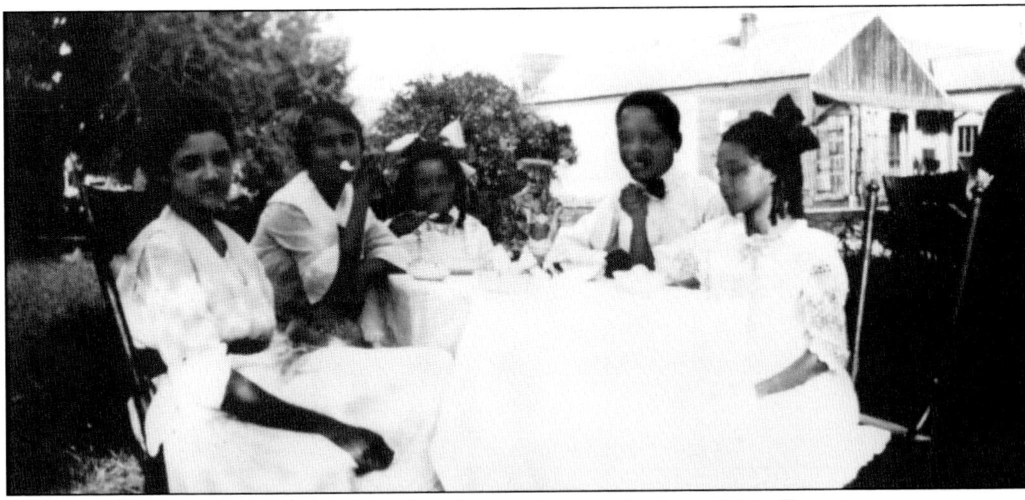

Balmy breezes on the Bluff brought friends together in the late 1910s. Enjoying ice cream are, from left to right, Josephine Prade, who is visiting from Louisiana, Juanita Garcia, Anita Mays, Charles Williams, and Alclair Mays. (Courtesy of the Corpus Christi Museum of Science and History, Alclair Pleasant Collection.)

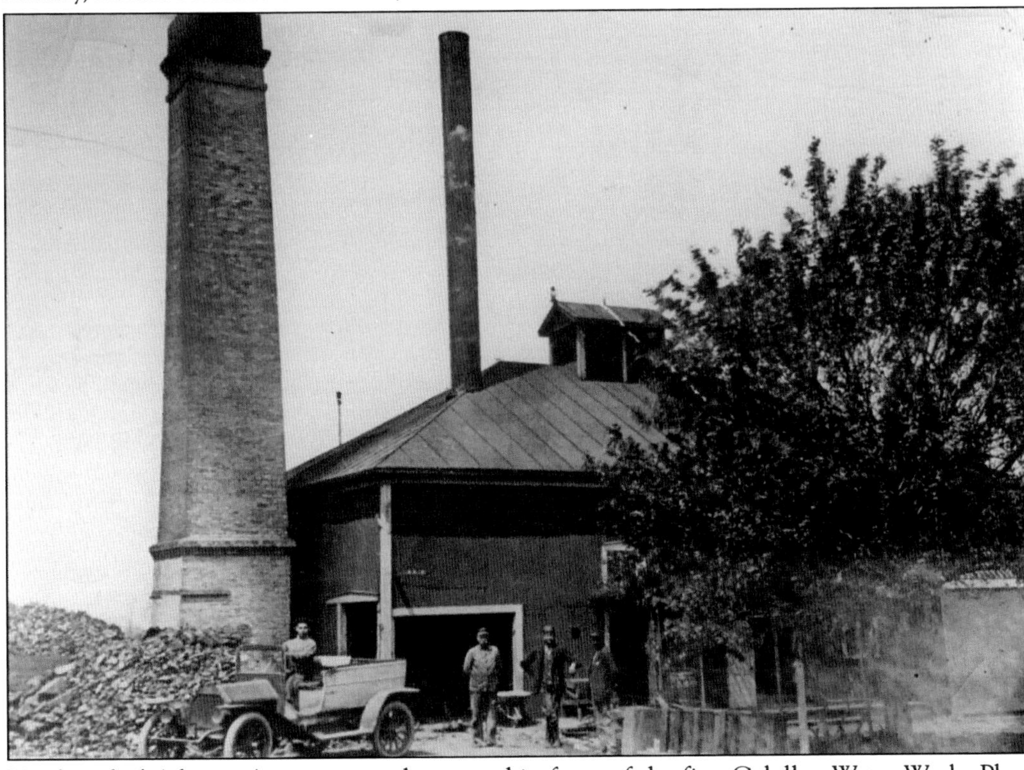

Unidentified African American workers stand in front of the first Calallen Water Works Plant where they are employed. Ground was broken for this building in June 1892, and it was completed over a year later. The Corpus Christi Supply Company furnished water to area residents and provided free water to the city for street watering and water troughs. This plant operated until 1915. (Courtesy of Texas A&M University-Corpus Christi Special Collections and Archives, Cunningham Collection 129.)

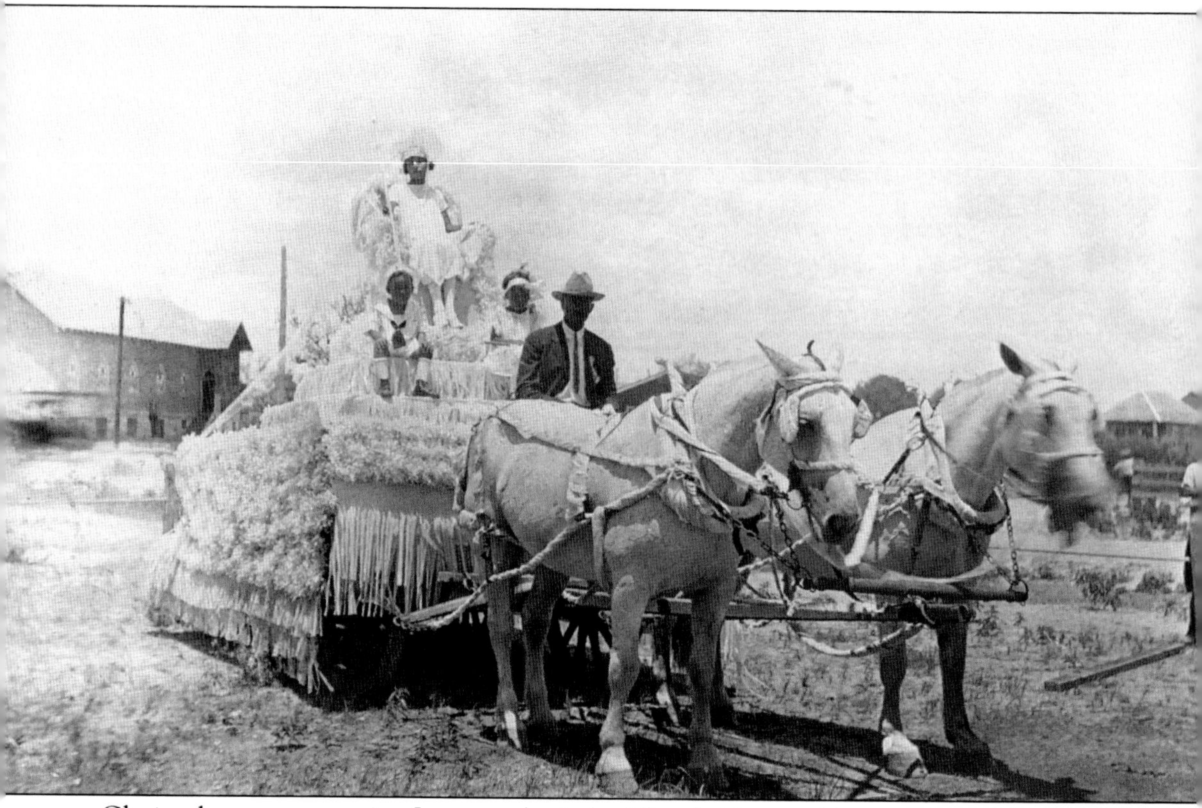

Gloriously commemorating Juneteenth, Anita Blanch Mays and her royal attendants ruled this annual celebration one summer in the 1920s. Riding in the parade with Queen Anita are Dorothy Kitchen Vaughn (right) and her brother L.C. Kitchen, the children of Mr. and Mrs. Walter Kitchen. The driver is unidentified. (Courtesy of the Corpus Christi Museum of Science and History, Alclair Pleasant Collection.)

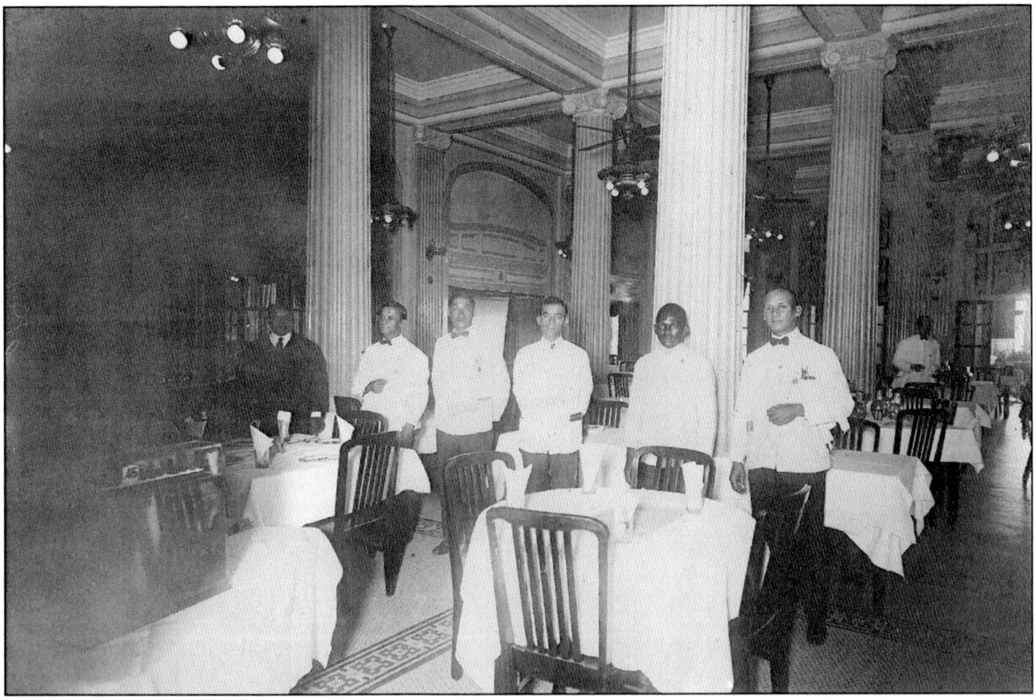

The skill and smoothness of the Nueces Hotel waiters were characteristic of the famous Corpus Christi hostelry. Pictured in its sumptuous dining room are, from left to right, Mr. Pratt (head waiter), Walter Mays, Roy Bohman (later head waiter), unidentified, Woodson Williams, and Mifflin Mays. (Courtesy of the Corpus Christi Museum of Science and History, Alclair Pleasant Collection.)

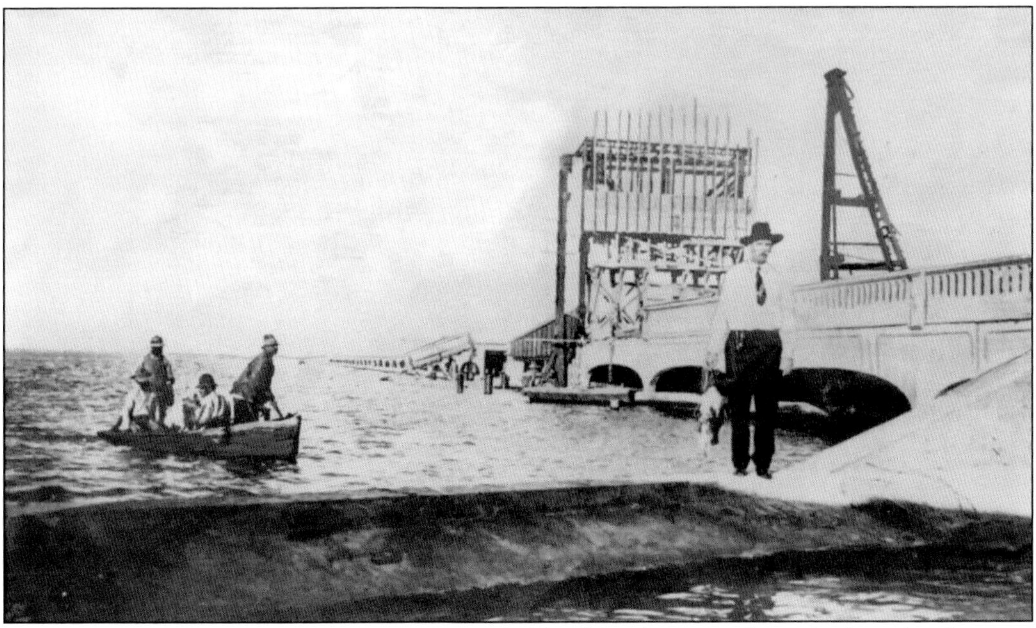

Fishing near the Nueces Bay Causeway provided food for dinner and supplied much relaxation and enjoyment, thanks to the cool, breezy days in this beautiful city. (Courtesy of the *Corpus Christi Caller-Times.*)

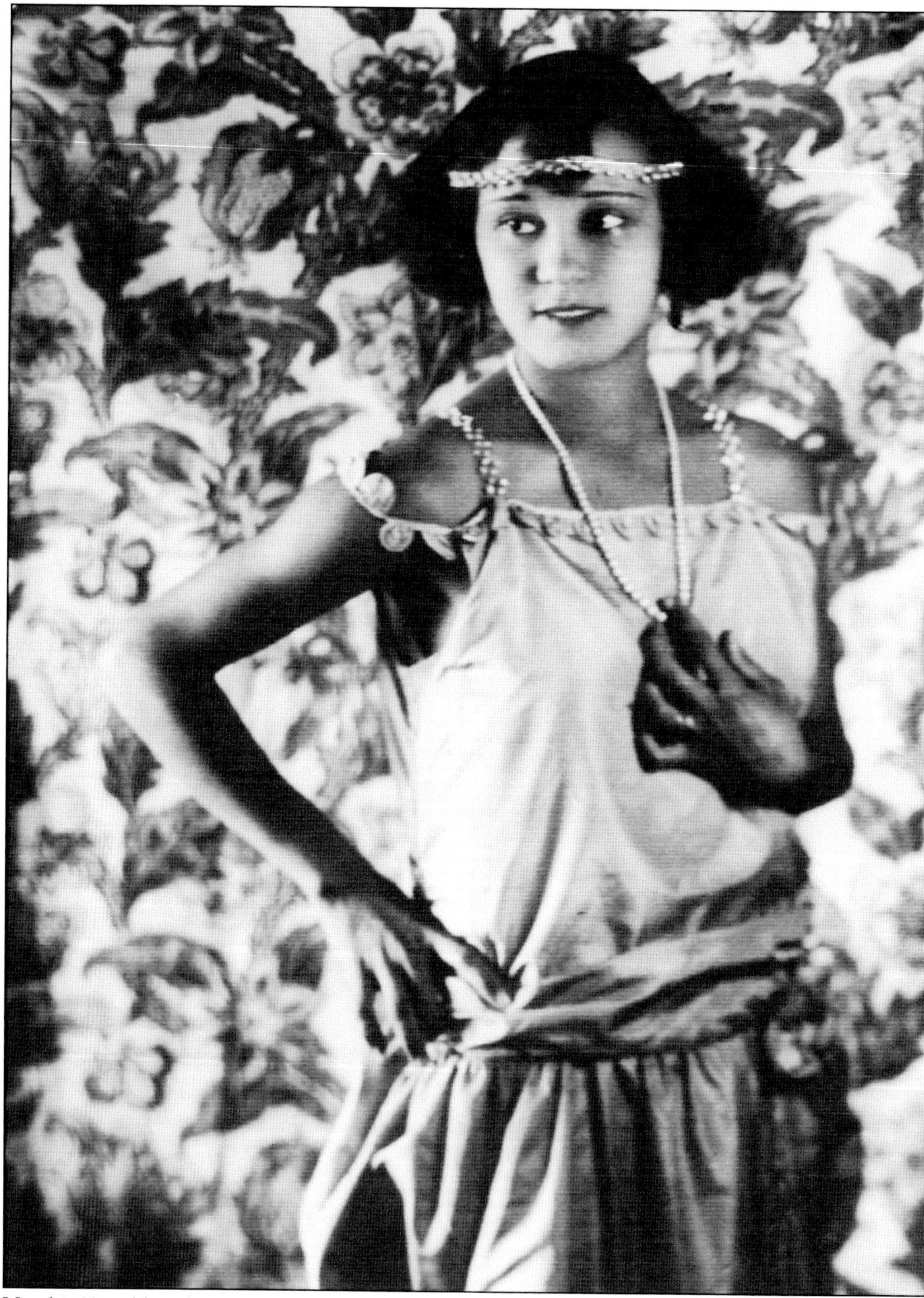

Until 1933, public education went only to 10th grade for African Americans in Corpus Christi. Many parents sent their children to Prairie View University to complete their high school educations. Alclair Mays attended the university and graduated with a teaching degree in 1925. (Courtesy of the Corpus Christi Museum of Science and History, Alclair Pleasant Collection.)

Two

Expanding Opportunities 1926–1940

The increased employment potential for African Americans in Corpus Christi that began following the hurricane of 1919 continued during the second half of the 1920s. By 1926, the residents of Corpus Christi had built a deepwater port. That improvement fueled a significant increase in Corpus Christi's black population, which more than doubled in size by the end of the decade. Other enhancements transpired; by 1930, considerable growth took place in the black sections of the city as well as in black-owned-and-operated businesses. The number of churches increased dramatically, and the illiteracy rate fell from 11.8 percent in 1920 to six percent 10 years later. This figure undoubtedly reflected the advantages that came with having a modern educational facility—the Solomon M. Coles School. By 1930, the majority of Nueces County blacks—80 percent—were urbanites; the total county black population stood at 2,640, with 1,951 residing in Corpus Christi.

The economic downfall and depression that floored the nation in the 1930s also affected blacks in Corpus Christi. The city continued to draw blacks to the community, increasing the black population but also bringing tensions from outside the community, such as white laborers who resented black competition for jobs. An advance occurred in 1934 when blacks could finally attend high school in Corpus Christi. Until then, those who sought a diploma moved elsewhere to places like Prairie View. The black community that emerged after 1926 attended cultural and recreational activities, such as Juneteenth and Buc Days celebrations, and enjoyed musicians and singers who featured Texas favorites in blues and jazz. Not all was well, however. As reported by Dr. H. Boyd Hall, "it was grim by 1937"; political bosses ensured Jim Crow's continued presence. The largest red-light district was located in the black residential area. That section was impacted by railroads, incinerators, and septic tanks. Most black residences were shanties with, at best, outhouses; rents were nevertheless expensive. Despite such conditions, African Americans of Corpus Christi stood ready to face new challenges, beginning with World War II. To begin to make changes, blacks in Corpus Christi organized a chapter of the NAACP as early as 1938.

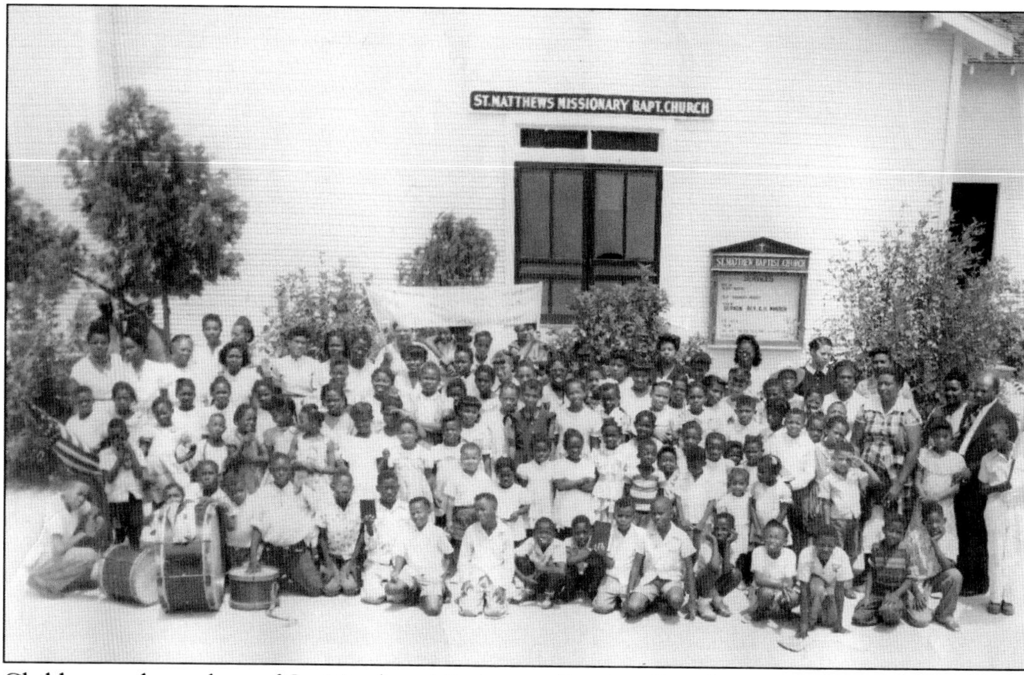

Children and members of St. Matthew Missionary Baptist Church pose in front of their house of worship. This institution traces its history back to the Freedman's Congregational Church of 1874 when the Baptists purchased the building. The church then became known as the Freedman Baptist Church but five years later, assumed the name of St. Matthew Missionary Baptist Church. (Courtesy of St. Matthew Missionary Baptist Church.)

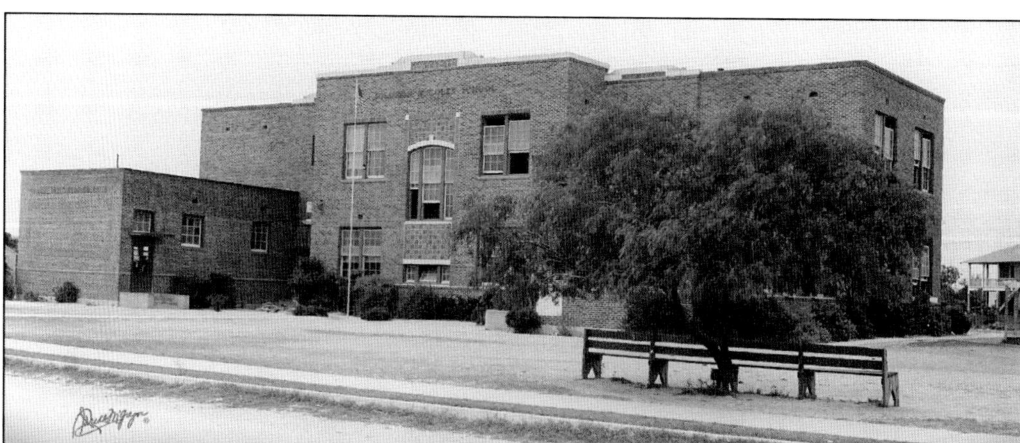

If religion was the source of spiritual strength for the Northside, the Solomon M. Coles School was its hope. Begun in 1877 as the Public Free School for Colored, the institution was renamed after the Reverend Solomon Melvin Coles, its founder and first principal, in 1925. (Courtesy of the Corpus Christi Museum of Science and History, John Fred'k "Doc" McGregor Photographic Collection.)

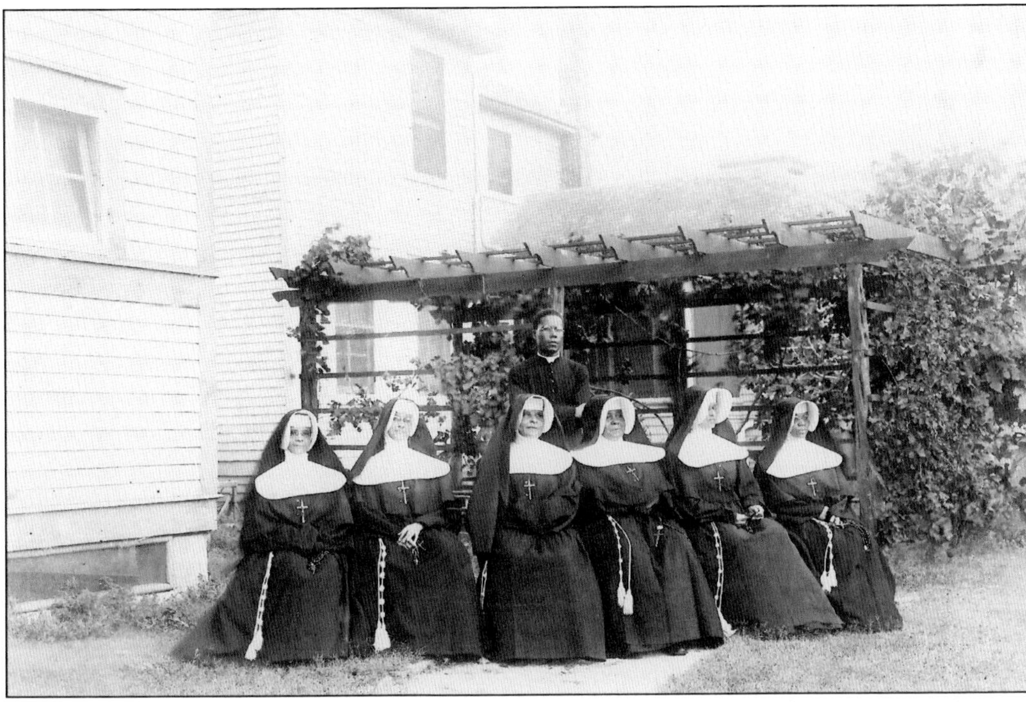

The Sisters of the Holy Family along with Rev. Joseph John, of the African Leonere Society, position themselves in the backyard of the Holy Cross Catholic Church. This group assumed the task of teaching the children of Holy Cross School for a few years. (Courtesy of the Diocese of Corpus Christi Archives.)

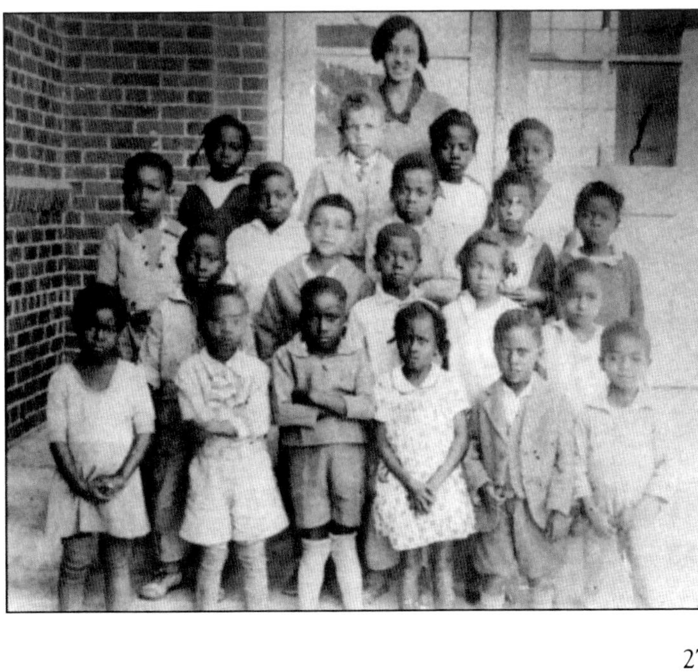

Alclair Pleasant stands with her first-grade class of 1930–1931 in front of Solomon M. Coles School. It was named after Solomon Melvin Coles, who arrived in Corpus Christi as a preacher and found a community lacking in educational opportunities. Coles began teaching in the evenings. By 1893, he became the principal of the Public Free School for Colored, and in recognition of his efforts, the school was named in his honor in 1925. (Courtesy of the *Corpus Christi Caller-Times*.)

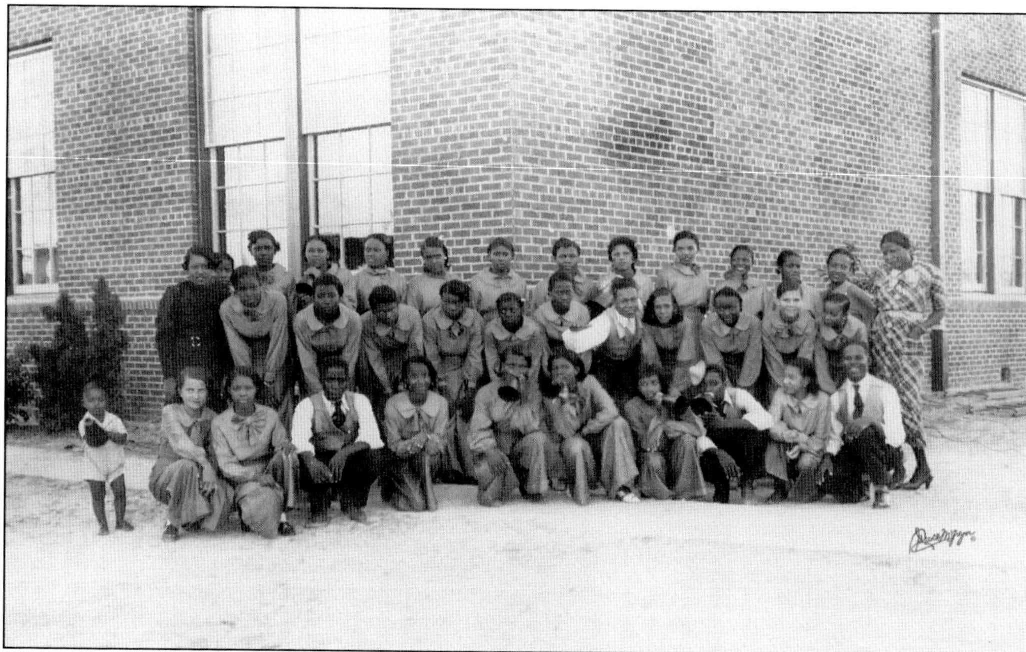

Shortly before this class picture was taken in 1934, the Solomon M. Coles School was granted full accreditation. It then offered complete elementary and secondary courses and occupied a massive brick structure on Winnebago Street. (Courtesy of the Corpus Christi Museum of Science and History, John Fred'k "Doc" McGregor Photographic Collection.)

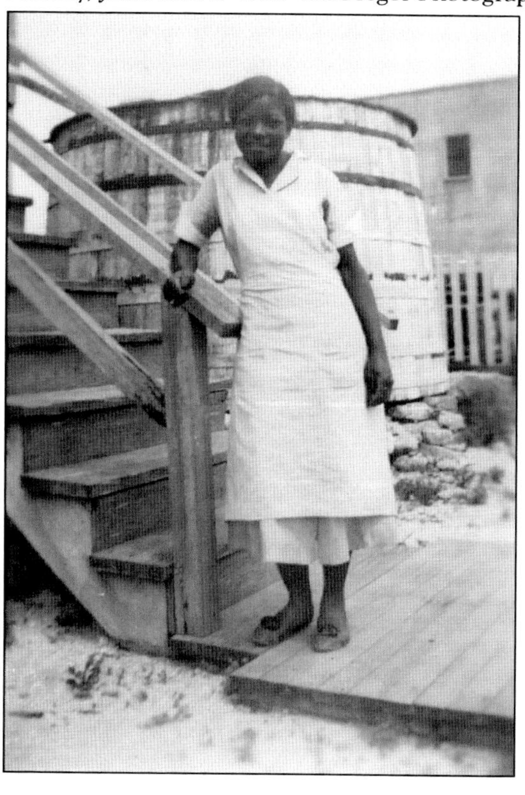

Gladys poses in the back of the Meuly residence on Water Street on a clear, spring day in 1936. Gladys kept the home clean and running smoothly. (Courtesy of Texas A&M Corpus Christi Special Collection and Archives, Meuly/Daimwood Collection.)

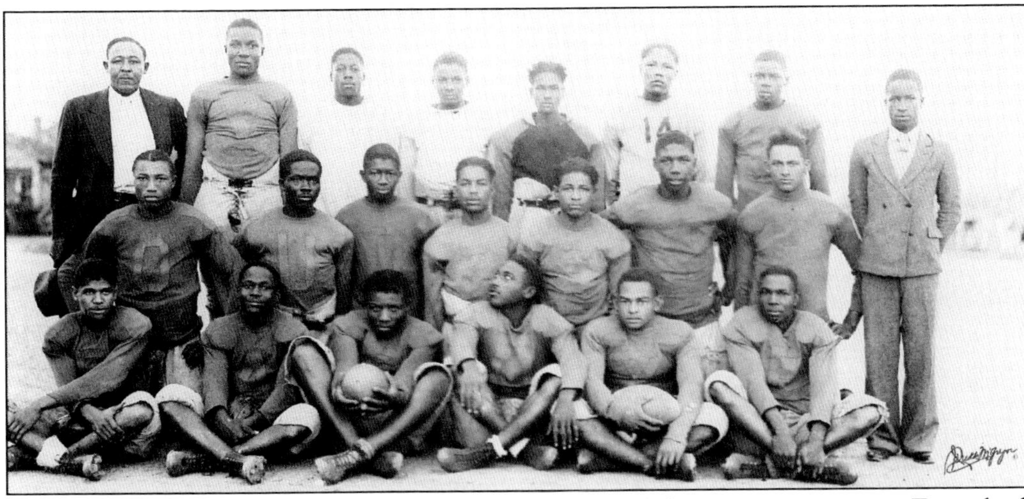

A significant advantage to full accreditation was the ability to participate in Texas high school sports. Pictured here is one of Solomon M. Coles School's earliest football teams. (Courtesy of the Corpus Christi Museum of Science and History, John Fred'k "Doc" McGregor Photographic Collection.)

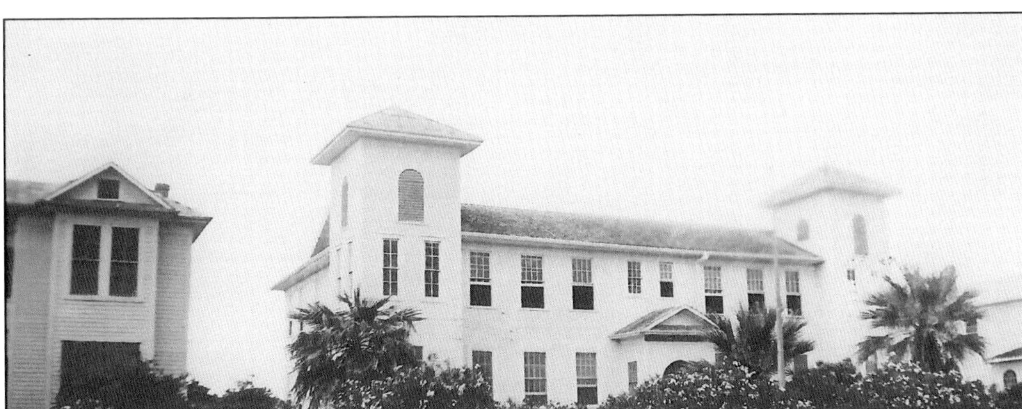

Holy Cross, established in 1917 as the first black Catholic school and church in the area, arose through the efforts of Sr. Katherine Drexel. An heiress who used her money for the benefit of African American and Native American children, Drexel purchased land for a two-story building that housed the church on the first floor and the school on the second floor. (Courtesy of the Diocese of Corpus Christi Archives.)

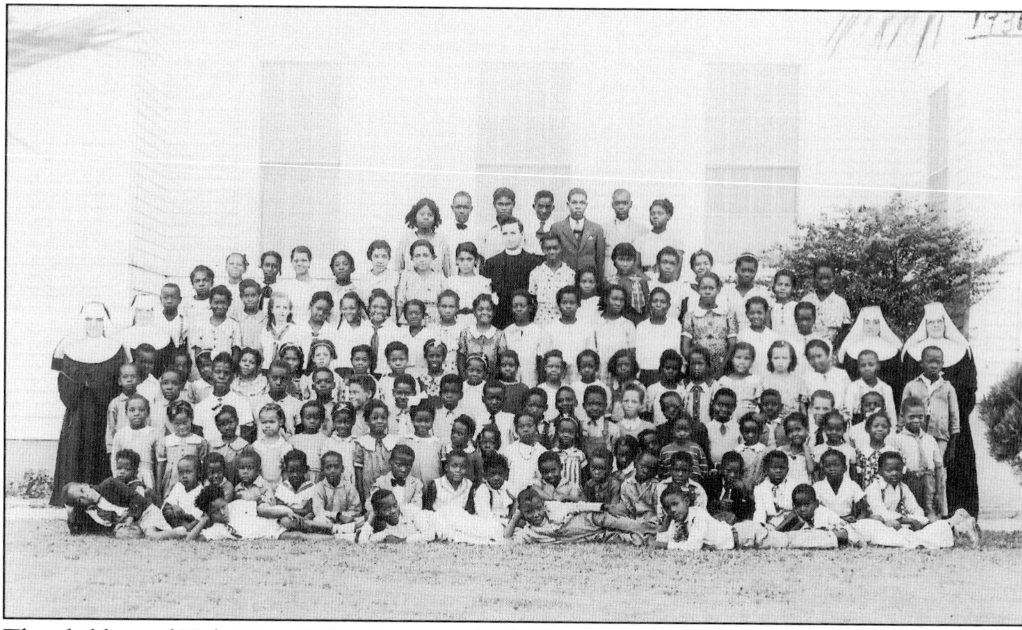

The children of Holy Cross School pose with their teachers in 1936. The school began in 1917, and five years later, the Sisters of the Holy Ghost of San Antonio (now known as the Sisters of the Holy Spirit) moved in and assumed school operations. This order managed the school until 1965, with only a brief two-year break. When enrollment declined, the school closed after 48 years. (Courtesy of the Diocese of Corpus Christi Archives.)

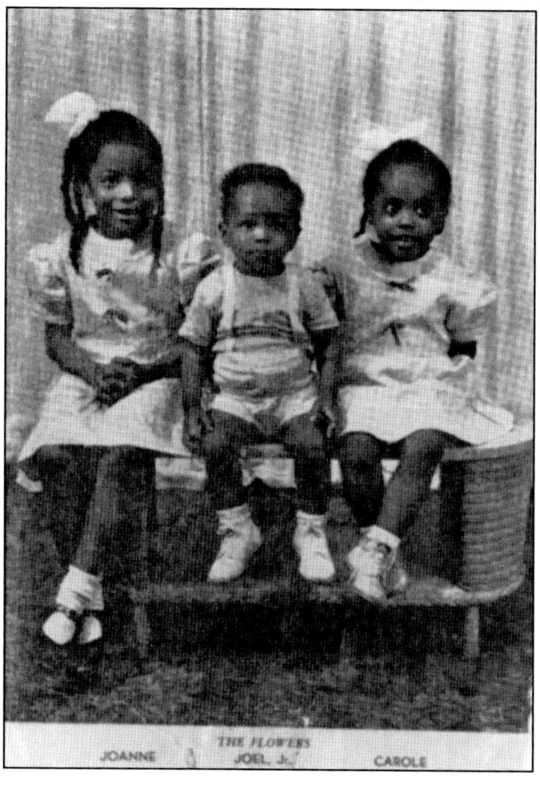

As charming in real life as in the photographer's studio, JoAnne Flowers (left), Joel Flowers Jr. (center), and Carole Flowers helped their parents advertise the Jackson and Flowers Funeral Home on Waco Street. (Courtesy of the Corpus Christi Museum of Science and History, Alclair Pleasant Collection.)

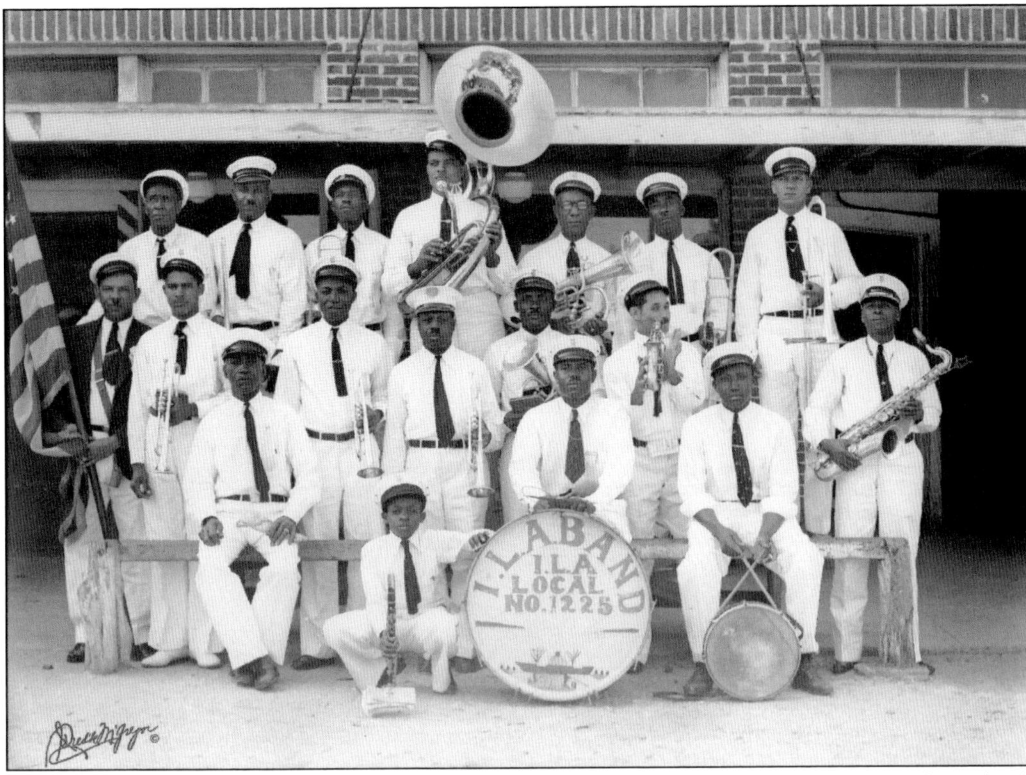

The International Longshoremen's Association Band was one of the most active groups of Northside musicians. Representing Local No. 1225, they participated in community events ranging from dedications to dances. (Courtesy of the Corpus Christi Museum of Science and History, John Fred'k "Doc" McGregor Photographic Collection.)

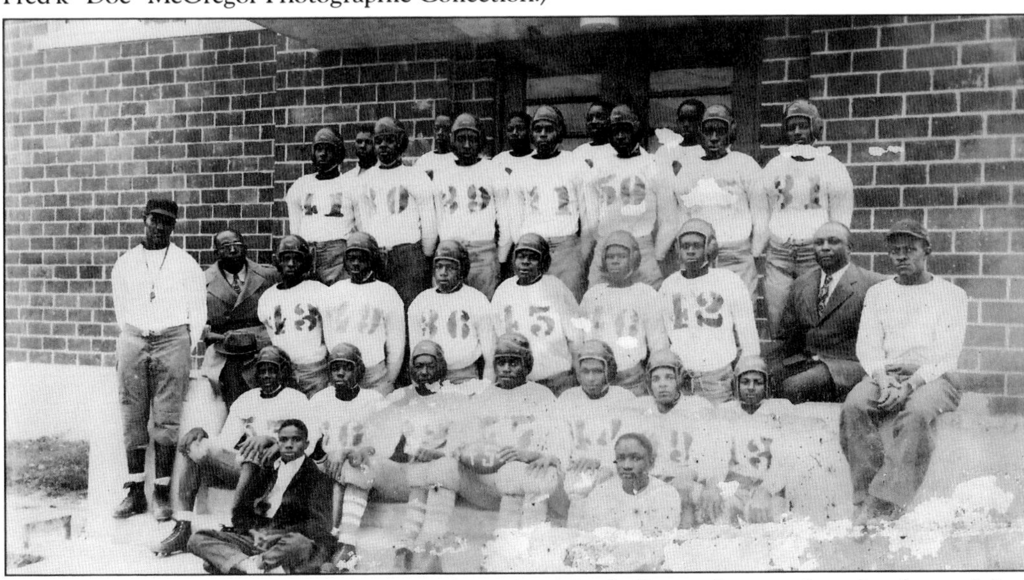

Players and staff with the Solomon M. Coles School football team have gathered in front of their school with principal and coach Harry Williams. Football practice, often strenuous, taught discipline and relieved stress after a hard day at school. (Courtesy of Solomon M. Coles School.)

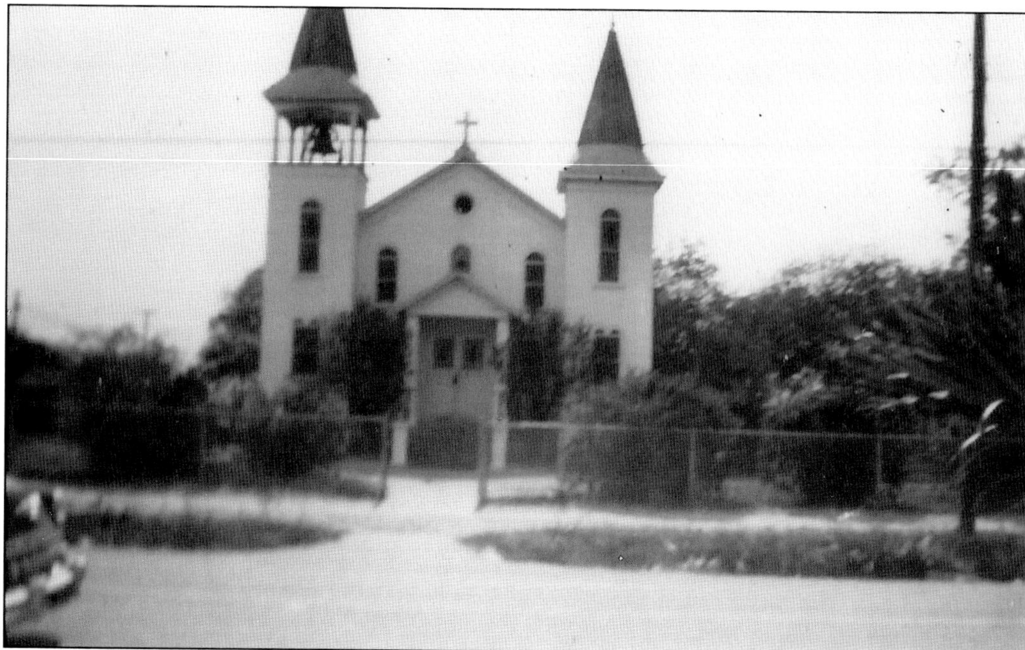

Holy Cross Church is the second oldest Catholic Church in the city. In 1923, the 20-year-old former Blessed Sacrament Hispanic Mission moved to its present location. The church relieved the pressure for space in the Holy Cross School, which contained both the church and school and held classes for several hundred children for a number of years. (Courtesy of Catholic Diocese of Corpus Christi Archives.)

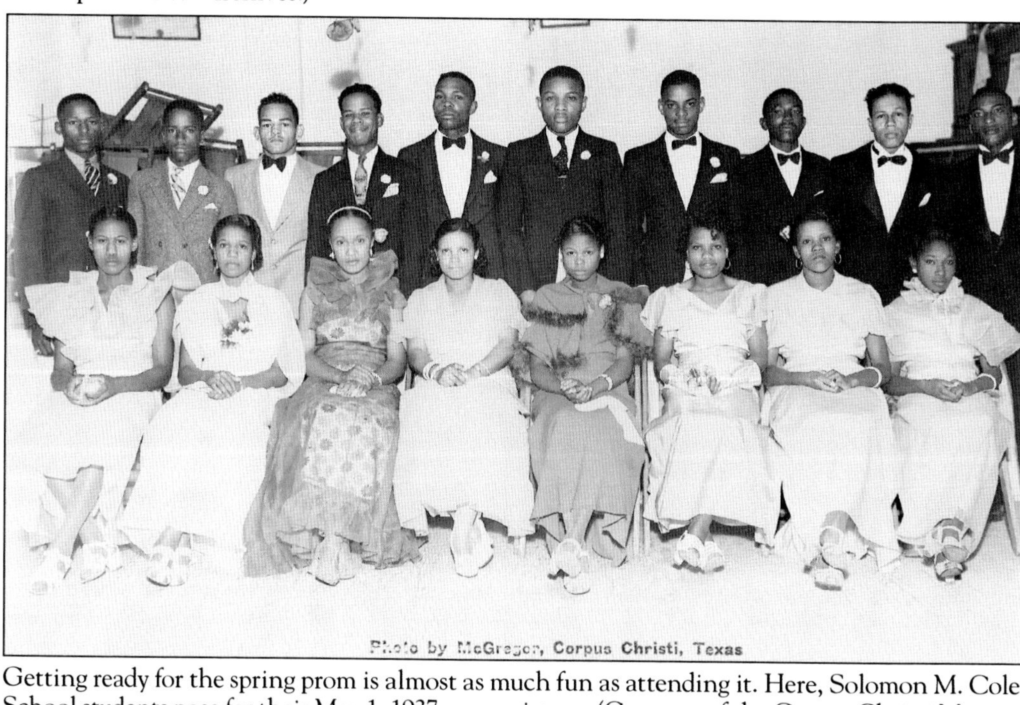

Getting ready for the spring prom is almost as much fun as attending it. Here, Solomon M. Coles School students pose for their May 1, 1937, prom picture. (Courtesy of the Corpus Christi Museum of Science and History, John Fred'k "Doc" McGregor Photographic Collection.)

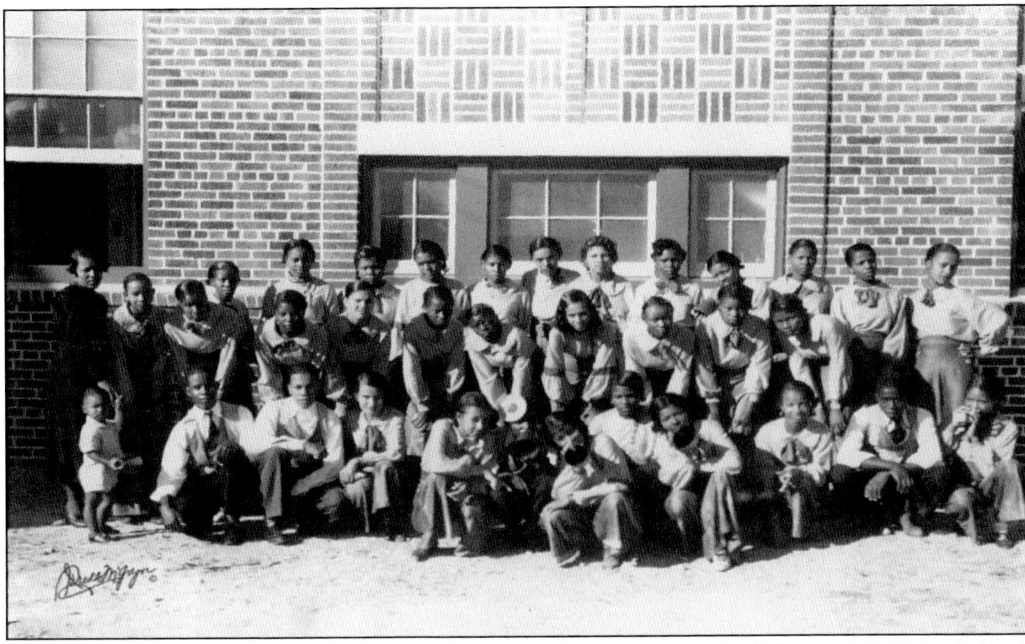

Everyone is dressed in his or her best for this 1934 class picture at the Solomon M. Coles School. (Courtesy of the Corpus Christi Museum of Science and History, John Fred'k "Doc" McGregor Photographic Collection.)

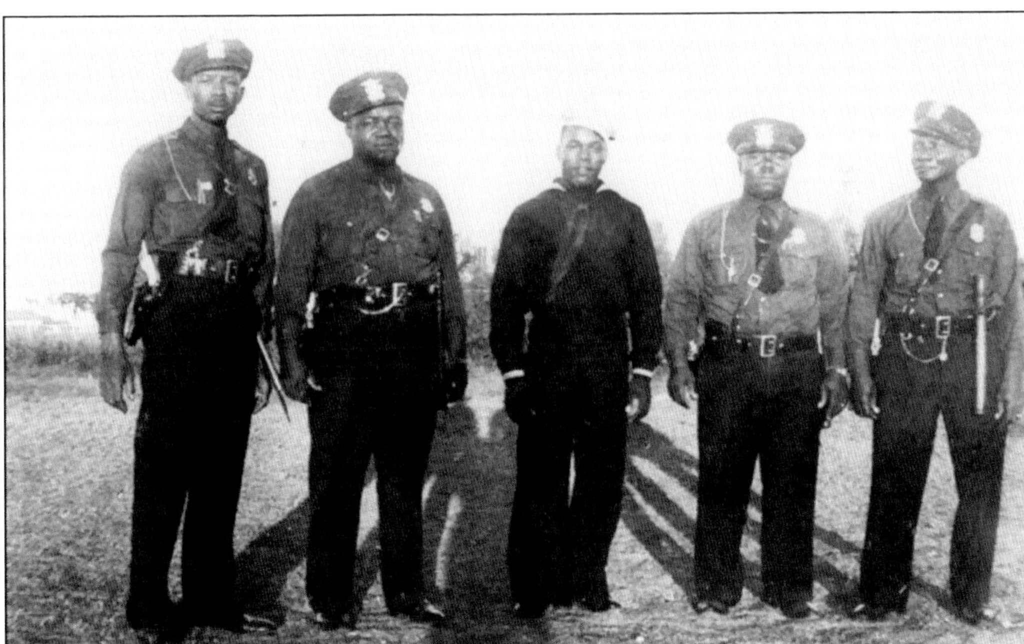

Officer Willie K. Brown (second from left), shown with three colleagues and a sailor, was one of the city's first full-time African American policemen. His patrol was primarily in the Northside (black) neighborhood. (Courtesy of the Corpus Christi Museum of Science and History, Alclair Pleasant Collection.)

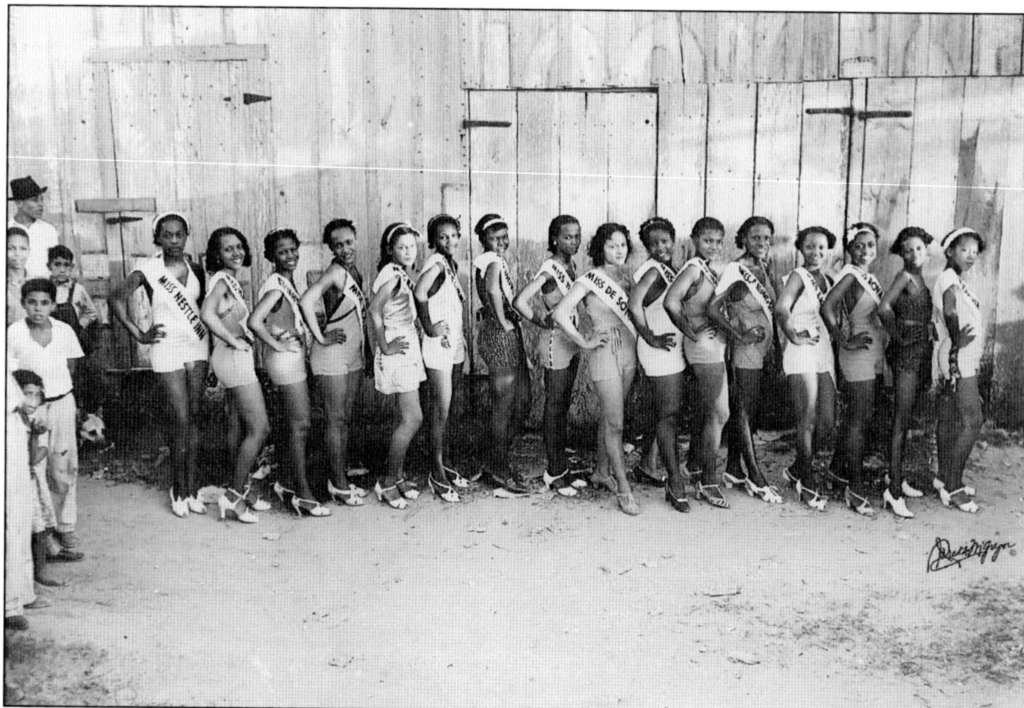

Juneteenth festivities in 1937 were special for these 16 young women. Representing different Northside organizations and businesses, they competed in the annual beauty contest. (Courtesy of the Corpus Christi Museum of Science and History, John Fred'k "Doc" McGregor Photographic Collection.)

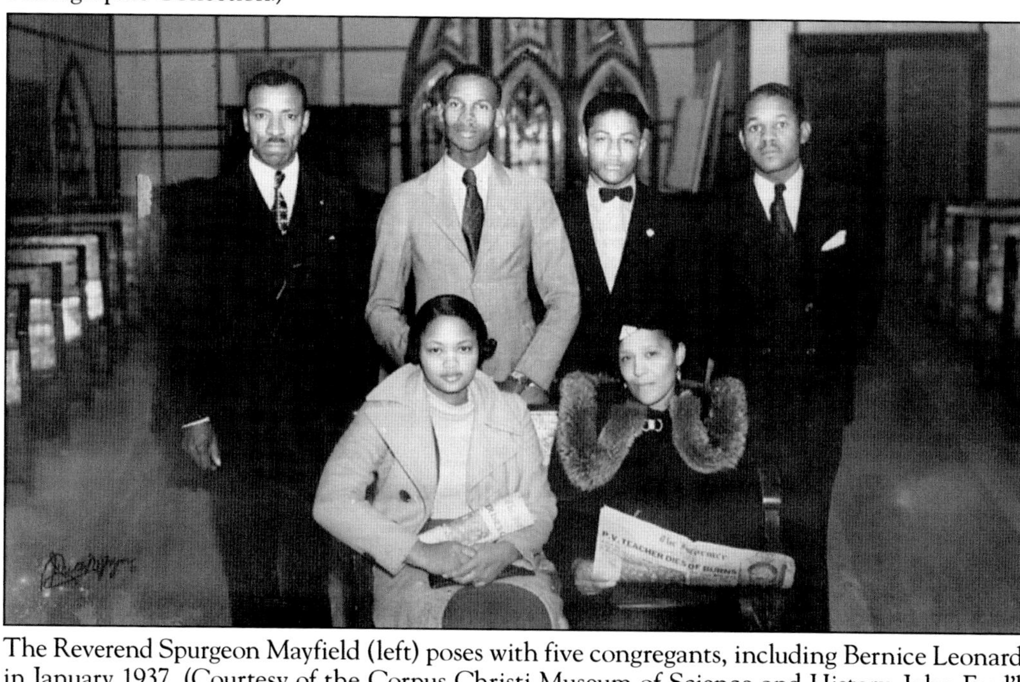

The Reverend Spurgeon Mayfield (left) poses with five congregants, including Bernice Leonard, in January 1937. (Courtesy of the Corpus Christi Museum of Science and History, John Fred'k "Doc" McGregor Photographic Collection.)

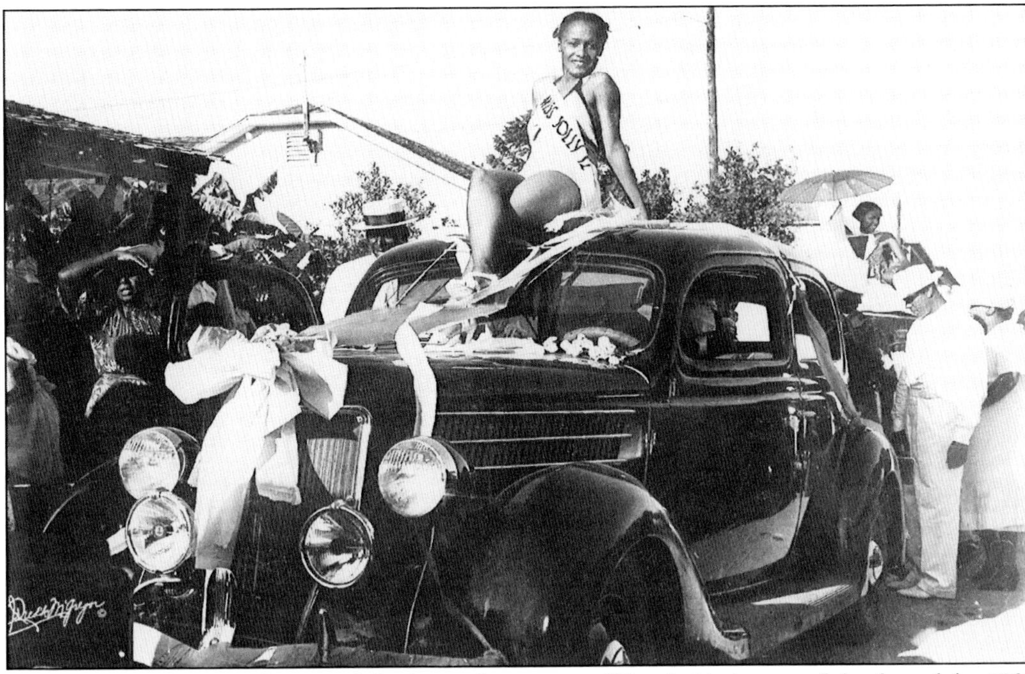

Riding a gaily decorated automobile down the streets of Northside is part of the fun of the 1937 Juneteenth celebration. (Courtesy of the Corpus Christi Museum of Science and History, John Fred'k "Doc" McGregor Photographic Collection.)

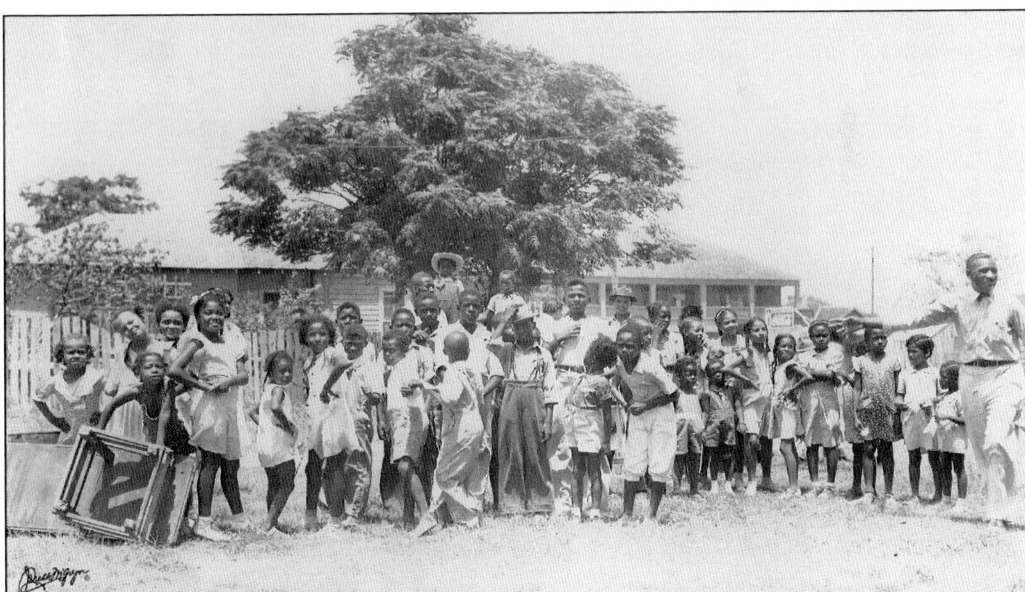

School is out, and summertime is here. A warm day in July 1937 brought many Northside youngsters to pose for the camera. (Courtesy of the Corpus Christi Museum of Science and History, John Fred'k "Doc" McGregor Photographic Collection.)

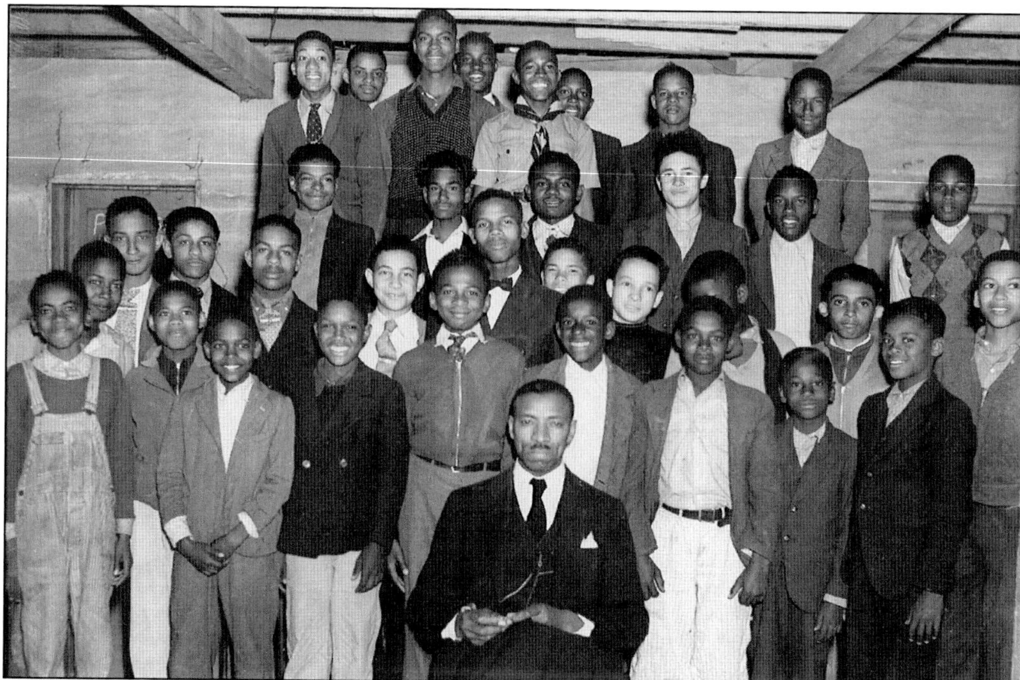

An active group of Cub Scouts, Boy Scouts, and an Eagle Scout posed with the Reverend Mayfield in February 1937. (Courtesy of the Corpus Christi Museum of Science and History, John Fred'k "Doc" McGregor Photographic Collection.)

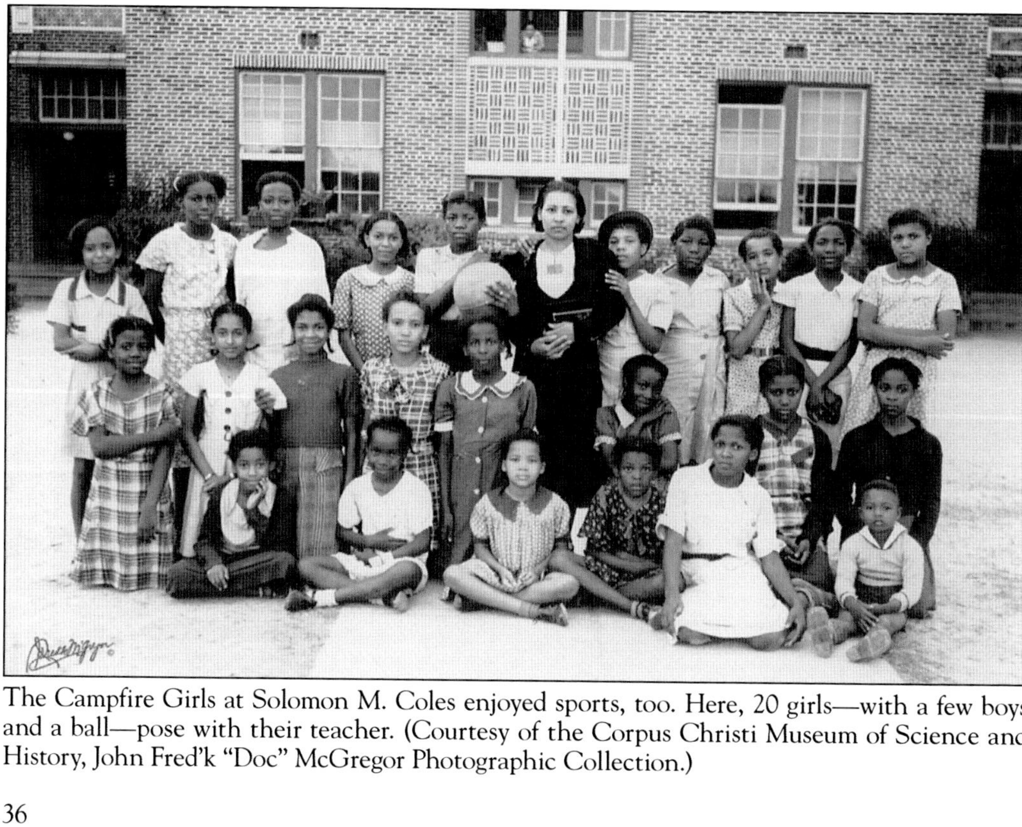

The Campfire Girls at Solomon M. Coles enjoyed sports, too. Here, 20 girls—with a few boys and a ball—pose with their teacher. (Courtesy of the Corpus Christi Museum of Science and History, John Fred'k "Doc" McGregor Photographic Collection.)

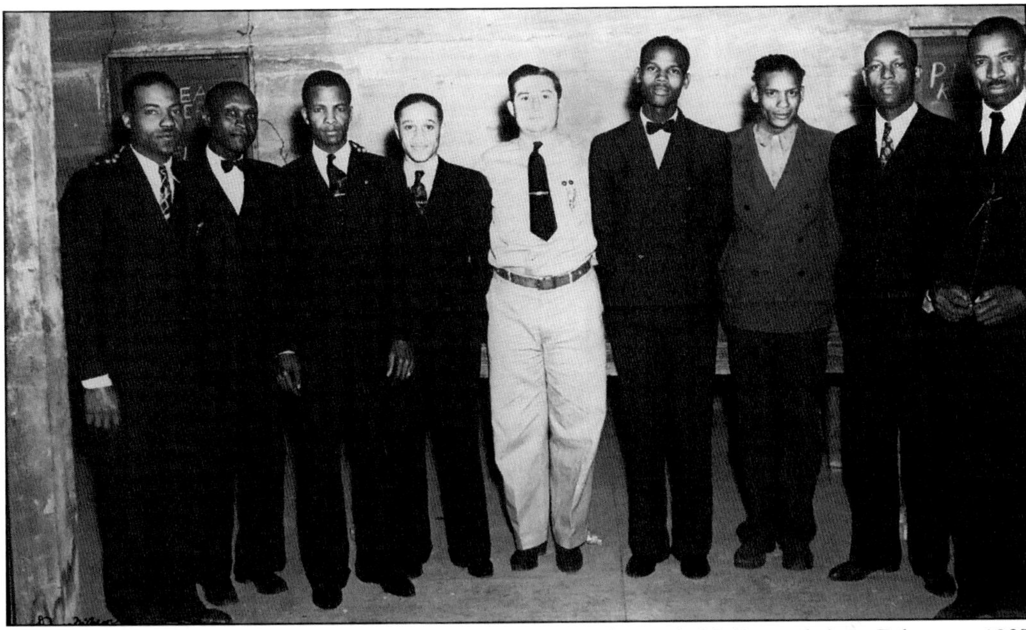

Northside community leaders pose with the Reverend Mayfield (far right) in February 1937. (Courtesy of the Corpus Christi Museum of Science and History, John Fred'k "Doc" McGregor Photographic Collection.)

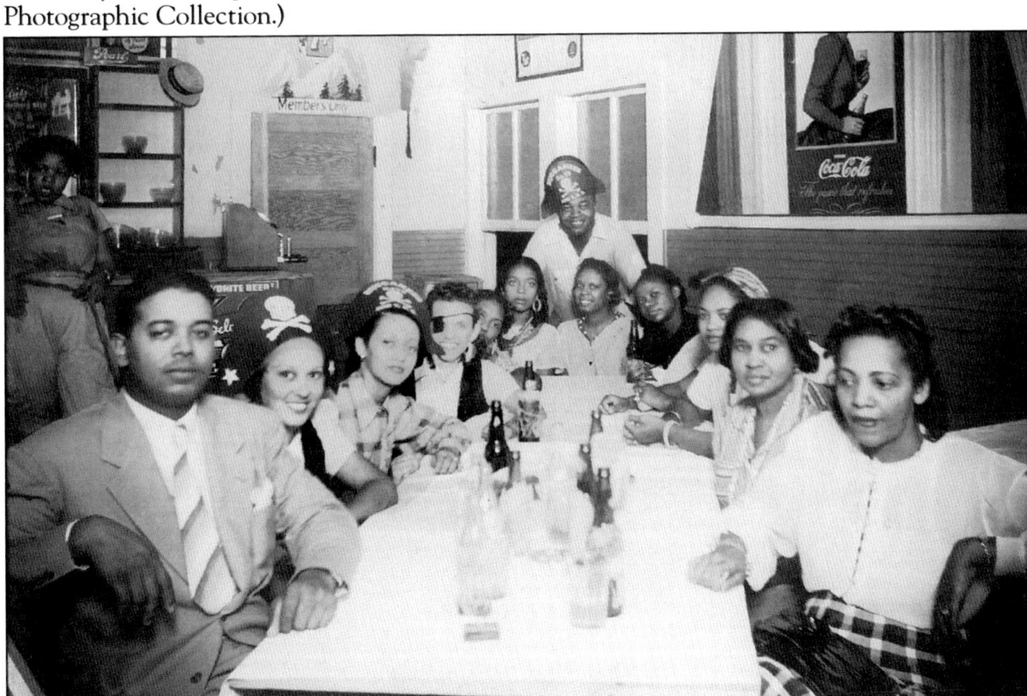

The year 1938 saw the beginning of the annual Buccaneer Days festival in Corpus Christi. Celebrating with pirate regalia are Alclair Pleasant (second from left), Juanita Kitchen Crecy (third from left), Willie K. Brown (in buccaneer hat at back), Florence Brooks (third from right), and several unidentified friends. (Courtesy of the Corpus Christi Museum of Science and History, Alclair Pleasant Collection.)

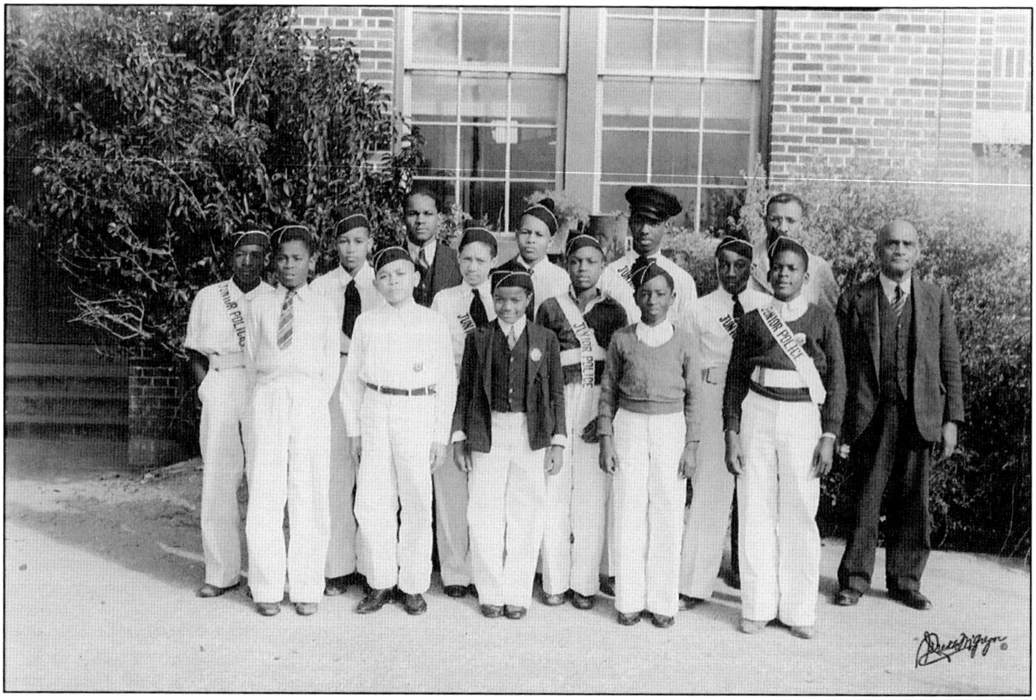

Starting off a brand-new year in 1938, the Junior Police Squad of Solomon M. Coles School poses with Principal T.C. Ayers (far right). (Courtesy of the Corpus Christi Museum of Science and History, John Fred'k "Doc" McGregor Photographic Collection.)

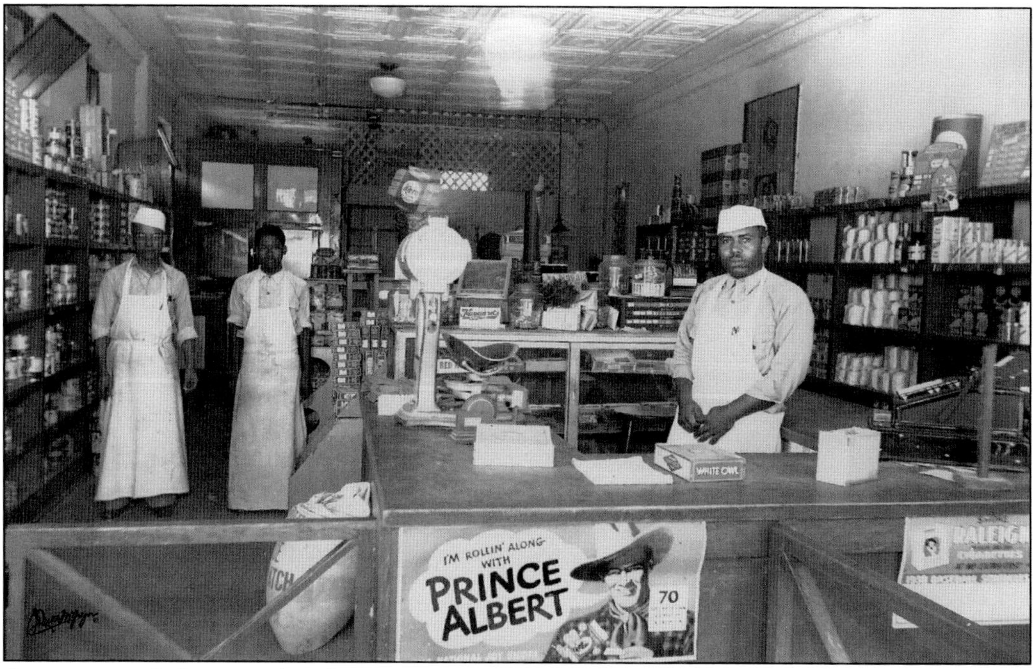

Canning jars, baking goods, tobacco, and candy are just a few of the items offered by this general store on the Bluff in August 1938. (Courtesy of the Corpus Christi Museum of Science and History, John Fred'k "Doc" McGregor Photographic Collection.)

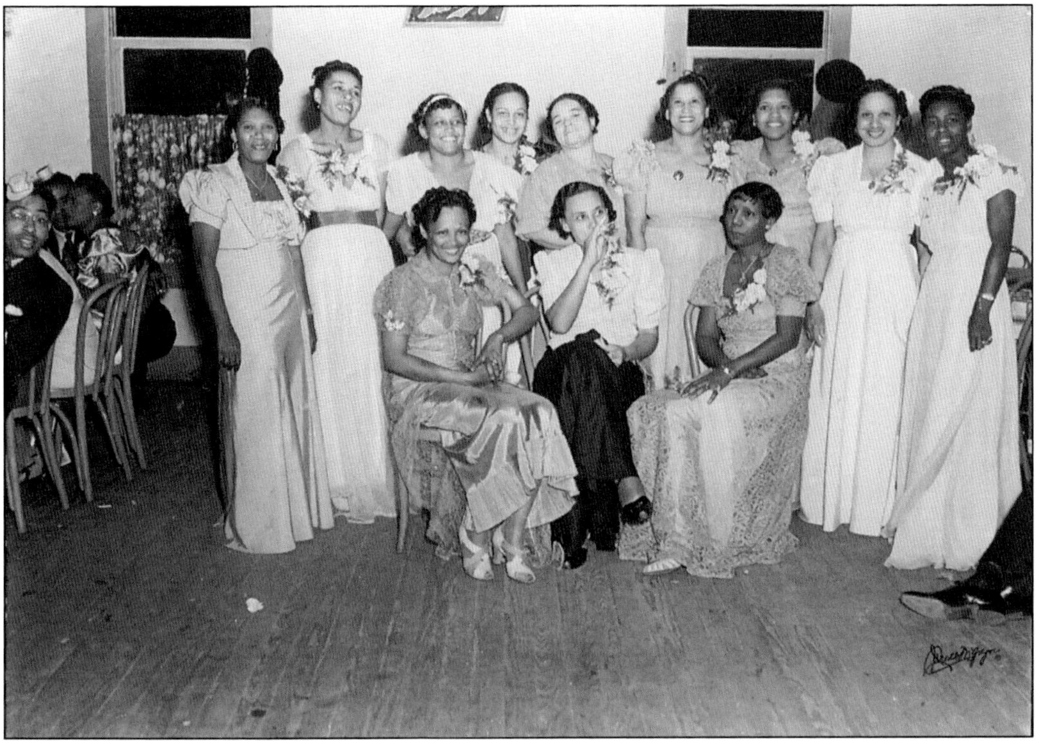

Springtime lends an exquisite air of excitement to the evening as ladies pose for a commemorative photograph at this May 1939 dance. (Courtesy of the Corpus Christi Museum of Science and History, John Fred'k "Doc" McGregor Photographic Collection.)

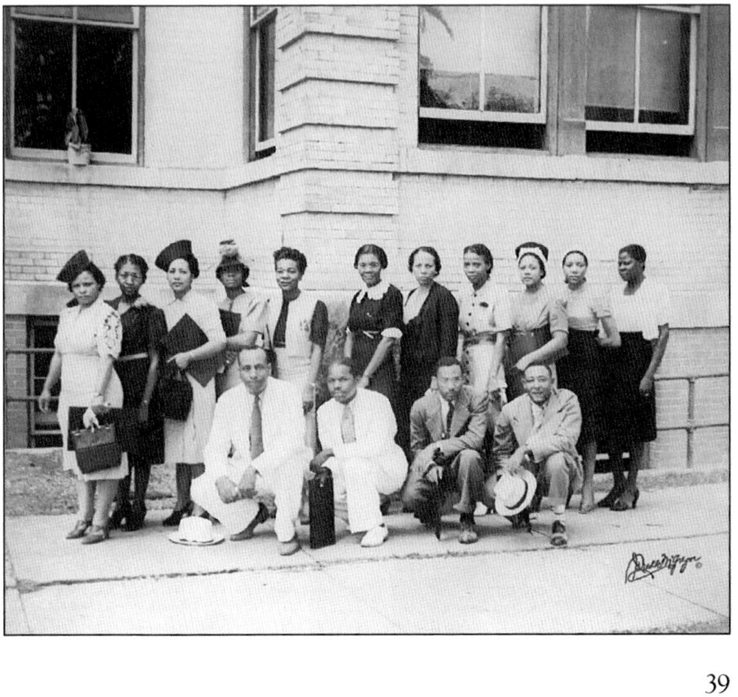

Pictured just as the new school year was beginning are 15 members of the Solomon M. Coles School faculty of 1939. (Courtesy of the Corpus Christi Museum of Science and History, John Fred'k "Doc" McGregor Photographic Collection.)

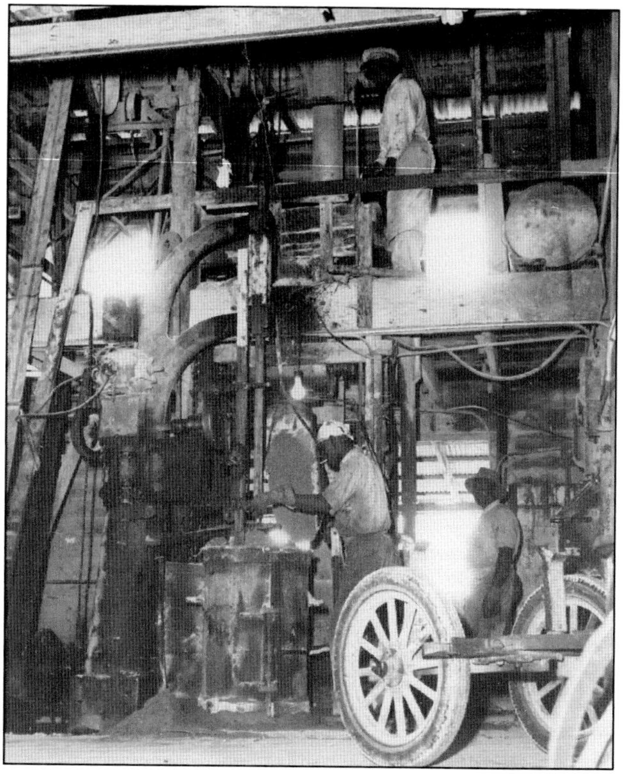

These workers for Southern Alkali Corporation are packing caustic soda. This business provided much-needed employment to the area and was the first big industry to arrive in Corpus Christi. (Courtesy of *Corpus Christi Caller-Times*.)

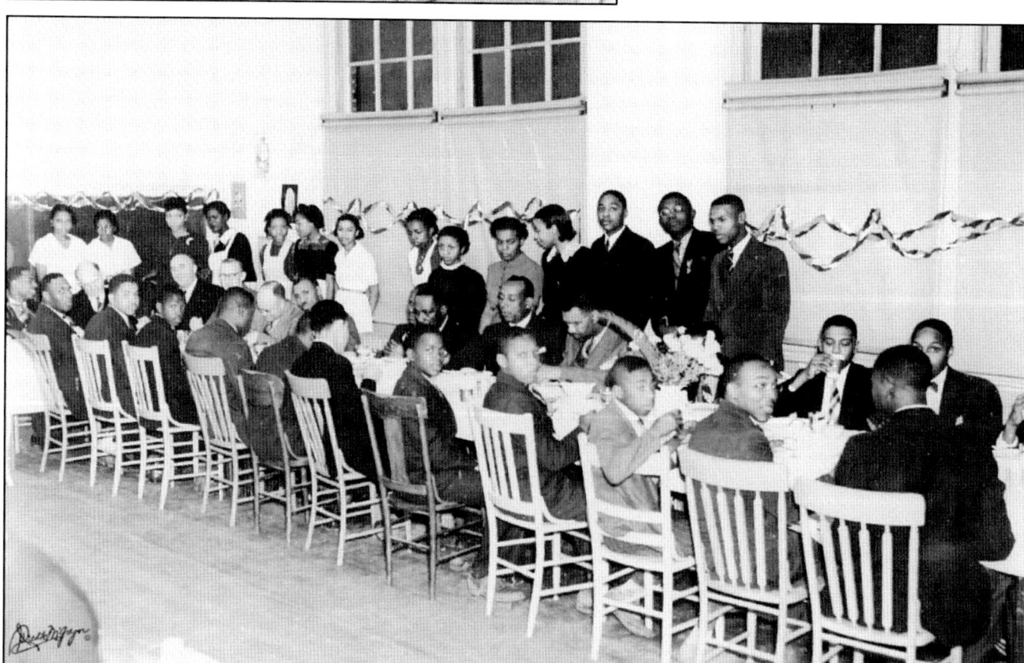

Congregants and visitors share a meal at the African Methodist Episcopal Brooks Chapel in February 1939. (Courtesy of the Corpus Christi Museum of Science and History, John Fred'k "Doc" McGregor Photographic Collection.)

Rev. Spurgeon Mayfield, pastor of the First Congregational Church from 1934 to 1939, worked tirelessly to improve his community. He implemented a department of religious education and began Boy Scout and Campfire Girls troops, a kindergarten, and a community library. Mayfield sought to improve race relations and spoke to both black and white groups. He worked with the International Longshoremen's Association and the Corpus Christi Hotel Men's Club and was president of the local NAACP. (Courtesy of the Corpus Christi Public Libraries.)

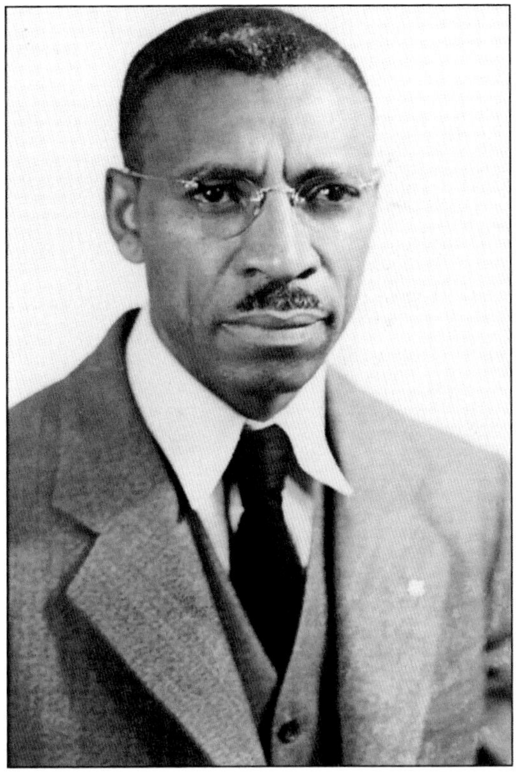

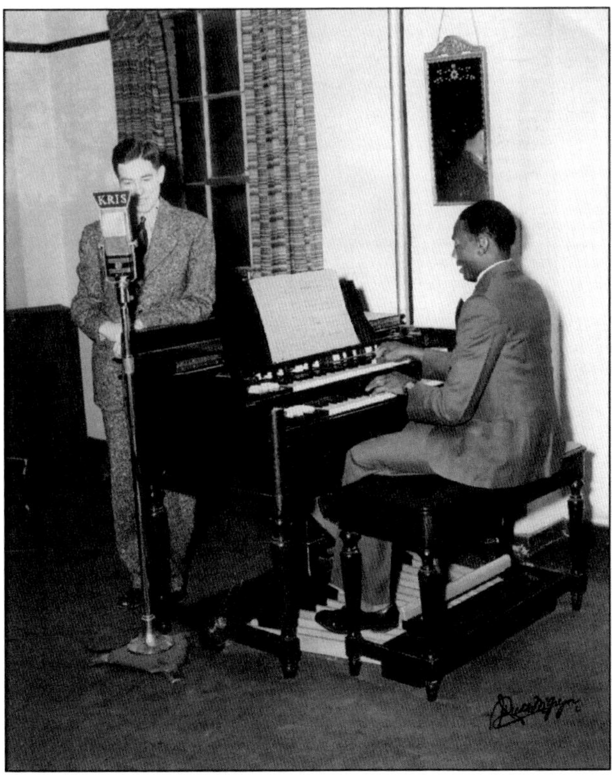

Exceptional organ music gave depth and resonance to the live broadcast presented by KRIS radio station in November 1939. (Courtesy of the Corpus Christi Museum of Science and History, John Fred'k "Doc" McGregor Photographic Collection.)

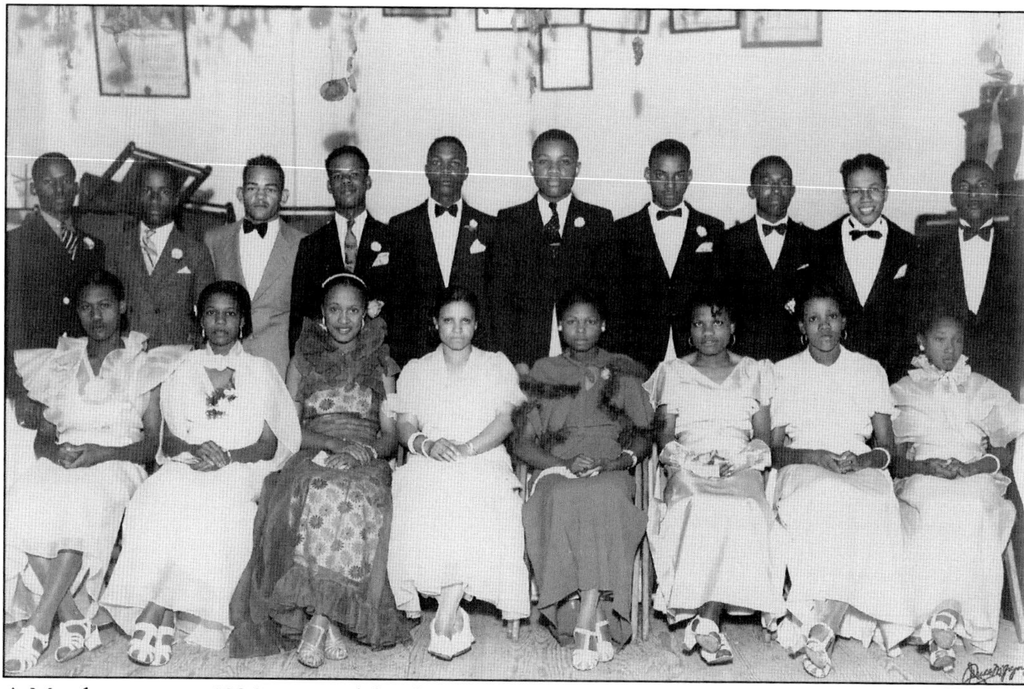

A Mayday prom in 1936 is special for this Coles class. (Courtesy of the Corpus Christi Museum of Science and History, John Fred'k "Doc" McGregor Photographic Collection.)

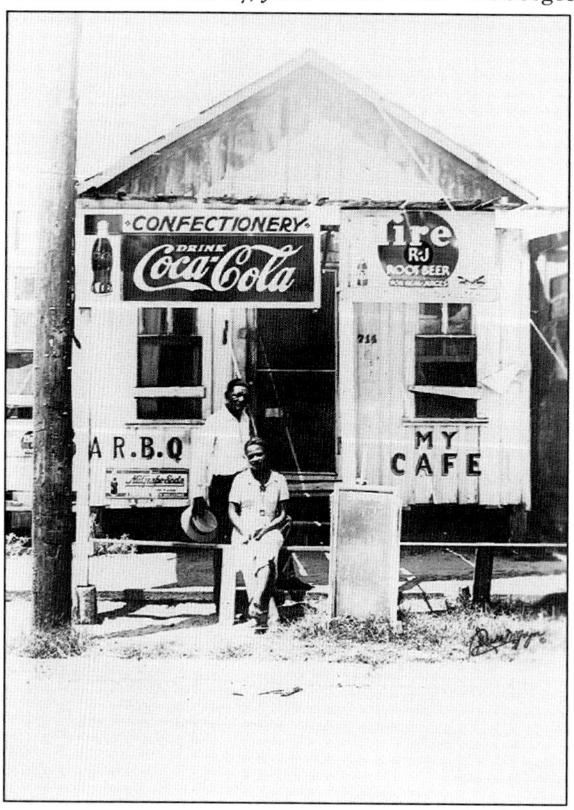

My Cafe was a popular eating place on the Bluff during the 1930s. (Courtesy of the Corpus Christi Museum of Science and History, John Fred'k "Doc" McGregor Photographic Collection.)

Myrtle Merryweather was a prominent Northside resident in the late 1930s. (Courtesy of the Corpus Christi Museum of Science and History, John Fred'k "Doc" McGregor Photographic Collection.)

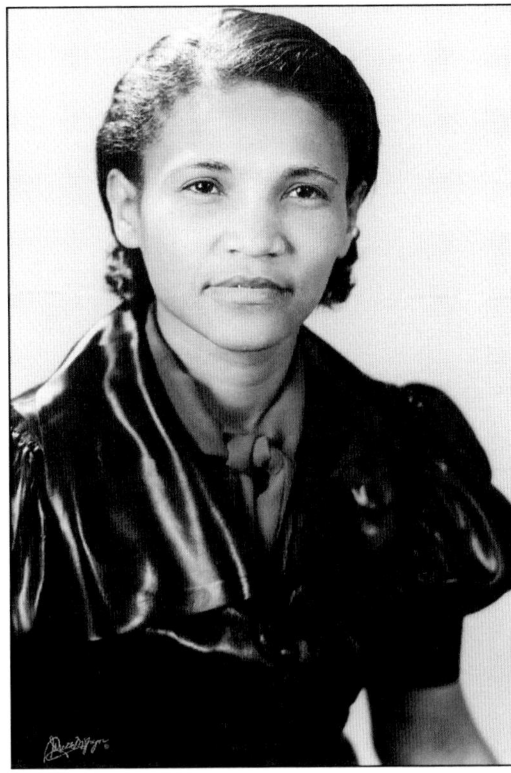

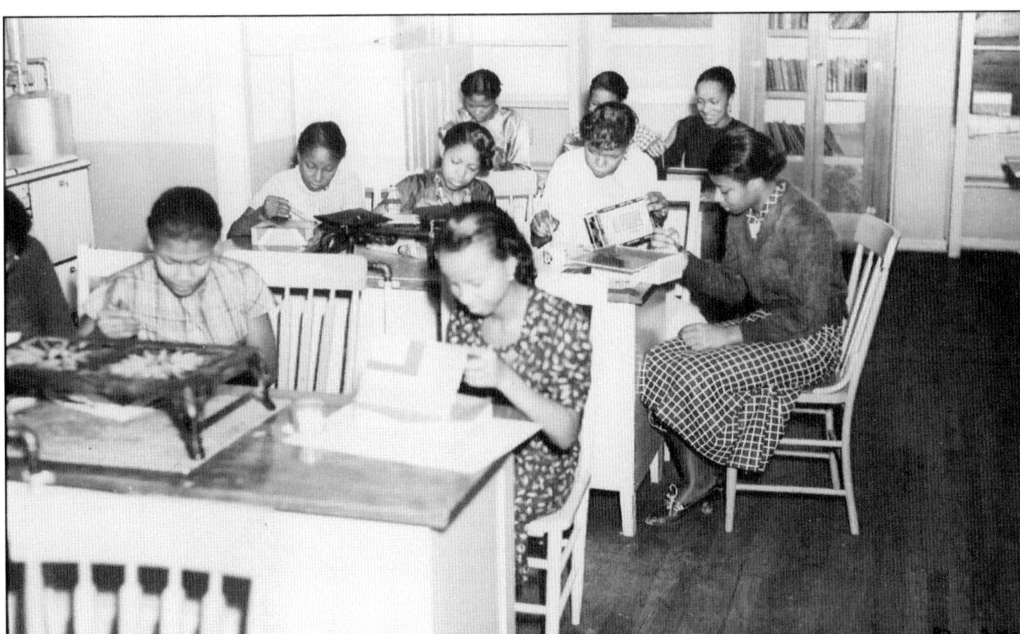

Pictured in mid-September of 1939, these Solomon M. Coles School students look ready for a new year. (Courtesy of the Corpus Christi Museum of Science and History, John Fred'k "Doc" McGregor Photographic Collection.)

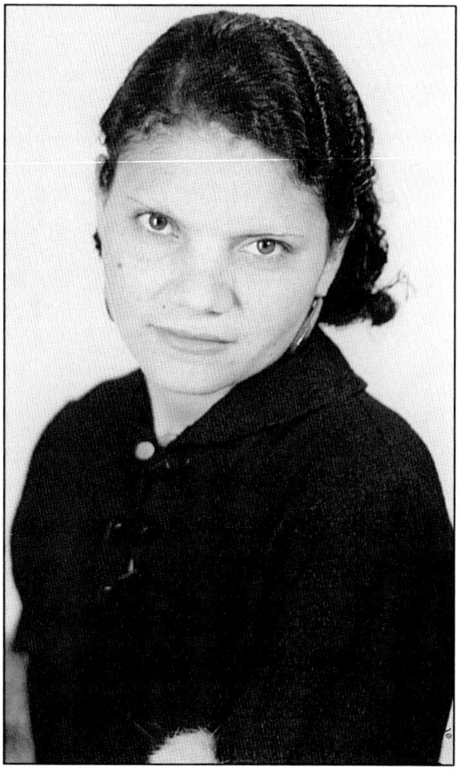

Dorothy Mason Hatch was another Northside community leader in the years leading to World War II. (Courtesy of the Corpus Christi Museum of Science and History, John Fred'k "Doc" McGregor Photographic Collection.)

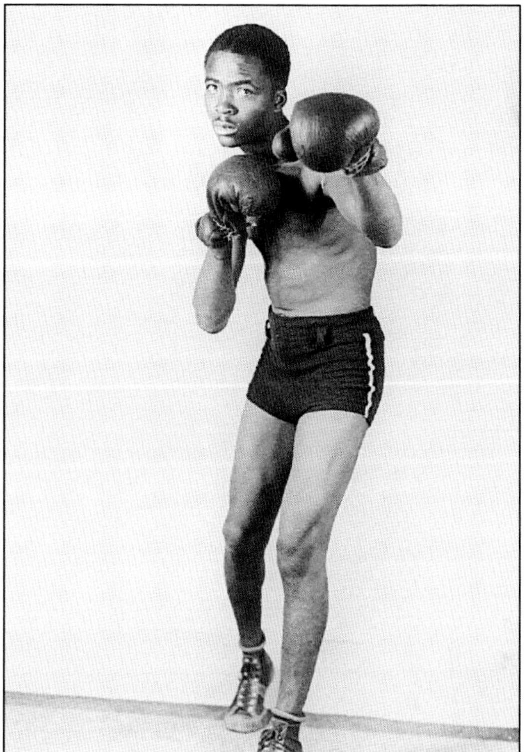

Boxing was a source of discipline and dexterity. It was highly popular among young Northside men in the late 1930s. This young man is unidentified. (Courtesy of the Corpus Christi Museum of Science and History, John Fred'k "Doc" McGregor Photographic Collection.)

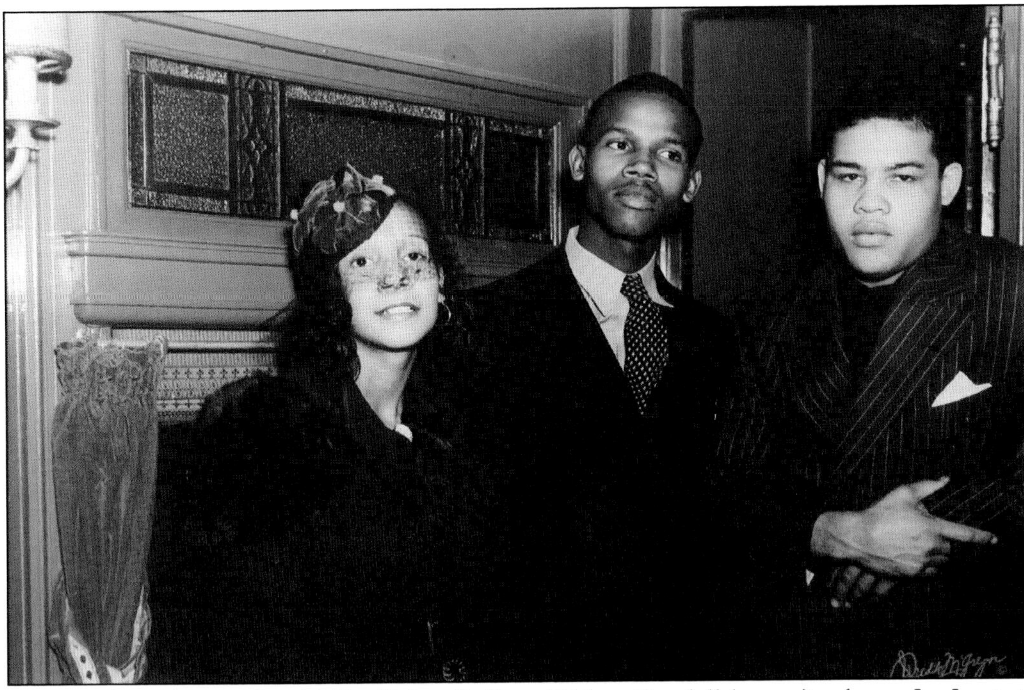

Corpus Christi boxing fans Mildred Mays (left) and Velton Randall (center) welcome Joe Louis to the Northside in March 1937. (Courtesy of the Corpus Christi Museum of Science and History, John Fred'k "Doc" McGregor Photographic Collection.)

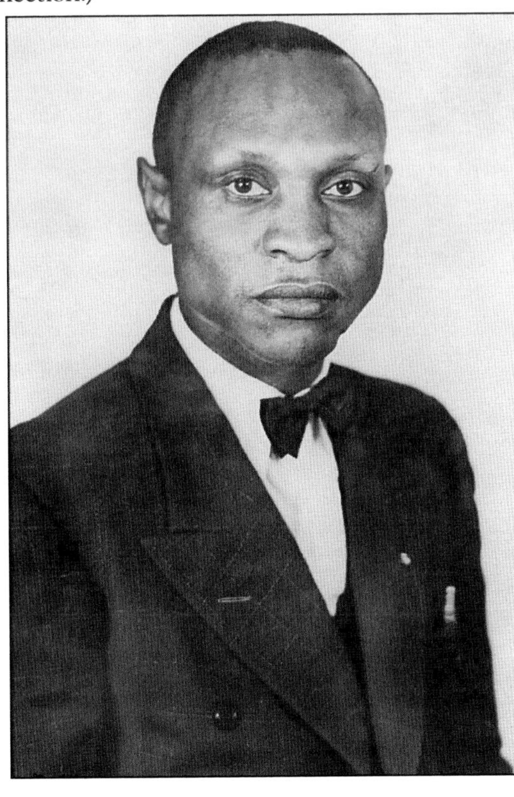

The Reverend Palmer provided spiritual and civic strength in his years on the Bluff. (Courtesy of the Corpus Christi Museum of Science and History, John Fred'k "Doc" McGregor Photographic Collection.)

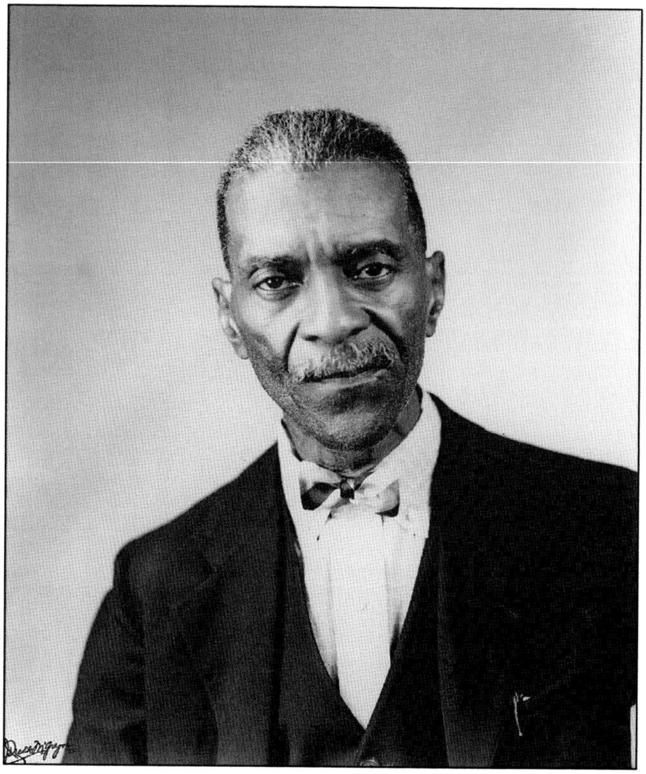

Proud and determined Corpus Christi resident Henry Holt poses for photographer "Doc" McGregor in 1937. (Courtesy of the Corpus Christi Museum of Science and History, John Fred'k "Doc" McGregor Photographic Collection.)

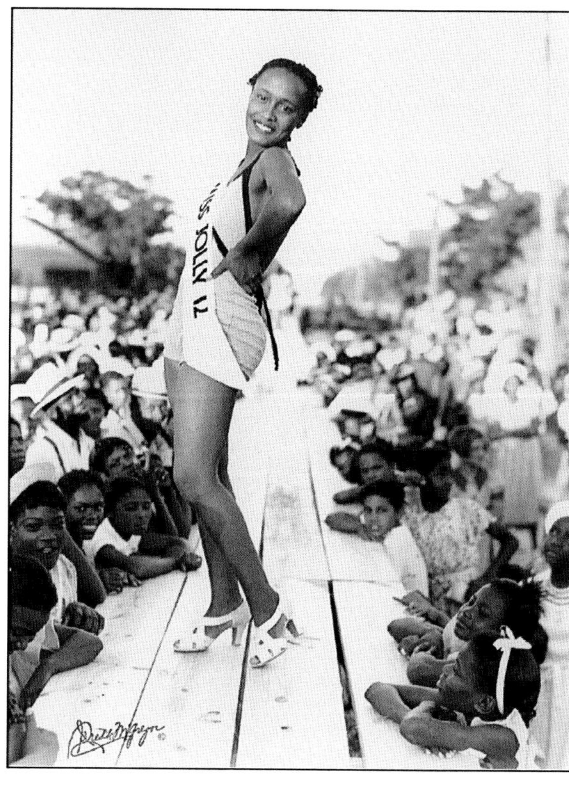

Willie Mae Branch is Miss Jolly 12 during the Juneteenth festivities in the summer of 1937. (Courtesy of the Corpus Christi Museum of Science and History, John Fred'k "Doc" McGregor Photographic Collection.)

Cleo Washington represents the Beauty Shoppe as she participates in the Miss Juneteenth Beauty Pageant of 1937. (Courtesy of the Corpus Christi Museum of Science and History, John Fred'k "Doc" McGregor Photographic Collection.)

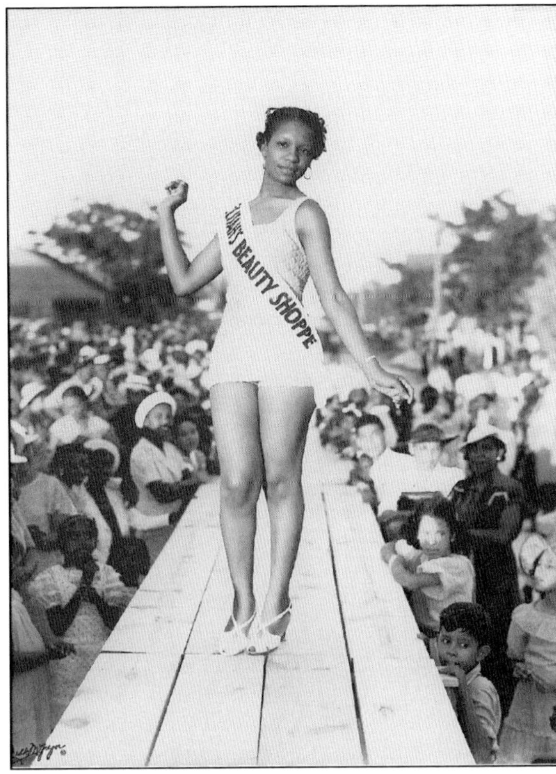

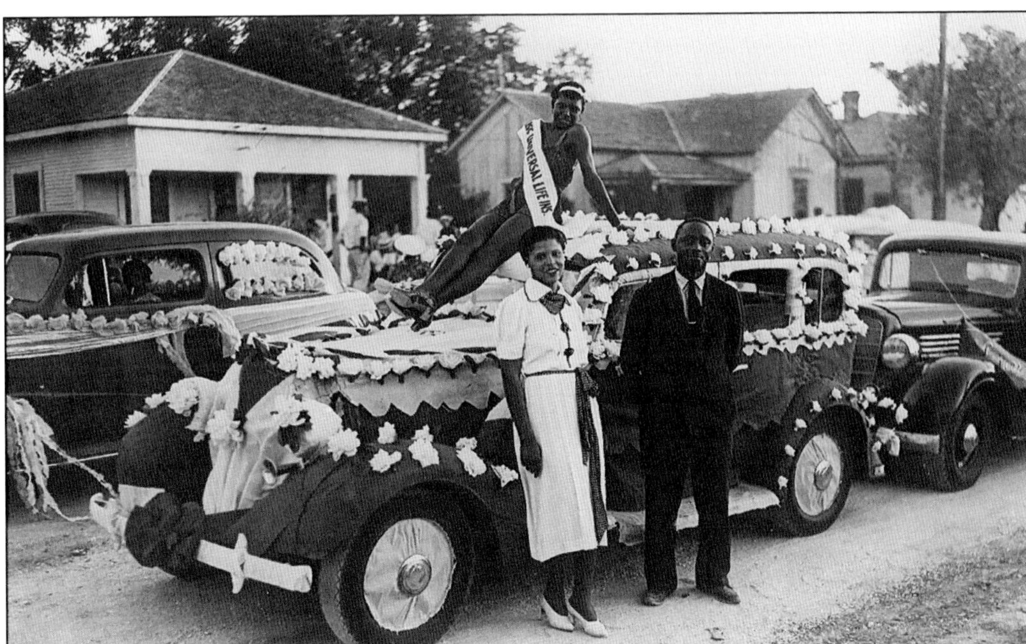

The local Universal Life Insurance Company sponsored Mildred Douglas (wearing sash) and her decorated car/float during one of Corpus Christi's annual Juneteenth celebrations. (Courtesy of the Corpus Christi Museum of Science and History, John Fred'k "Doc" McGregor Photographic Collection.)

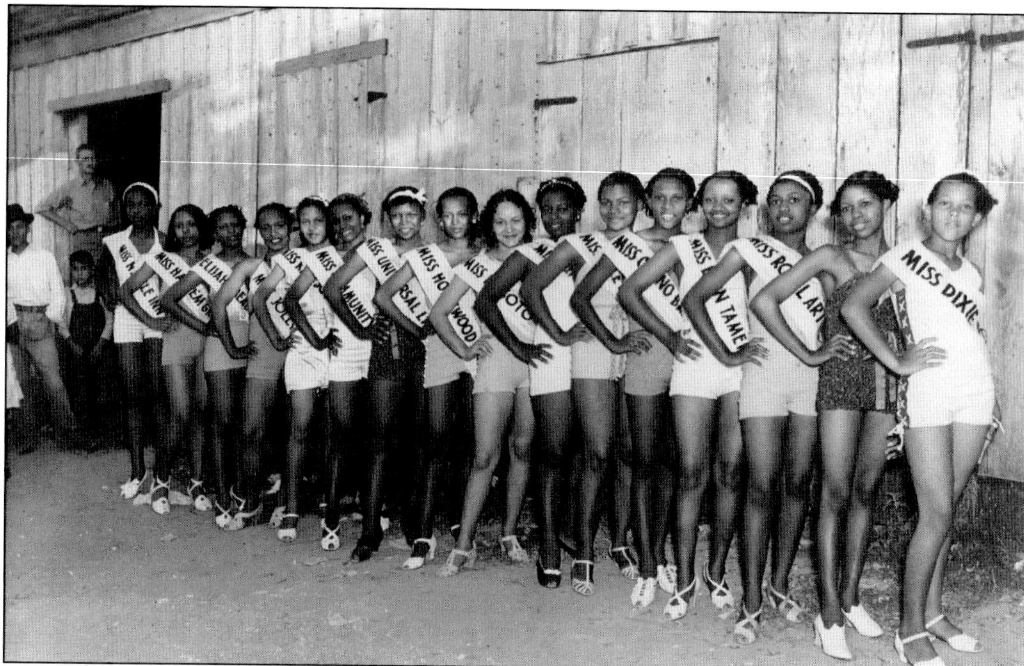

Some of the excited contestants participating in the 1937 Juneteenth Beauty Pageant include, in no particular order, Beatrice Booker, Myrtle Eester Bell, Zeola Hardeman, Mildred Douglas, and Willie Mae Branch. (Courtesy of the Corpus Christi Museum of Science and History, John Fred'k "Doc" McGregor Photographic Collection).

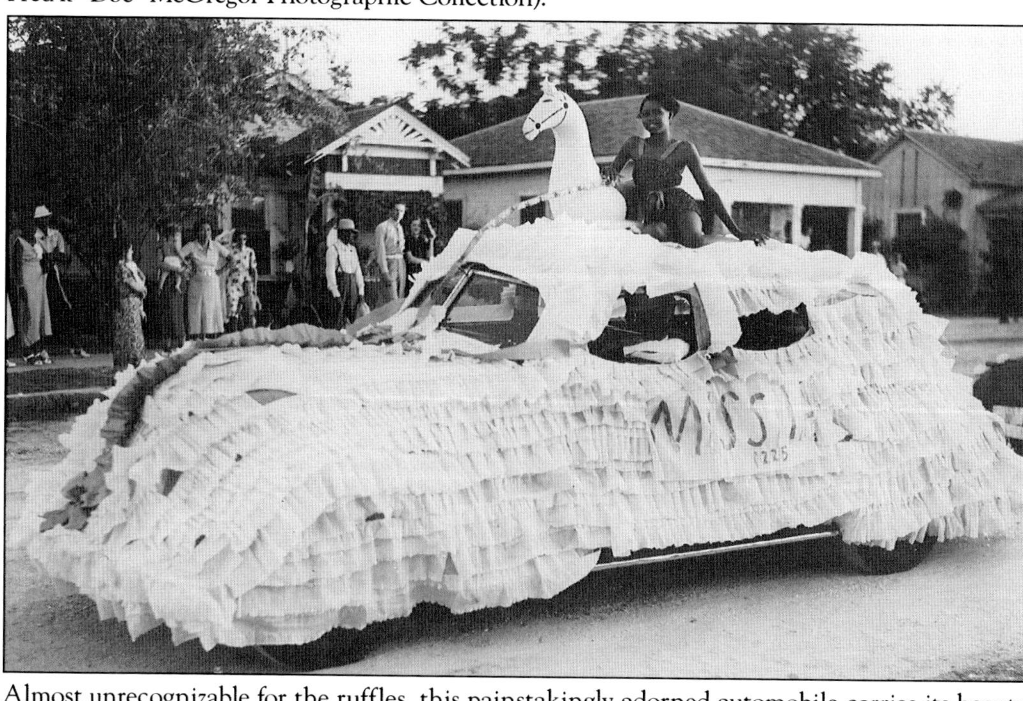

Almost unrecognizable for the ruffles, this painstakingly adorned automobile carries its beauty contestant and her "steed" through the 1937 Juneteenth Parade. (Courtesy of the Corpus Christi Museum of Science and History, John Fred'k "Doc" McGregor Photographic Collection.)

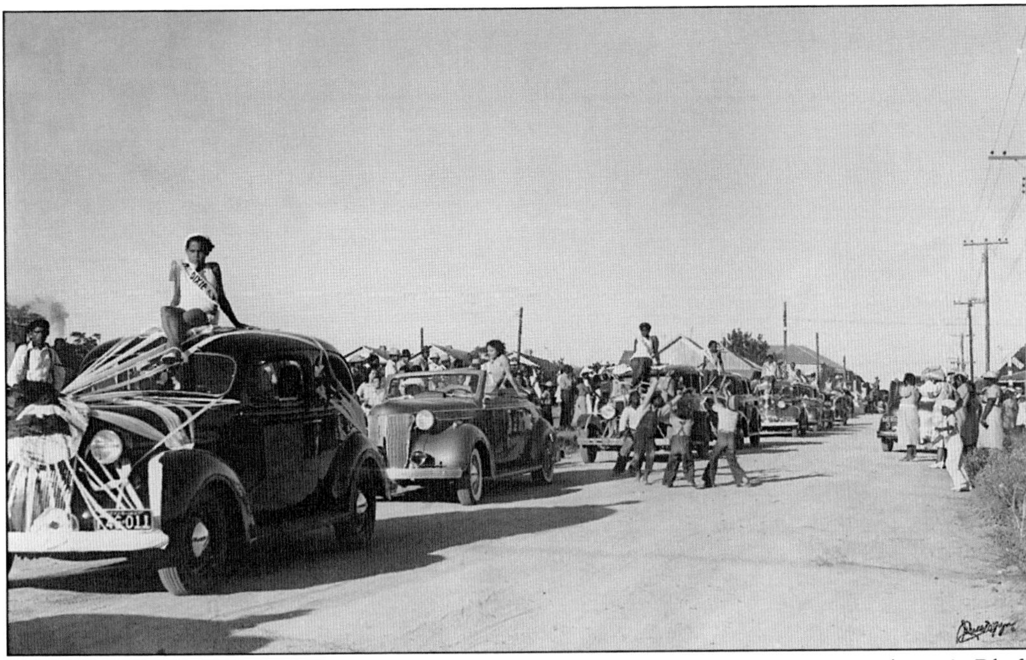

Neighbors and friends line the 1937 Juneteenth Parade route on Corpus Christi's Bluff. (Courtesy of the Corpus Christi Museum of Science and History, John Fred'k "Doc" McGregor Photographic Collection.)

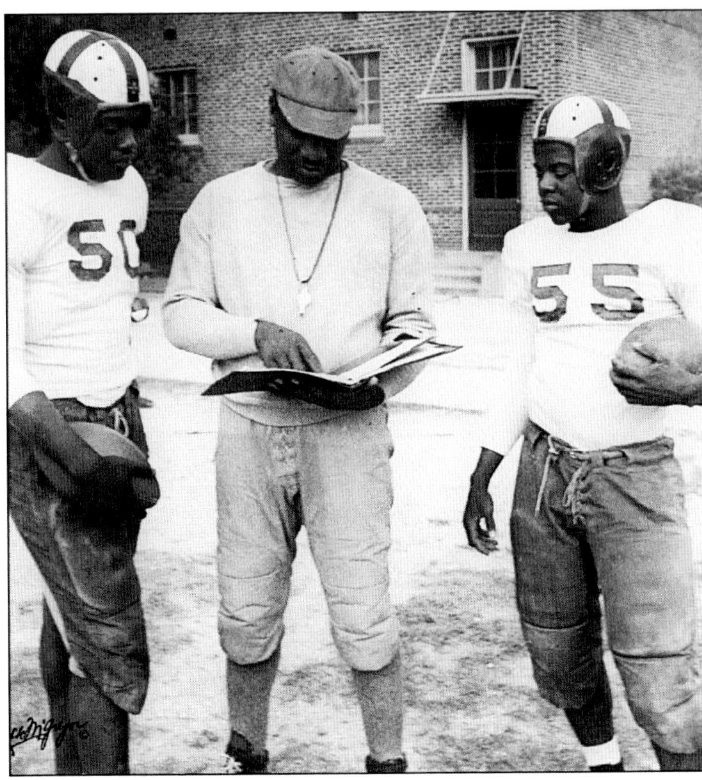

Heading into homecoming, the coach outlines plays with two members of the 1941 Solomon M. Coles School football team. No one is identified in this photograph. (Courtesy of the Corpus Christi Museum of Science and History, John Fred'k "Doc" McGregor Photographic Collection.)

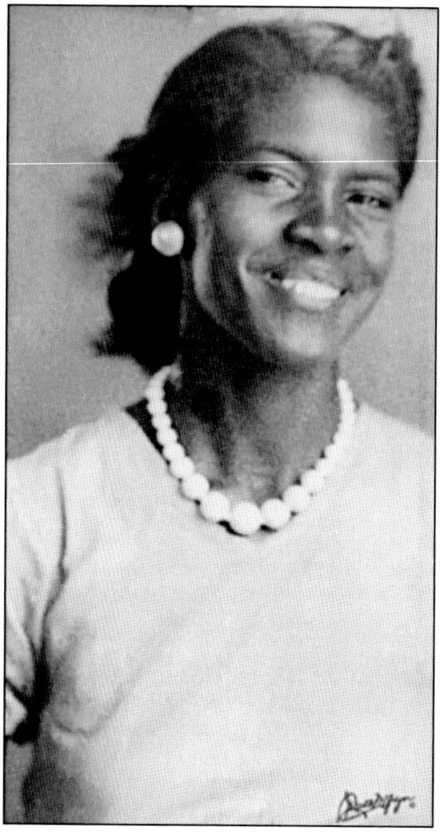

A favorite Solomon M. Coles School junior high teacher was Ardalia Thompson. (Courtesy of the Corpus Christi Museum of Science and History, John Fred'k "Doc" McGregor Photographic Collection.)

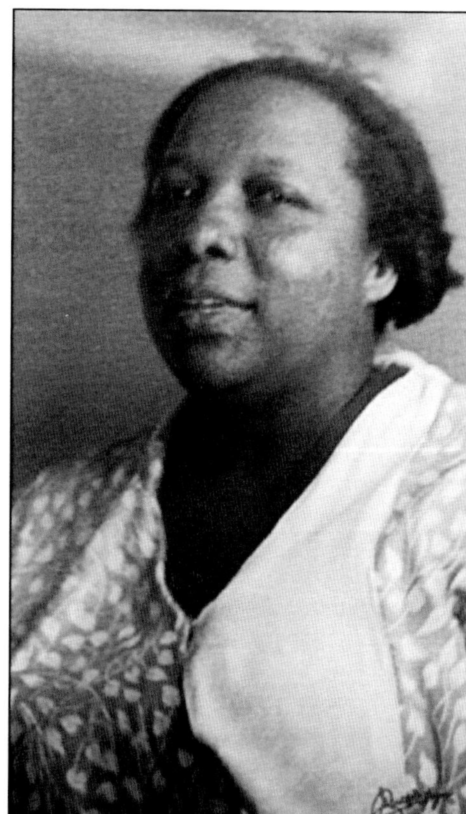

Mytris Ayers worked alongside her husband, Prof. T.C. Ayers, to teach the children of Solomon M. Coles School. (Courtesy of the Corpus Christi Museum of Science and History, John Fred'k "Doc" McGregor Photographic Collection.)

Principal and professor T.C. Ayers was a guiding light at Solomon M. Coles School. (Courtesy of the Corpus Christi Museum of Science and History, John Fred'k "Doc" McGregor Photographic Collection.)

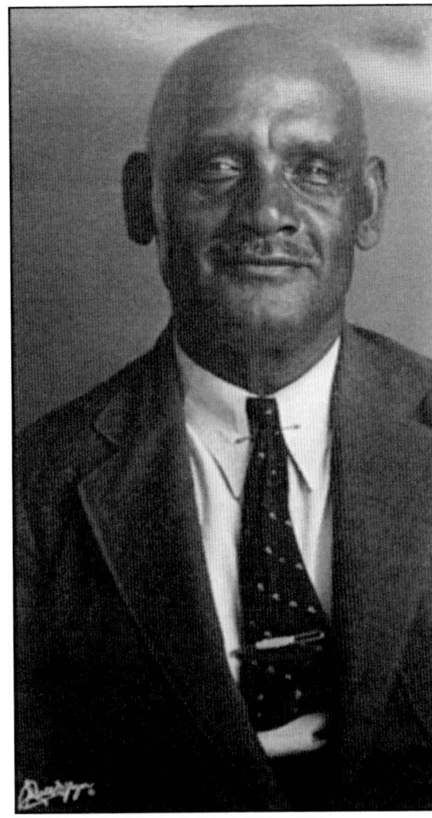

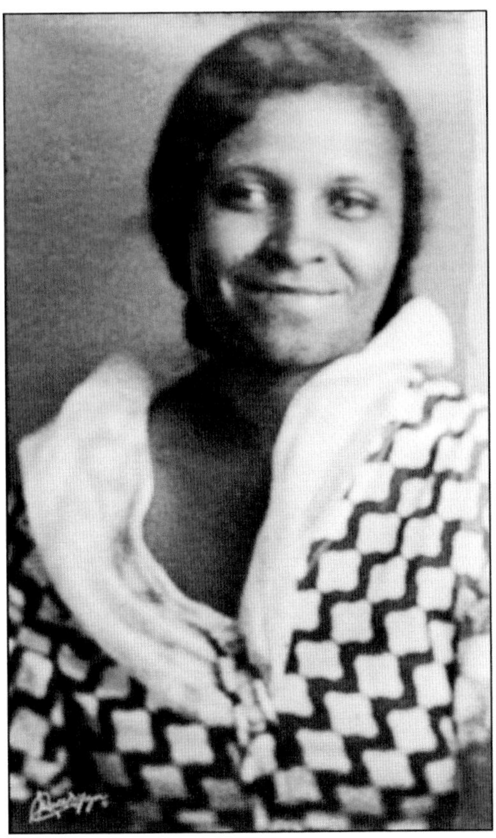

Another devoted Solomon M. Coles School instructor was P.D. Moore. (Courtesy of the Corpus Christi Museum of Science and History, John Fred'k "Doc" McGregor Photographic Collection.)

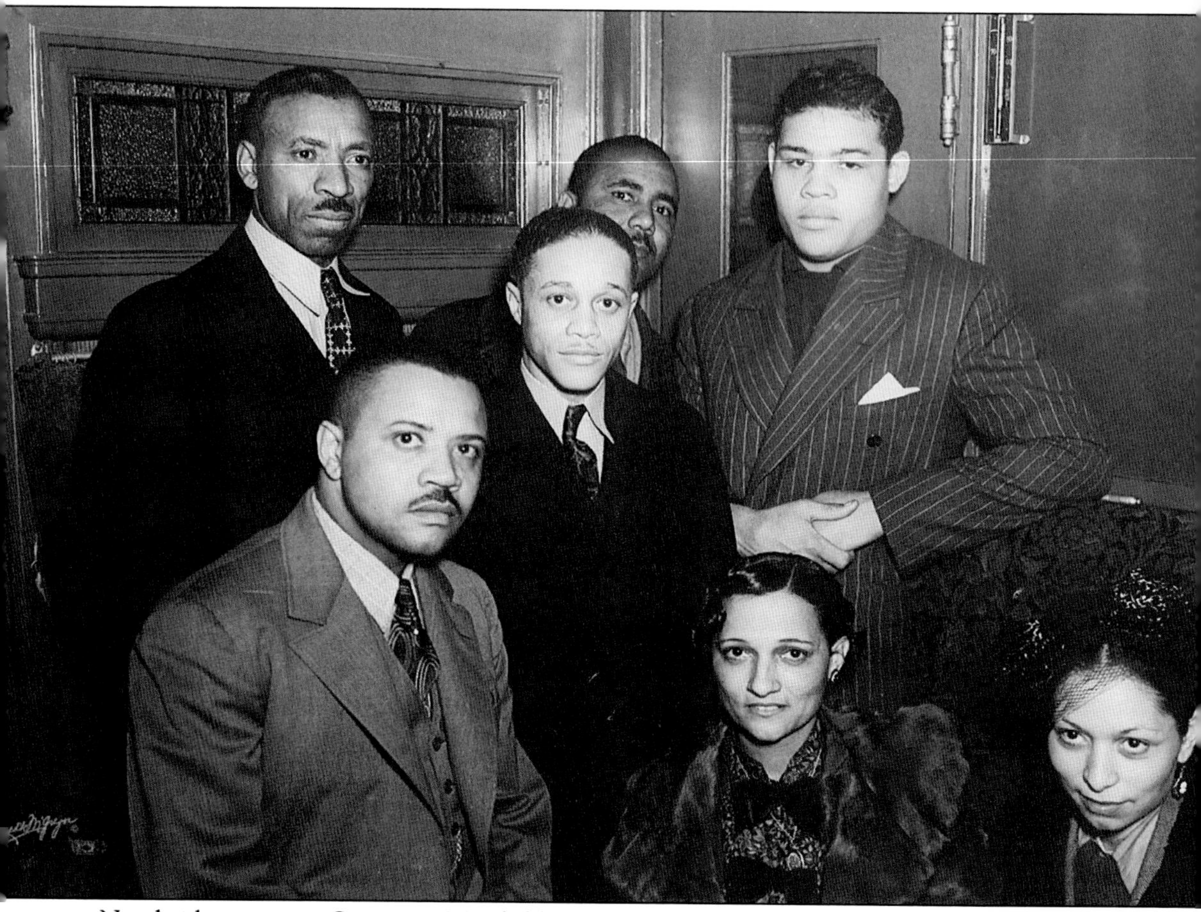

Northside ministers Spurgeon Mayfield (standing, left) and R.L. Palmer (standing, center) are among those hosting professional boxer and heavyweight champion Joe Louis (standing, right) during his 1937 visit to Corpus Christi. The others in this photograph are unidentified. (Courtesy of the Corpus Christi Museum of Science and History, John Fred'k "Doc" McGregor Photographic Collection.)

Three

Challenging Segregation 1941–1954

The 1940s started out dramatically for African Americans in Corpus Christi. Their population exploded, more than doubling in size to 4,545. To confront discriminatory behavior by white supremacists, Corpus Christi blacks capitalized on the local charter of the National Association for the Advancement of Colored People (NAACP)—considered the most important black civil rights organization. The Harlem Theater, a movie establishment for black patrons, opened in 1941, and the United States entered World War II in December of that year.

Nationally, and in Corpus Christi, African Americans were determined not only to fight for America in the war, but also to work for their own civil and political rights. World War II offered opportunities to all residents of Corpus Christi. It brought renewed emphasis on oil and gas production, on cotton crops, on port tonnage, and on improvements to the urban center. African Americans saw increased employment opportunities. At the end of the war, blacks, frequently led by H. Boyd Hall, continued their struggle for equitable living and working conditions.

On both the state and local levels, blacks challenged segregation. With *Smith v. Allwright* in 1944, the US Supreme Court struck down the nefarious white primary. Blacks could attend law school after Heman Marion Sweatt won his 1950 case against the University of Texas. In 1952, Del Mar College admitted black students even before the US Supreme Court's 1954 *Brown v. Board of Education* decision. Other changes occurred in Corpus Christi. The segregated lines at the IRS were abolished, black postal workers were hired, and facilities at the naval station desegregated. This was a time of transition for black residents of Corpus Christi.

Opportunities for recreation increased. The Harlem Theater continued to provide entertainment for black patrons. In 1950, the multicultural Galvan Ballroom opened, and well-known black entertainers, such as Duke Ellington, performed at the venue. Even though blacks could not socialize with white patrons, they could rent the ballroom for private parties and did so. Mostly, however, blacks still congregated in their churches, as well as local cafés, bars, and other segregated venues. Nonetheless, social changes began to occur as blacks in Corpus Christi asserted their rights in the years after the *Brown* decision.

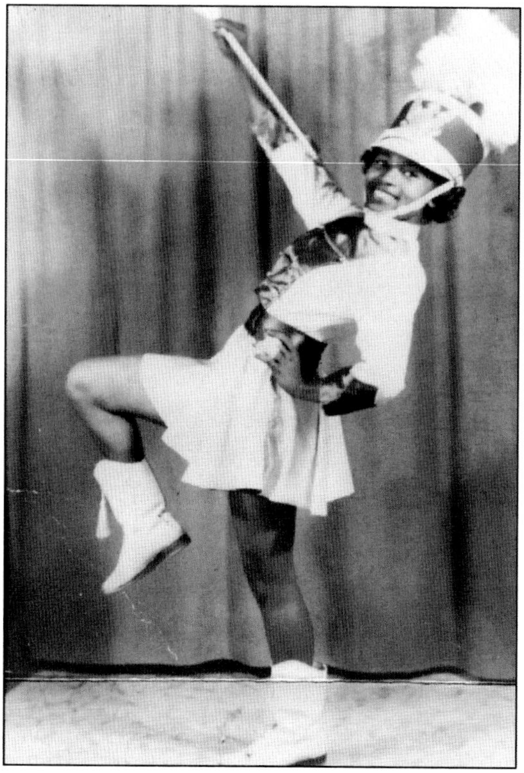

A 1954 graduate of Solomon M. Coles School, Helen Alexander (Crenshaw) poses in her typical stance for the stage camera. The leading school majorette for six years, she also danced, sang, and played piano. After graduation, she played with various professional artists and later became Corpus Christi's first black female drag racer, receiving over 20 trophies for racing victories. (Courtesy of Solomon M. Coles School.)

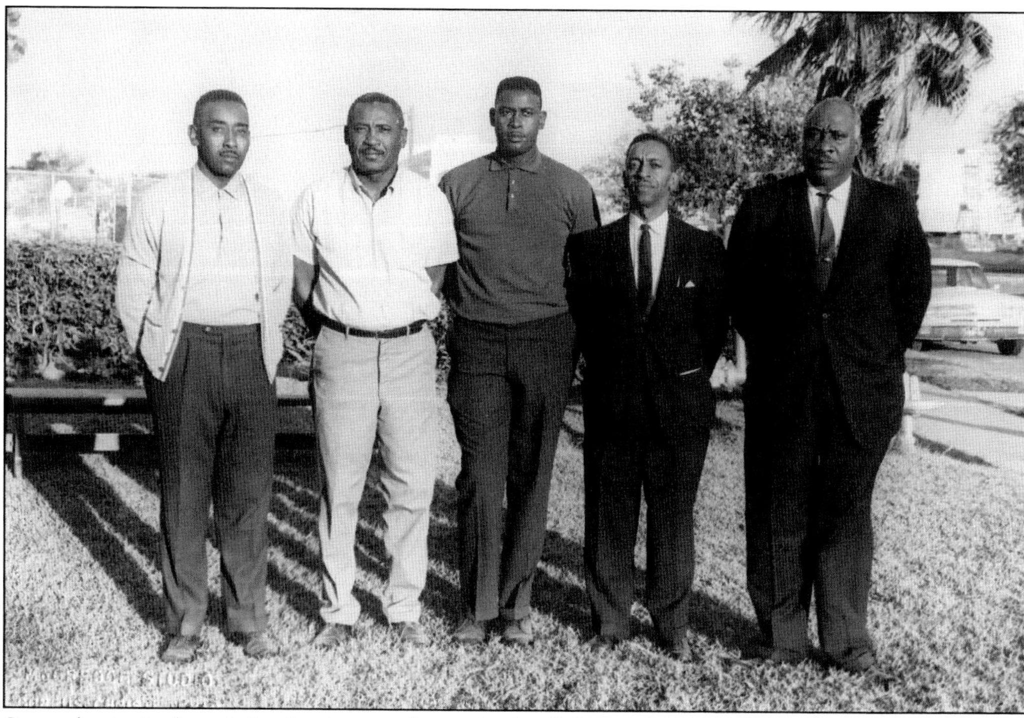

Several principals and dignitaries stand outside the Solomon M. Coles School, including William Johnson, George Hillman, and Bob Campbell. (Courtesy of Solomon M. Coles School.)

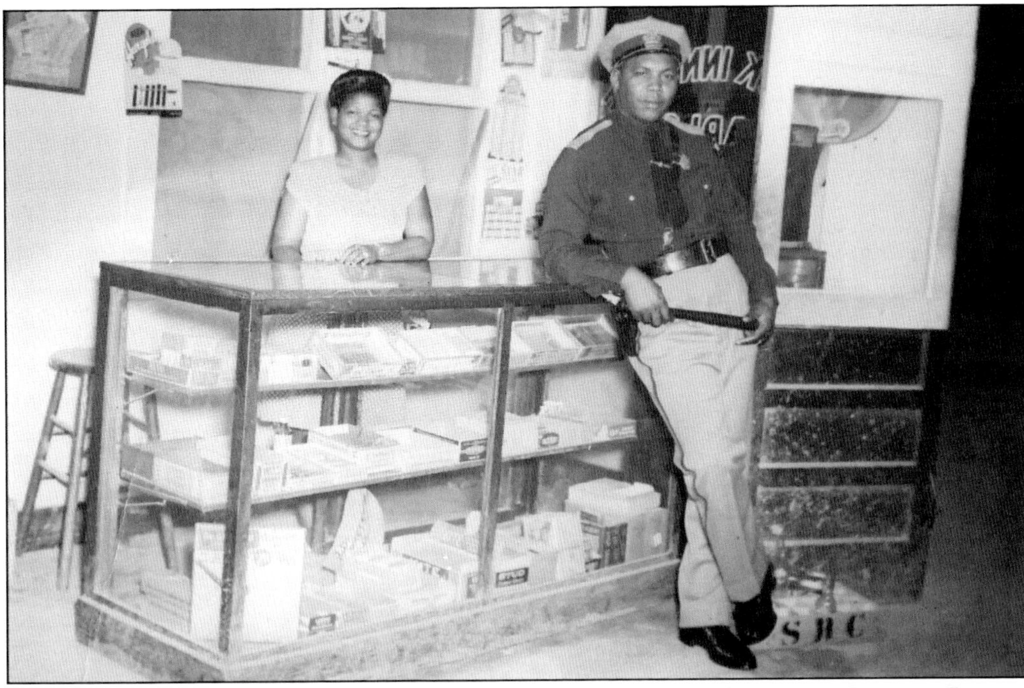

Vida Scott stands behind the counter of her establishment, the Harlem Liquor Store, on Ramirez Street. Local law enforcement, also pictured, often visited the business to ensure its security. (Courtesy of Dr. Gloria Randle Scott.)

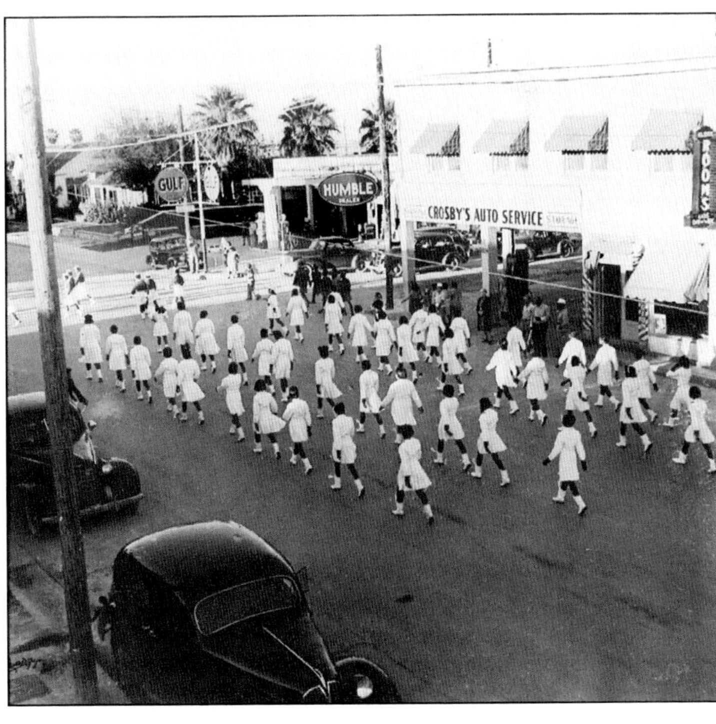

Northside neighbors cheer for participants in the Solomon M. Coles School homecoming parade on November 4, 1941. (Courtesy of the Corpus Christi Museum of Science and History, John Fred'k "Doc" McGregor Photographic Collection.)

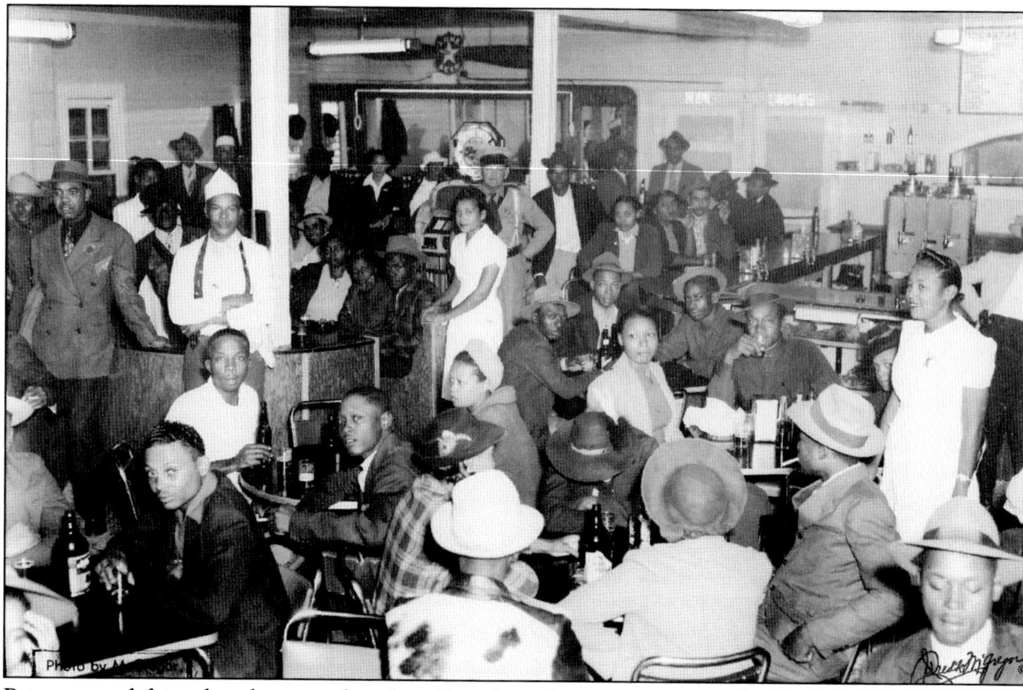

Patrons and friends relax at a local café and exchange news on the happenings of the day. (Courtesy of the Corpus Christi Museum of Science and History, John Fred'k "Doc" McGregor Photographic Collection.)

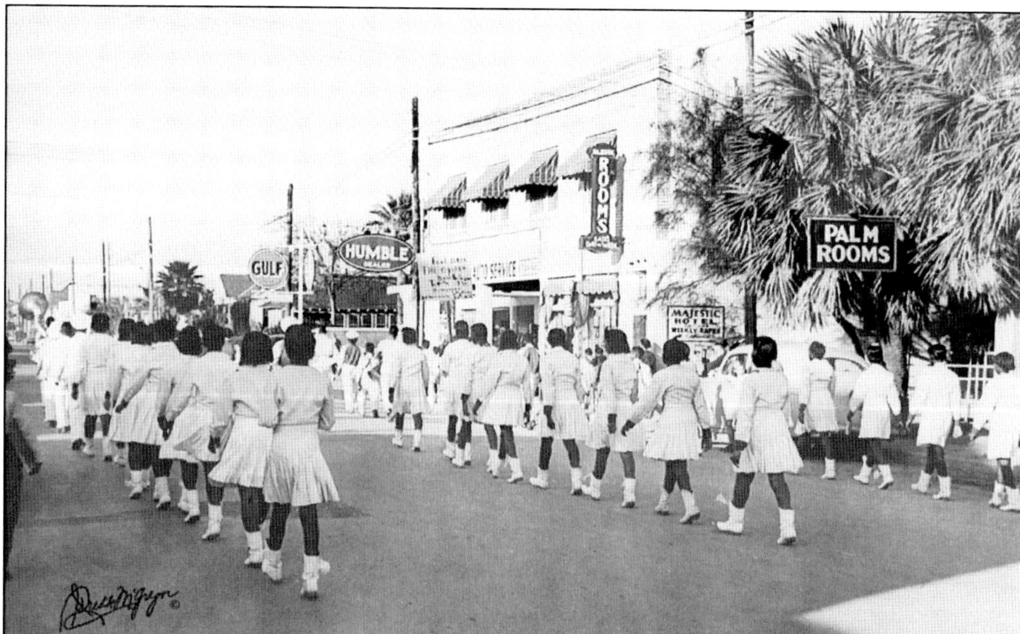

On December 30, 1941, the Solomon M. Coles pep squad marches down Northside for a New Year's Eve parade. Since the group's homecoming parade appearance six weeks earlier, the United States had gone to war, and the members' lives would change drastically. (Courtesy of the Corpus Christi Museum of Science and History, John Fred'k "Doc" McGregor Photographic Collection.)

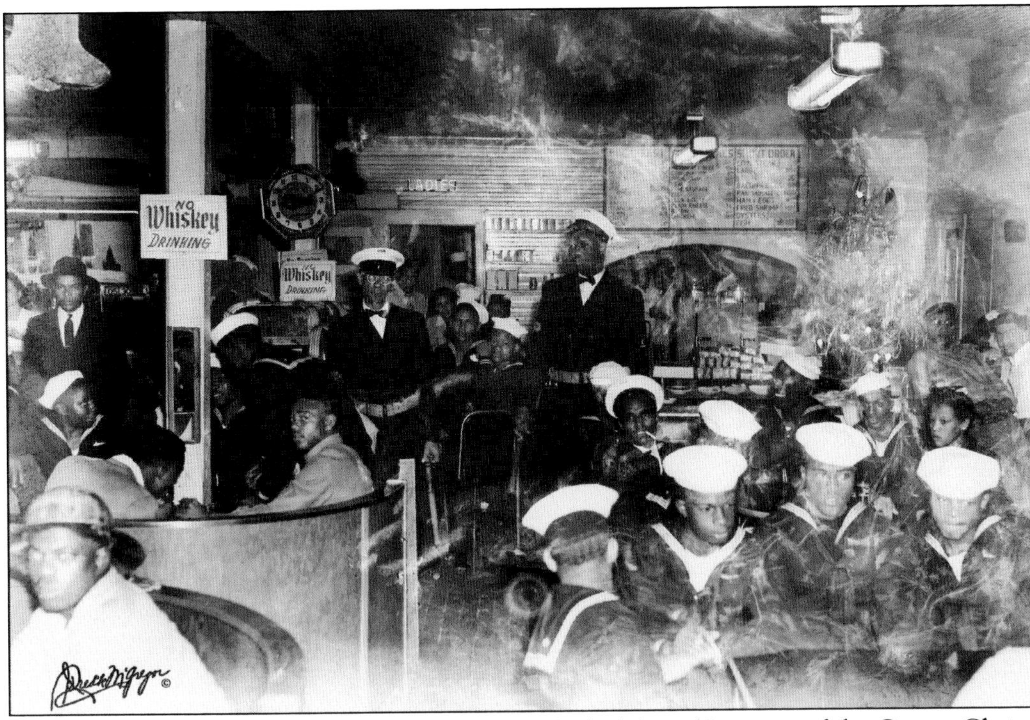

Military men enjoy dinner at a local café during the holidays. (Courtesy of the Corpus Christi Museum of Science and History, John Fred'k "Doc" McGregor Photographic Collection.)

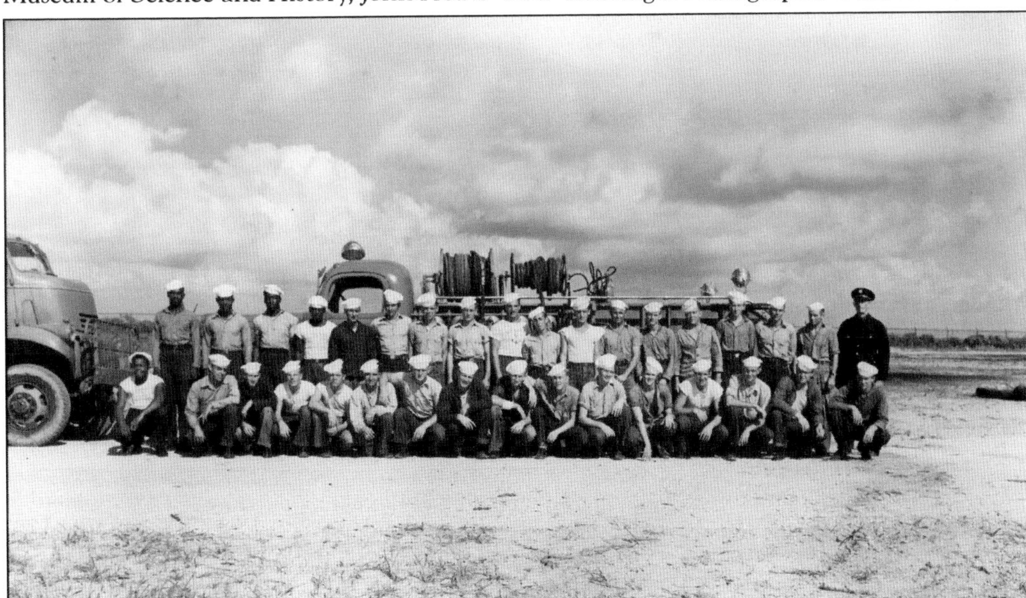

Unidentified sailors pose in front of their heavy equipment at Naval Air Station Corpus Christi. Although the Navy was the first of the armed forces to integrate, at the time of this photograph black sailors experienced various forms of segregation but still diligently worked with their peers to get the job done. (Courtesy Texas A&M University-Corpus Christi Special Collections and Archives, Smylie Collection 29.21.)

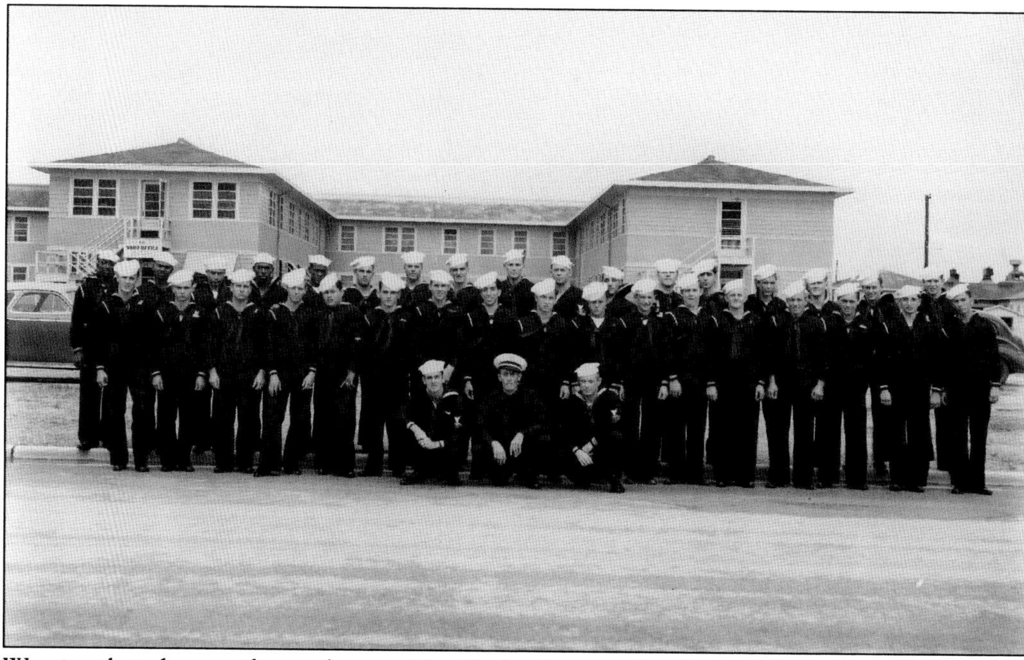

Wearing their dress uniforms, these unidentified sailors stand in front of the barracks at Naval Air Station Corpus Christi. Pres. Franklin Delano Roosevelt approved the proposal for the building of the base, and it was dedicated on March 12, 1941. (Courtesy Texas A&M University-Corpus Christi Special Collections and Archives, Smylie Collection 29.21.)

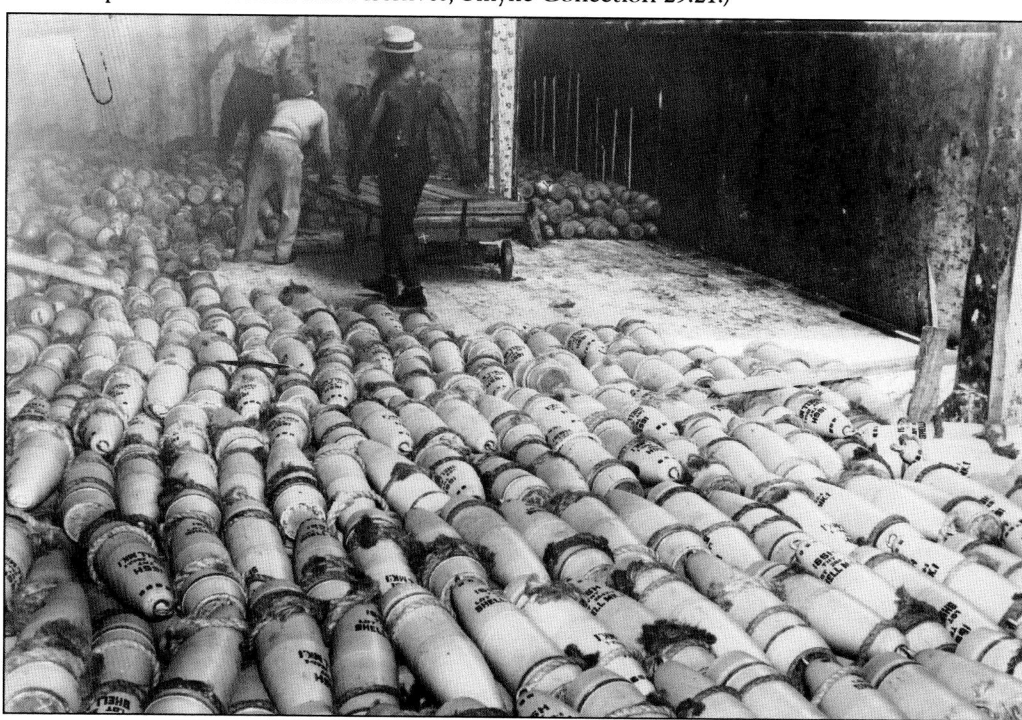

These men have the daunting task of loading these armaments at the port. (Courtesy of Texas A&M University-Corpus Christi Special Collections and Archives, Smylie Collection 29.21.)

Many local men found employment in rebuilding the Nueces Bay Causeway. This causeway had to be rebuilt several times because of storms, flooding, and general usage. (Courtesy of the *Corpus Christi Caller-Times*.)

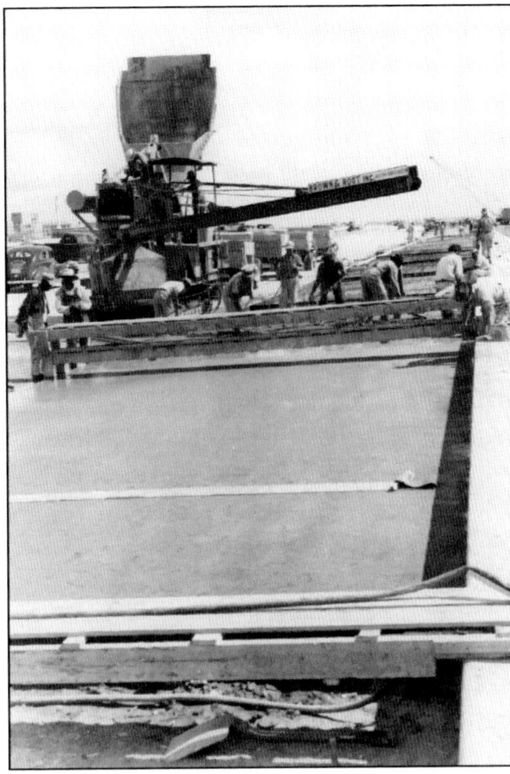

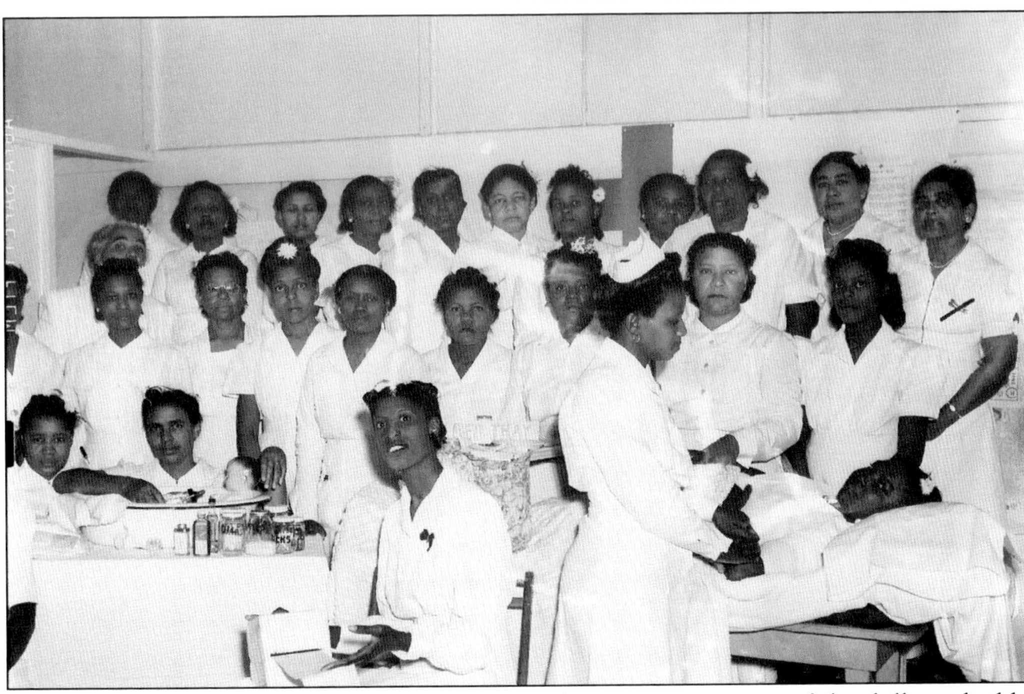

Observing patients and practicing pediatric procedures were just some of the skills studied by these unidentified nursing students in early 1945. (Courtesy of the Corpus Christi Museum of Science and History, John Fred'k "Doc" McGregor Photographic Collection.)

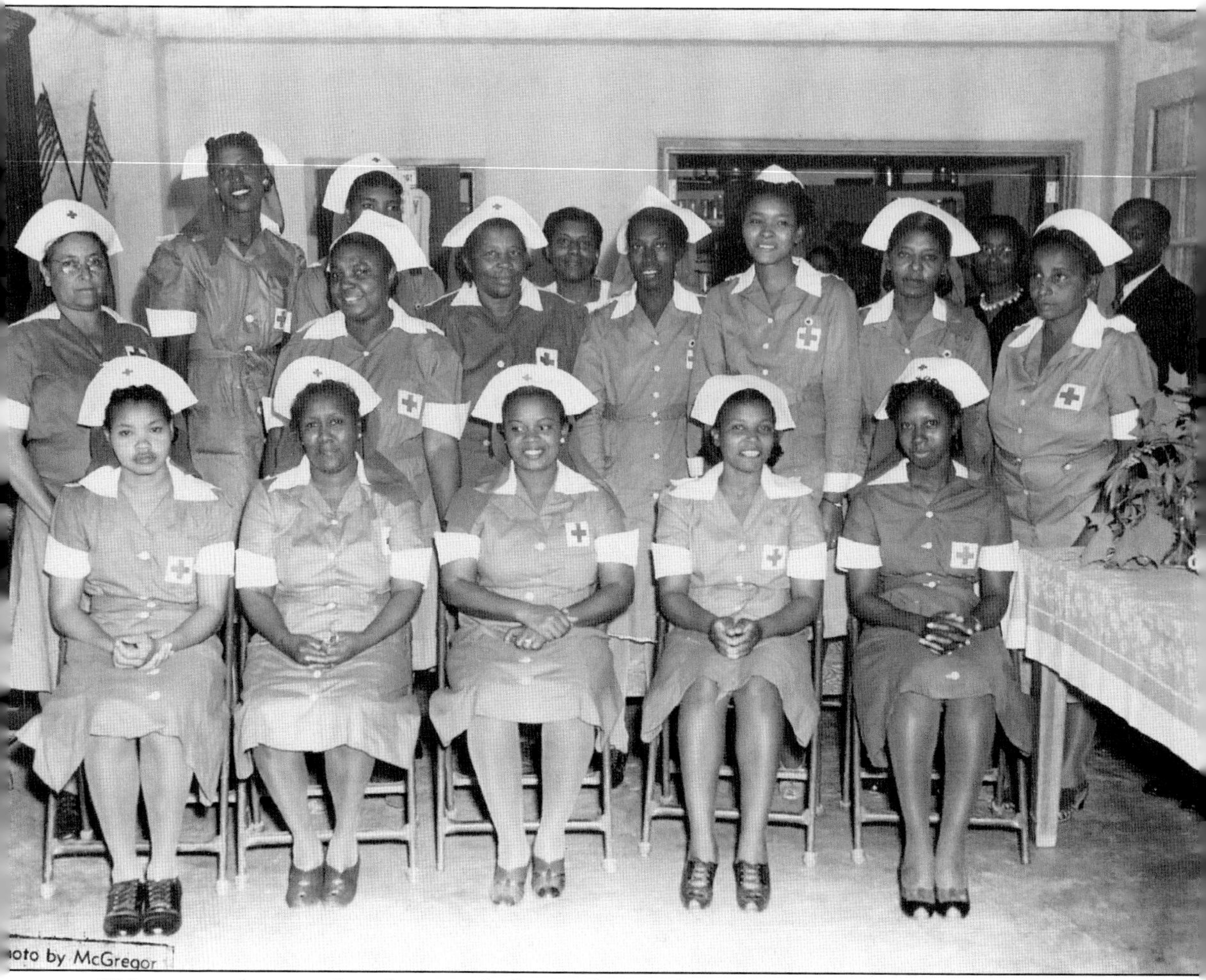

Taken at graduation, this photograph shows a happy class of licensed nursing professionals ready to help the war effort in hospitals and on the home front. No one is identified in this photograph. (Courtesy of the Corpus Christi Museum of Science and History, John Fred'k "Doc" McGregor Photographic Collection.)

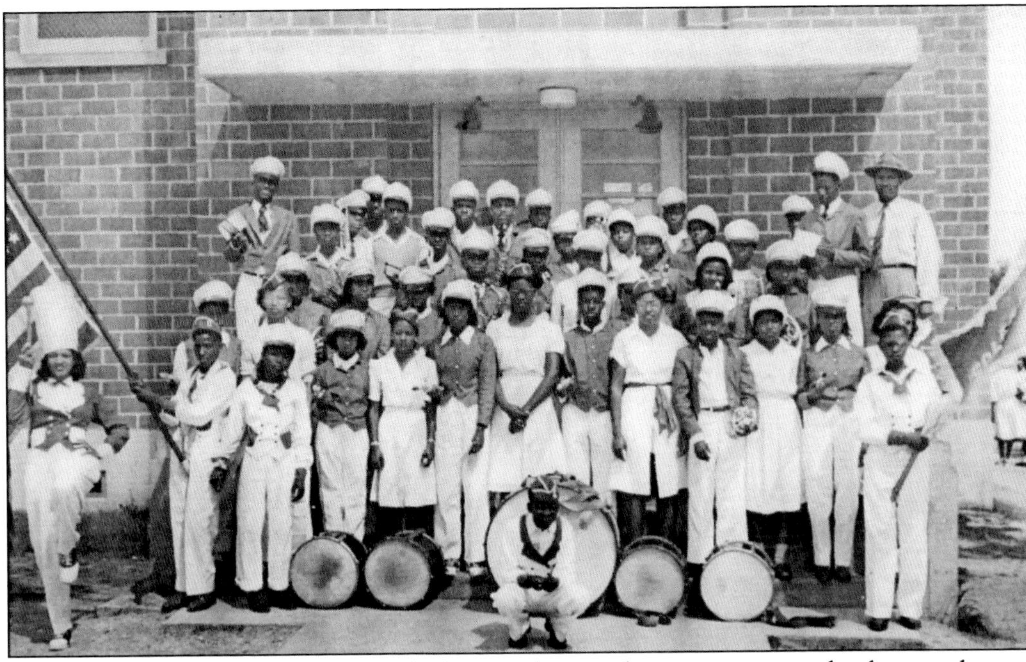

The Solomon M. Coles School band of 1948, along with its majorette and color guard, poses proudly in front of the school. (Courtesy of Solomon M. Coles School.)

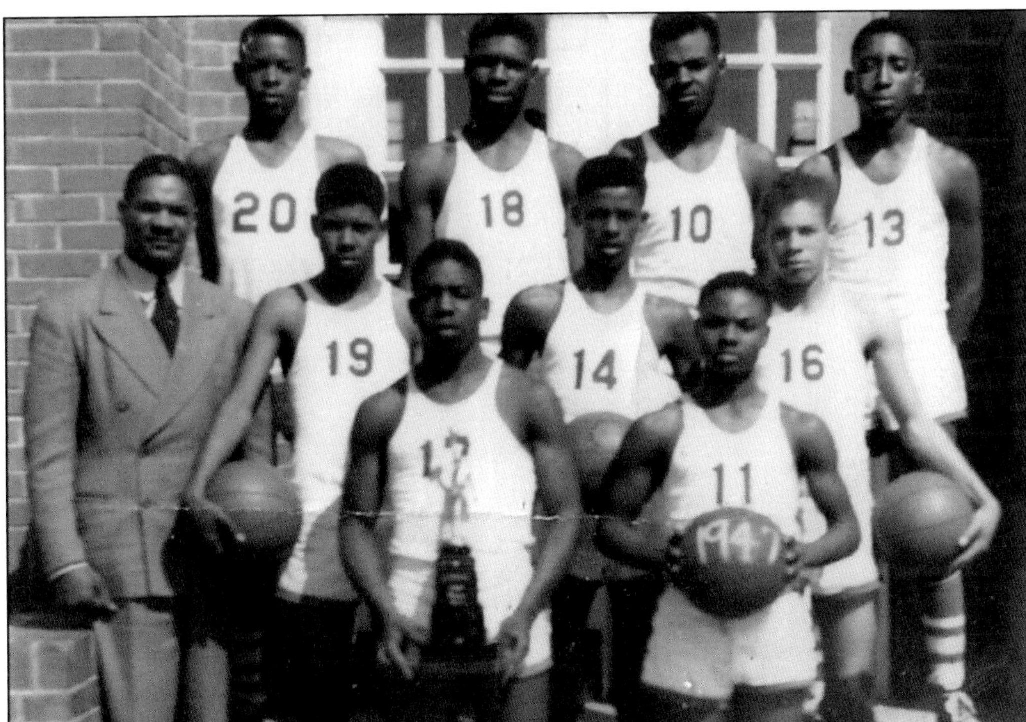

The 1947 basketball team and its coach stand proudly displaying their trophy in front of Solomon M. Coles School. No one is identified. (Courtesy of the Corpus Christi NAACP.)

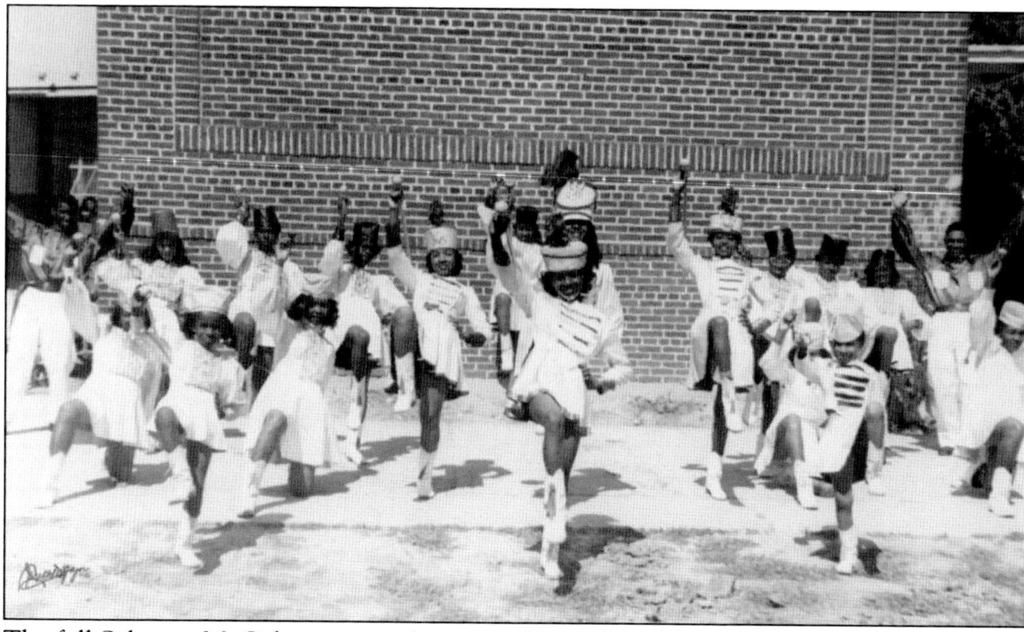

The full Solomon M. Coles pep squad poses in front of the school in October 1951. (Courtesy of the Corpus Christi Museum of Science and History, John Fred'k "Doc" McGregor Photographic Collection.)

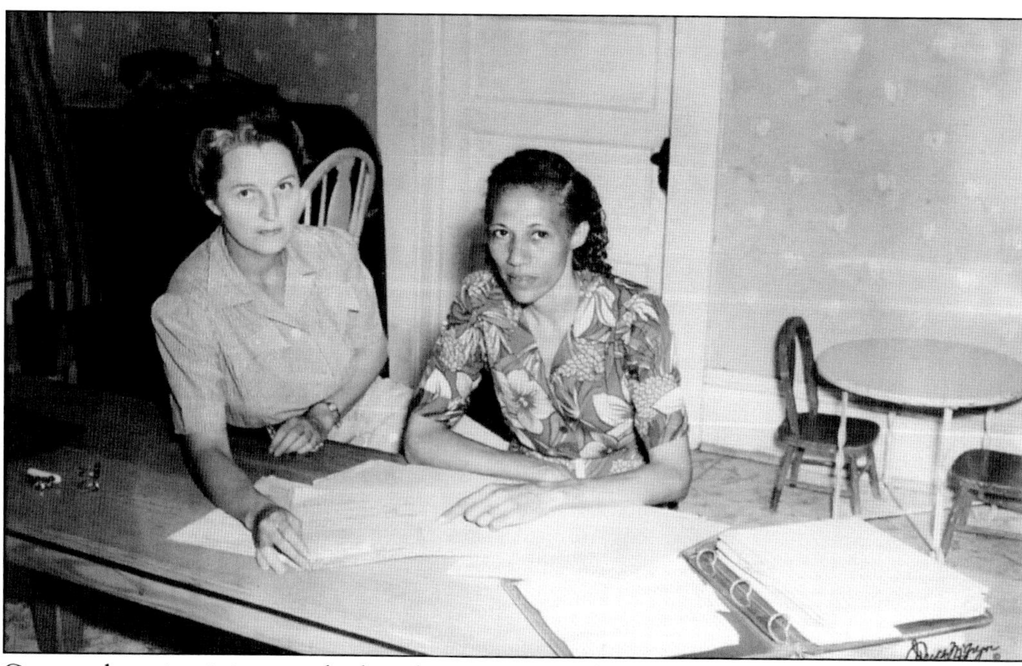

Constantly maintaining standards in her capacity as director of the Bethune Day Nursery on the Northside, Bernice Leonard (right) is shown going over papers in the fall of 1942 with an unidentified woman. (Courtesy of the Corpus Christi Museum of Science and History, John Fred'k "Doc" McGregor Photographic Collection.)

Providing one of the most important services on the Northside has been the Bethune Day Nursery. Young children receive hot meals and warm attention while their mothers work away from home. (Courtesy of the Corpus Christi Museum of Science and History, John Fred'k "Doc" McGregor Photographic Collection.)

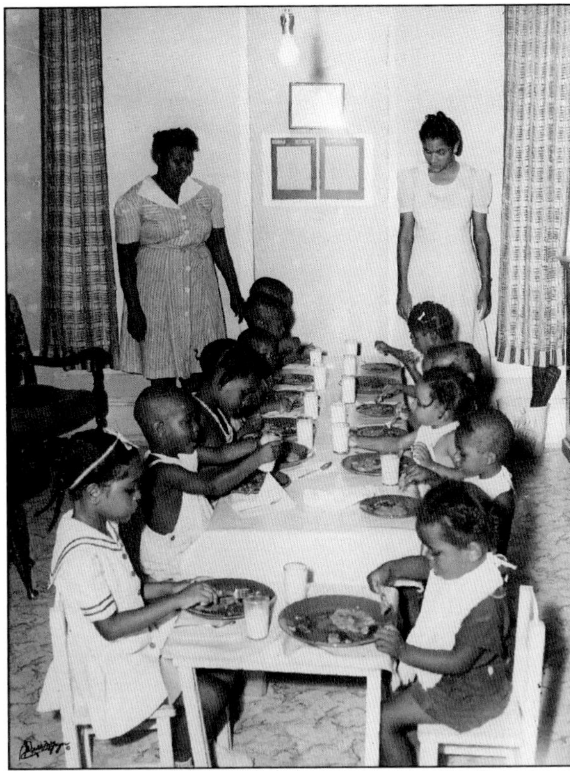

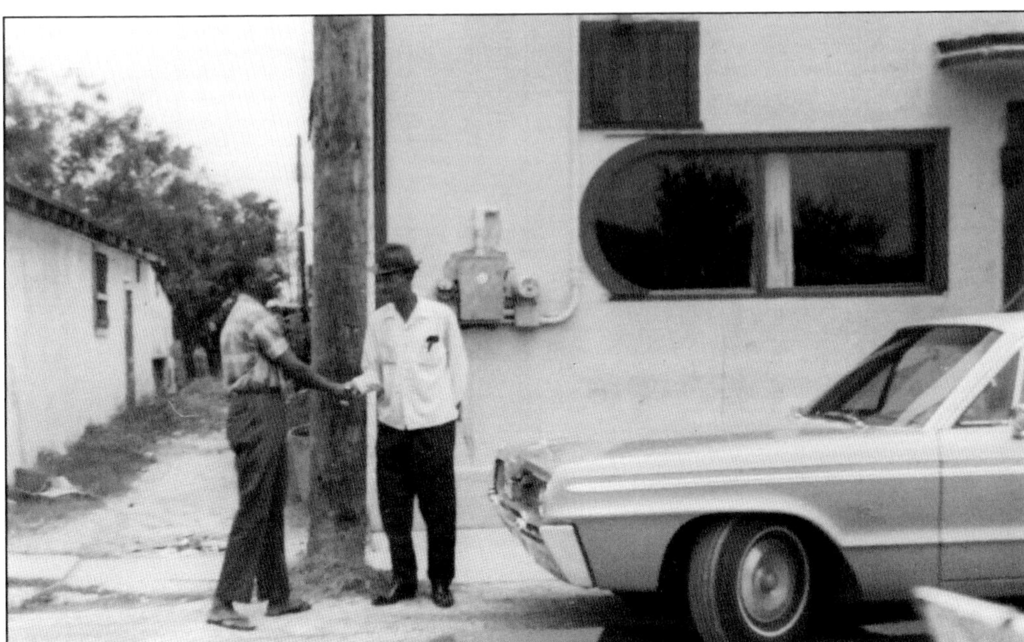

Will Scott Sr. (right) and Will B. Scott shake hands in front of the Cotton Club on Ramirez Street. The Cotton Club was a well-known gathering place for many in the neighborhood. The building to the left housed the Harlem Liquor Store owned by Will Sr. (Courtesy of Dr. Gloria Randle Scott.)

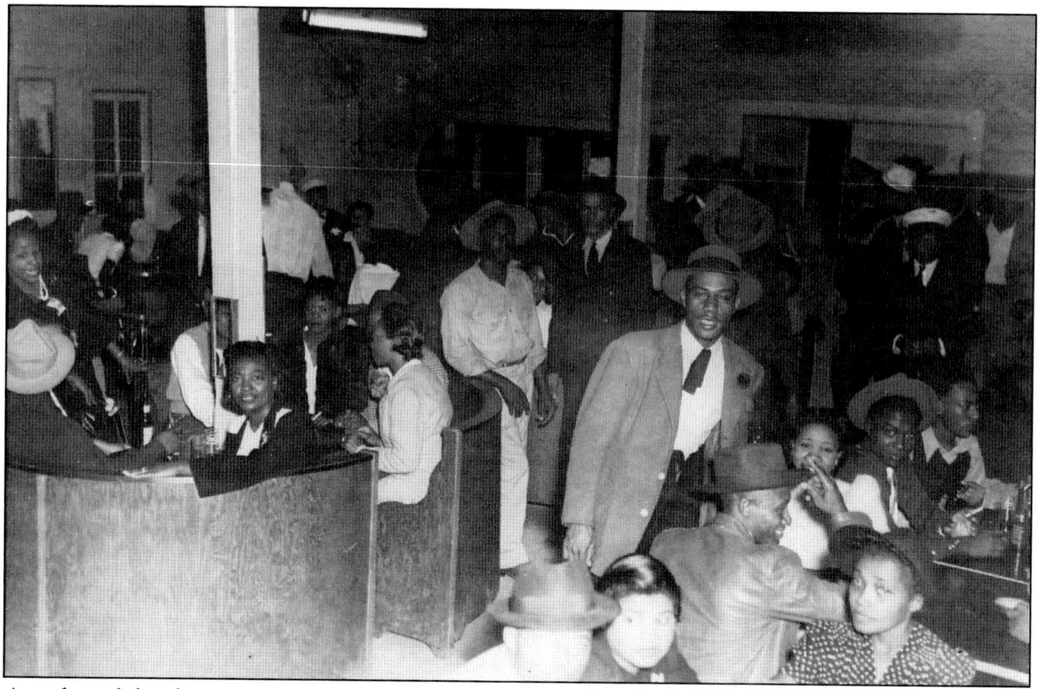

Another club of interest was Crecy's Place, commonly known as the Down Beat Club. Many gathered at this establishment to meet friends and enjoy each other's company. (Courtesy of Texas A&M University-Corpus Christi Special Collections and Archives, Smylie Collection 26.6.)

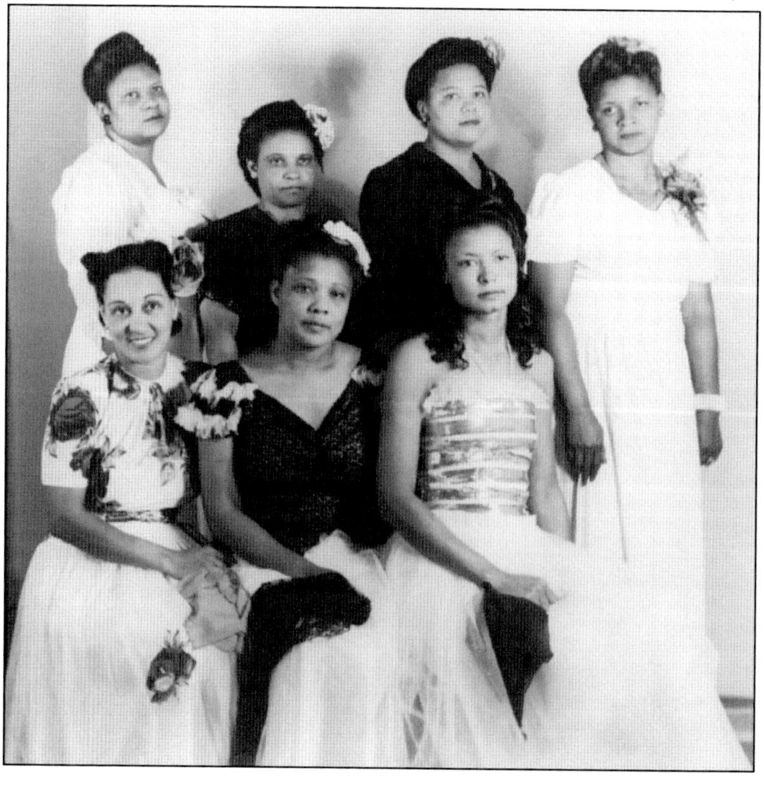

Social events enlivened the Progressive Women's Club work, including formal dances like the one these women are posing at in 1947. (Courtesy of the Corpus Christi Museum of Science and History, Alclair Pleasant Collection.)

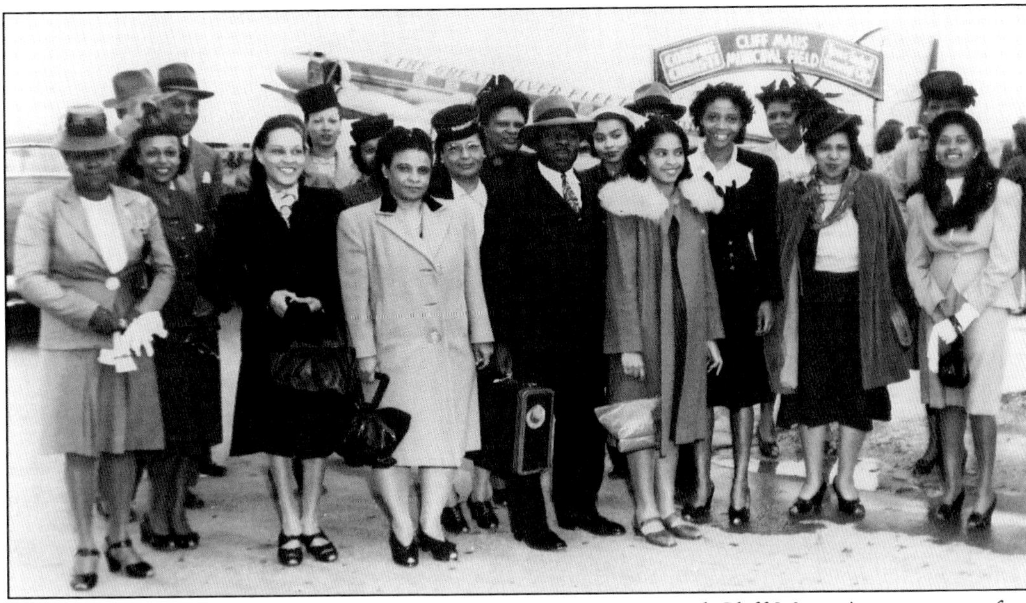

Out-of-town speakers broadened the Northside experience, and Cliff Maus Airport was often their arrival point. Here, a sizeable gathering—including, in no particular order, Alma Henderson, Alclair Pleasant, Portia Moore Hervey, Annie Bohman, the Reverend Sidney Smith, Helen Corline, the Reverend Claud Black, Margie Callahan, Fela Sweatt, and Gertrude Booker Woodson—welcomes a guest. (Courtesy of the Corpus Christi Museum of Science and History, Alclair Pleasant Collection.)

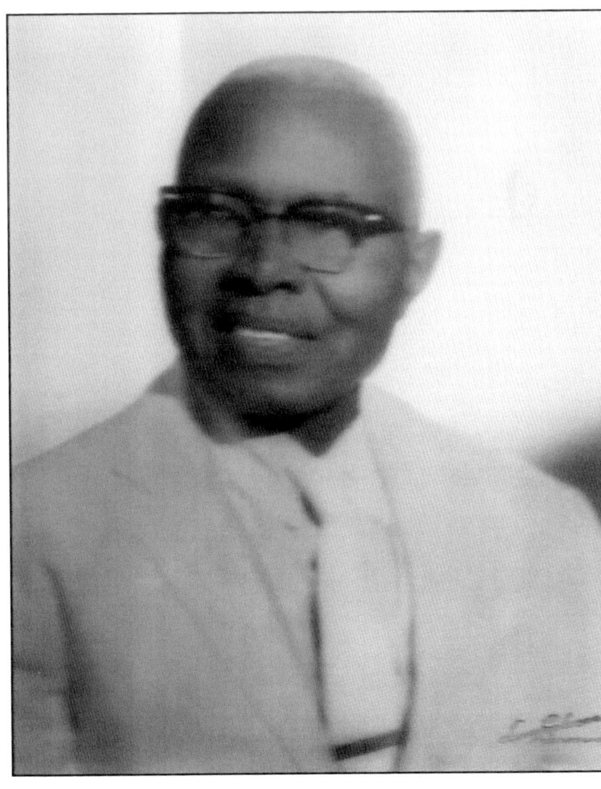

Rev. Edward Ray Russell organized the Rising Star Baptist Church in 1948. The congregation met in his home for a few years before moving to Deacon Collin's tool shed and later to yet another home before a church could be built. Russell pastored Rising Star until 1966 and enlarged the church to include 36 members. (Courtesy of Rising Star Baptist Church.)

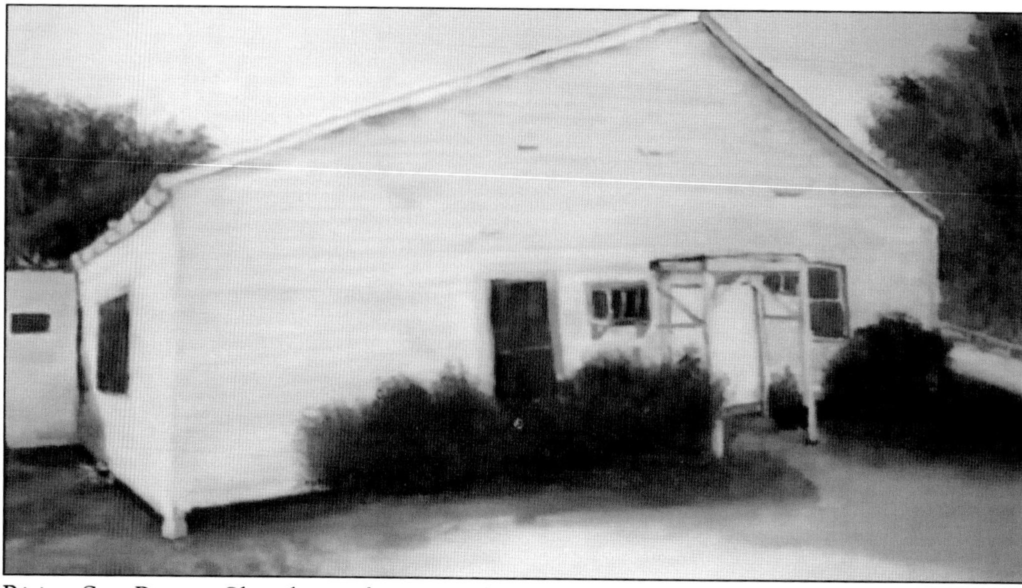

Rising Star Baptist Church was first started by Reverend Russell in 1948 and moved to this building in 1953. This house of worship stood at 4733 Barrera Street. Because of the church's presence, Barrera Street was the first street paved in the Molina area. (Courtesy of Rising Star Baptist Church.)

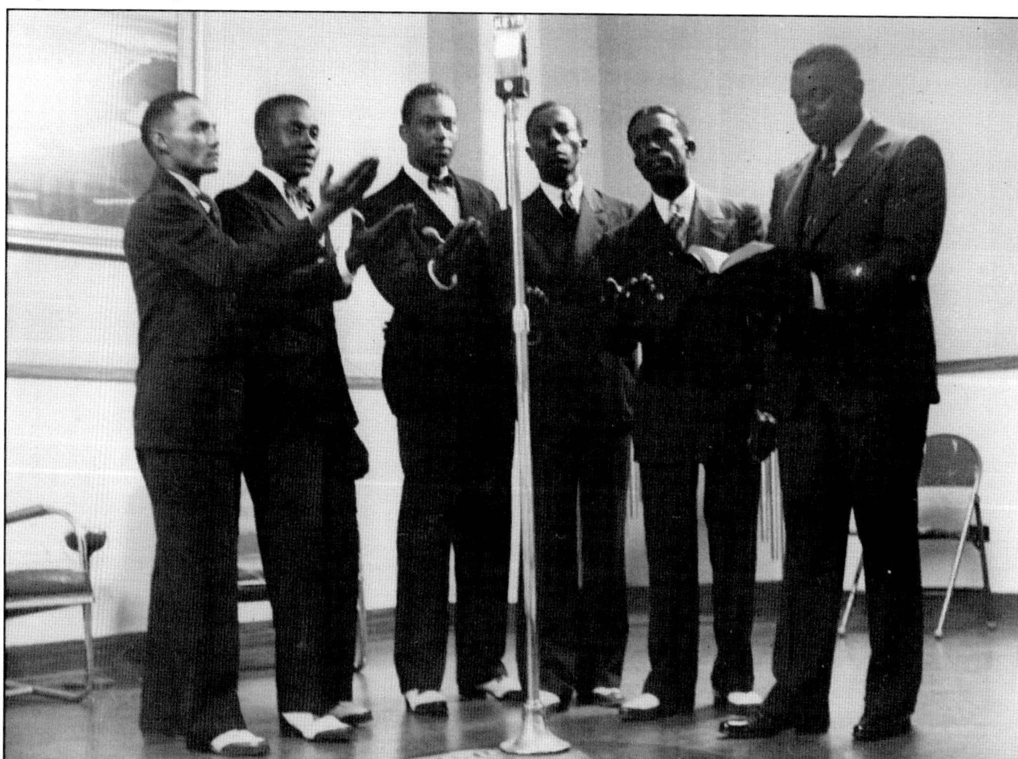

This unidentified group sings gospel over the radio at the KEYS radio station. (Courtesy of Texas A&M University-Corpus Christi Special Collections and Archives, Smylie Collection 28.32.)

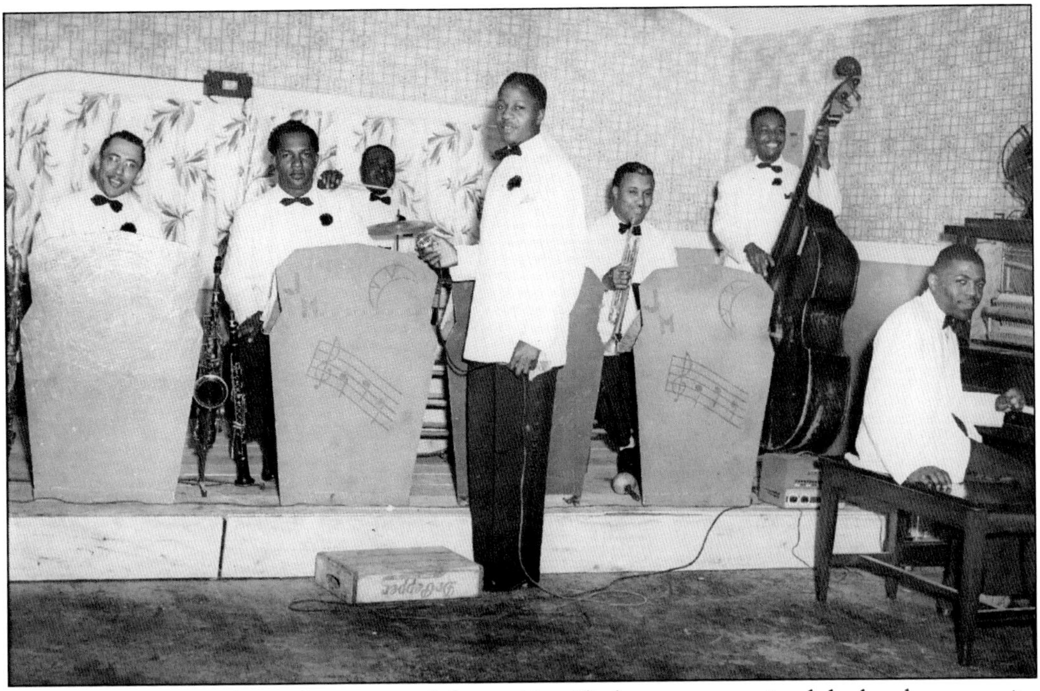

Band music was popular at this time, and this unidentified group entertained the local community and provided music for dances and other occasions. (Courtesy of Texas A&M University-Corpus Christi Special Collections and Archives, Smylie Collection 28.5.)

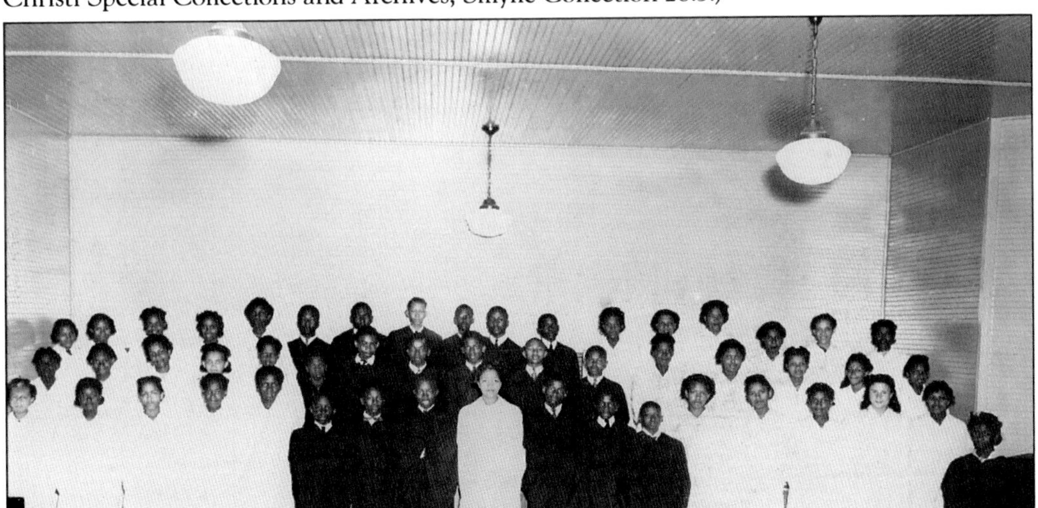

St. Matthew Missionary Baptist Church choir members pose in their gowns for this 1941 picture. (Courtesy of the Corpus Christi Museum of Science and History, John Fred'k "Doc" McGregor Photographic Collection.)

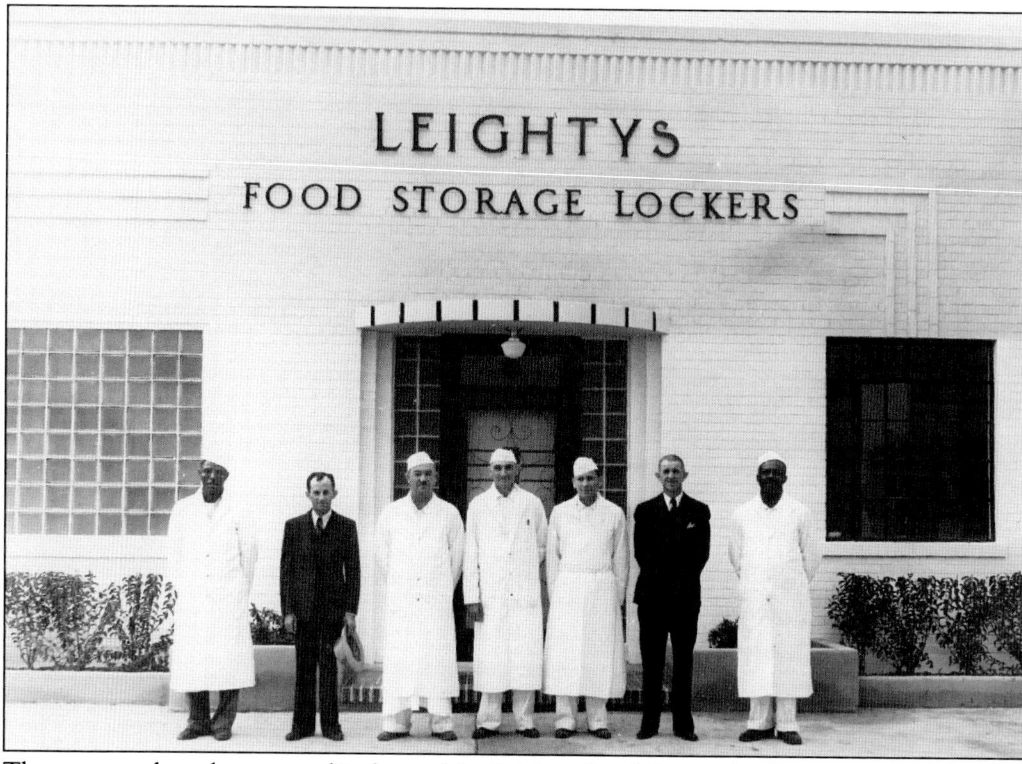

The owner and employees stand in front of the Leightys Food Storage Lockers. No one is identified in this photograph. (Courtesy of Texas A&M University-Corpus Christi Special Collections and Archives, Smylie Collection 26.6.)

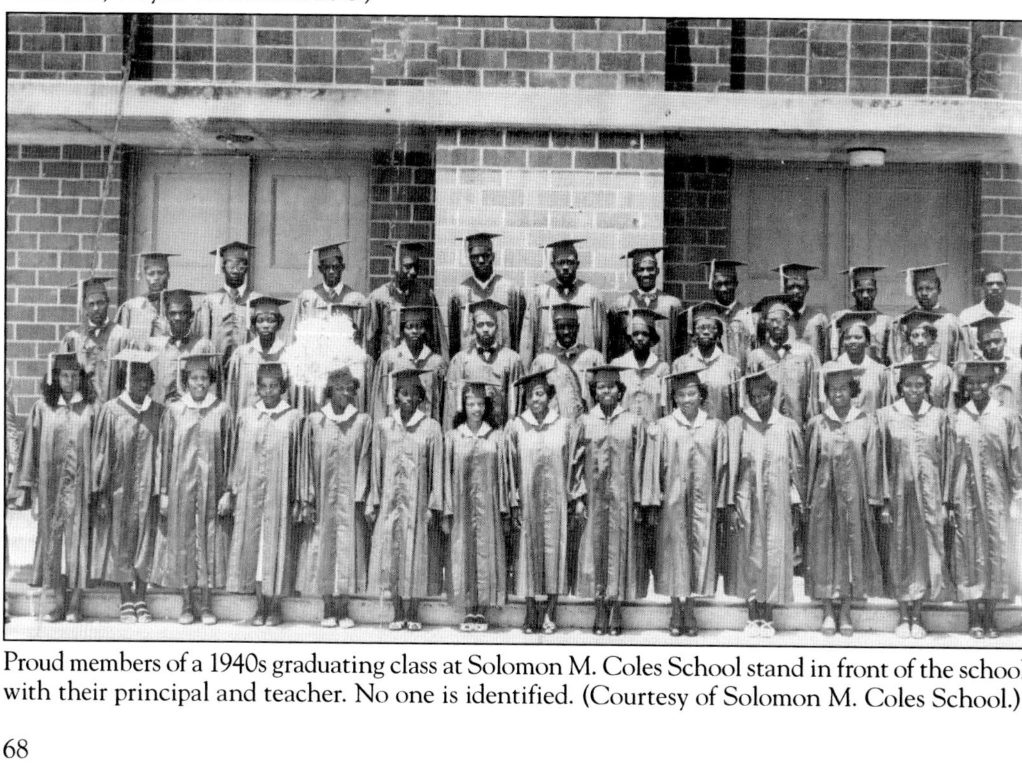

Proud members of a 1940s graduating class at Solomon M. Coles School stand in front of the school with their principal and teacher. No one is identified. (Courtesy of Solomon M. Coles School.)

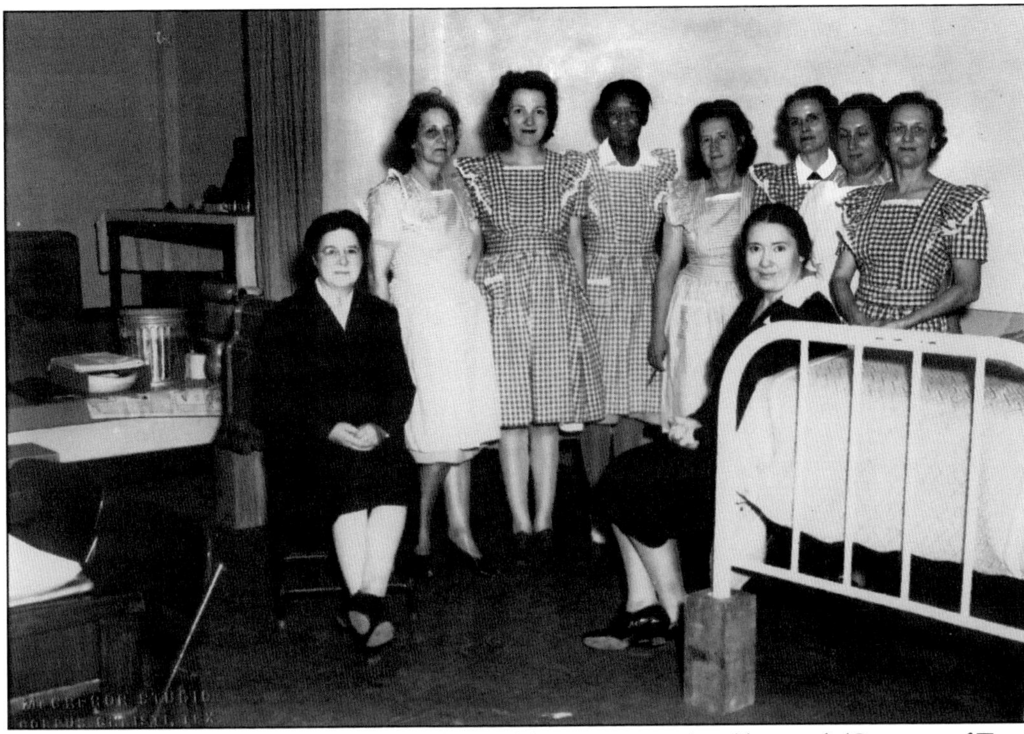

Unidentified hospital volunteers pose in front of the camera at a local hospital. (Courtesy of Texas A&M University-Corpus Christi Special Collections and Archives, Smylie Collection 28.14.)

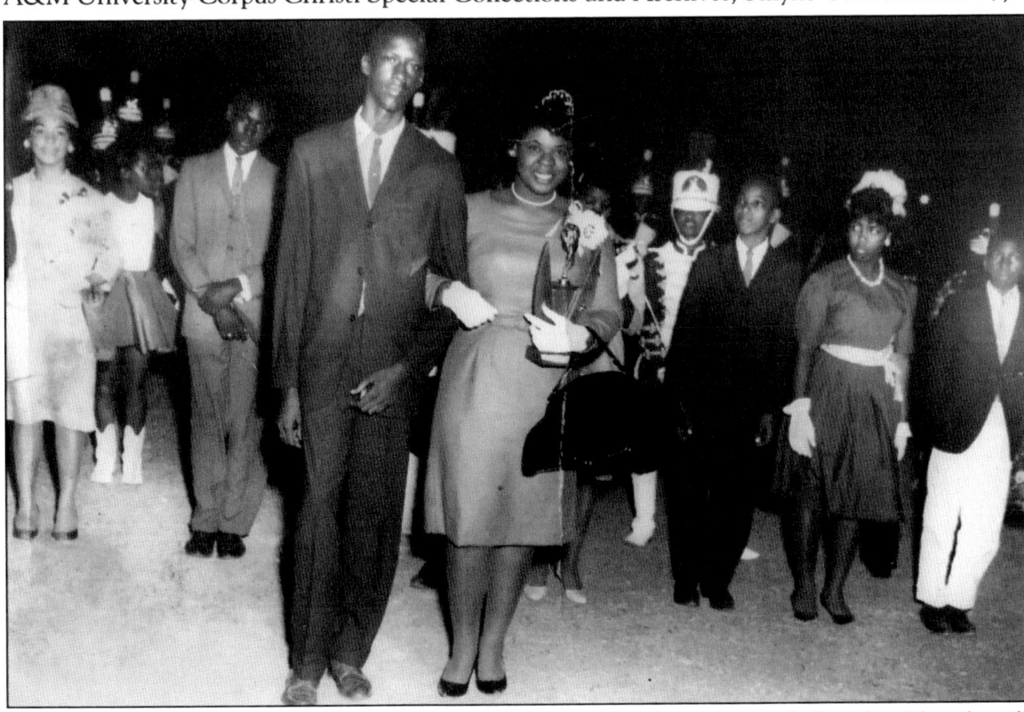

An unidentified homecoming king and queen, along with classmates and the school band, walk off the field after receiving their crown and trophy. (Courtesy of Solomon M. Coles School.)

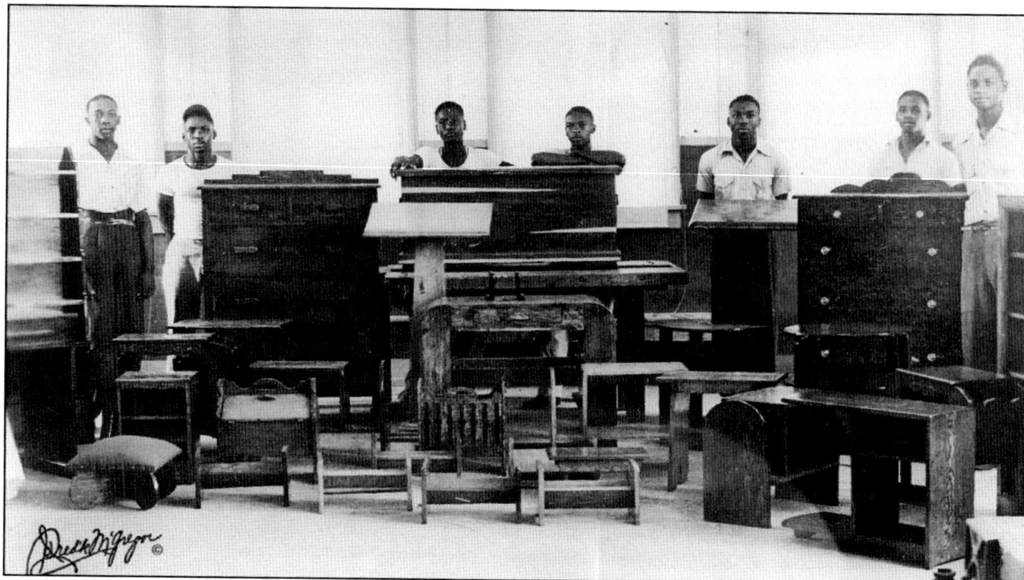

Surrounded by their craftsmanship are unidentified members of the Solomon M. Coles School woodworking class in 1943. (Courtesy of the Corpus Christi Museum of Science and History, John Fred'k "Doc" McGregor Photographic Collection.)

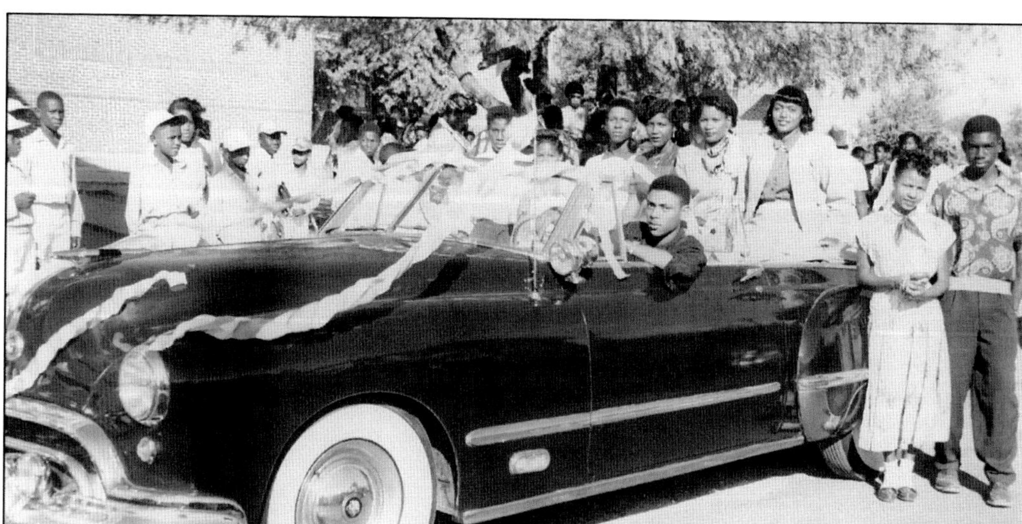

Decorated automobiles were part of the 1950s Solomon M. Coles School football parades. (Courtesy of the Corpus Christi Museum of Science and History, John Fred'k "Doc" McGregor Photographic Collection.)

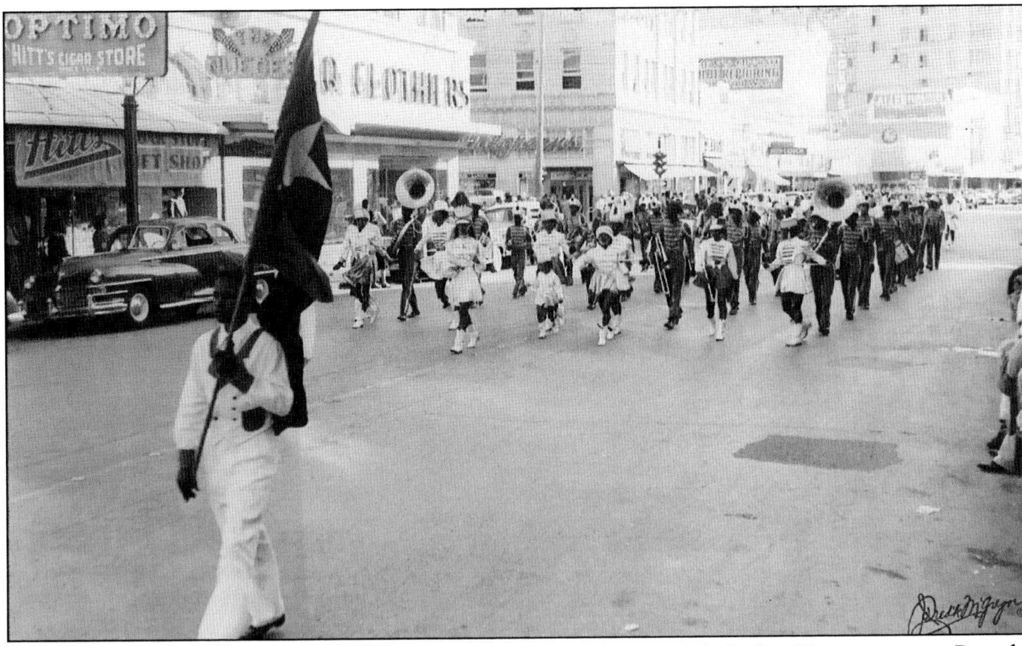

The flag corps and the pep squad head the 1950 Solomon M. Coles Homecoming Parade. (Courtesy of the Corpus Christi Museum of Science and History, John Fred'k "Doc" McGregor Photographic Collection.)

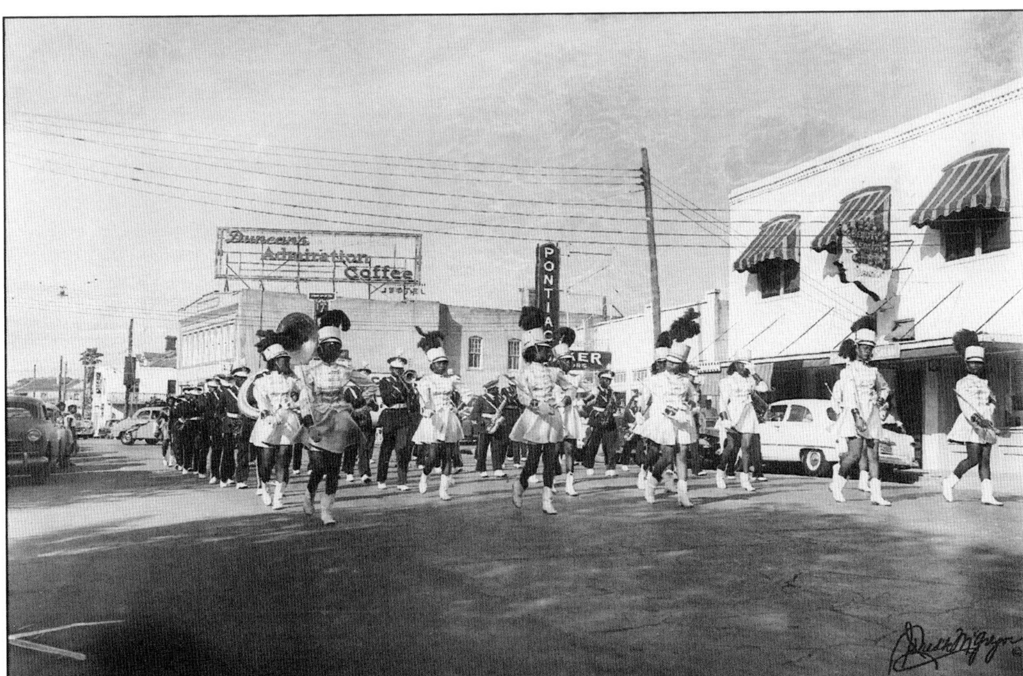

The Solomon M. Coles School marching band leads the homecoming parade of 1951 through the streets of Northside. (Courtesy of the Corpus Christi Museum of Science and History, John Fred'k "Doc" McGregor Photographic Collection.)

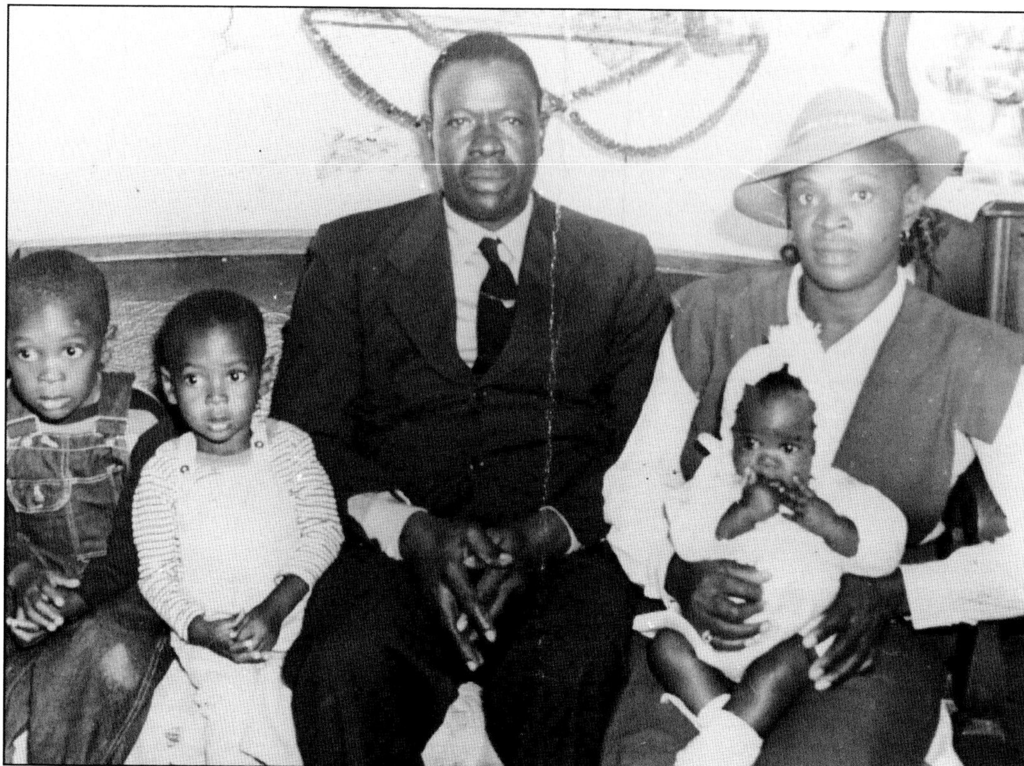

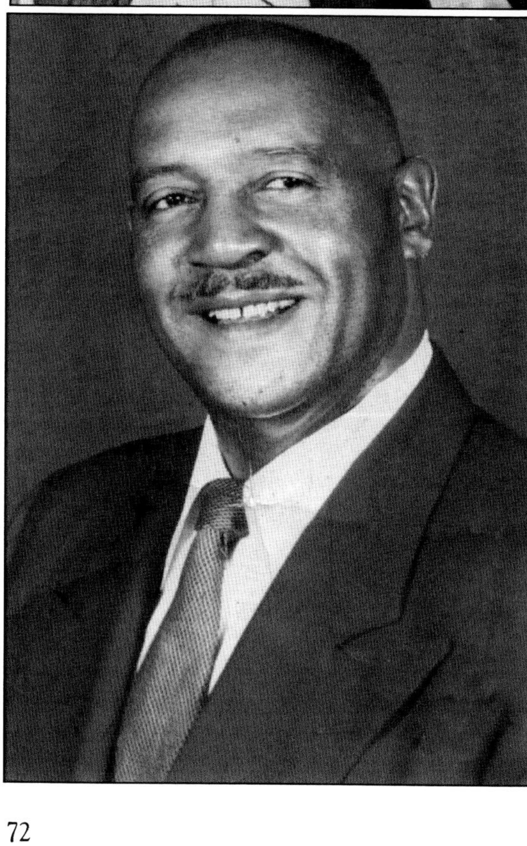

Stephney "Tony" Lott (center) poses with his family, who are, from left to right, Stephney Jr., Fletcher, wife Mary, and baby Shirley Doris Lott (later Rhodes). Tony worked as a cowboy from the age of 12 and helped his father on the Welder Ranch. Tony retired from the O'Connor's ranch and moved to Corpus Christi. He continued to ride horses until well after he turned 88 years old. He eventually became pastor of Westhaven Baptist Church. (Courtesy of Shirley Doris Lott Rhodes.)

Dr. Henry Boyd Hall was born in Palestine, Texas. In 1937, he moved from Seguin with his wife and teacher, Olivia Williams, to Corpus Christi, where he practiced dentistry for more than 36 years. A noted community activist, Hall spearheaded the local branch of the NAACP and later became state president. He was instrumental in desegregating housing and schools as well as state and federal facilities in Corpus Christi. (Courtesy of the Meharry Medical College Archives.)

Four

Asserting Rights 1955–1974

A year following the 1954 *Brown* decision, the Corpus Christi Independent School District continued the attendance zones around segregated neighborhoods, thus creating a dual school system in which Anglos had their schools and African and Mexican American students shared schools. Ultimately, in *Cisneros v. CCISD* (1970), a case supported by the United Steelworkers Union and 24 Mexican American parents, a federal judge found Mexican Americans to be an identifiable minority and held that the racial and ethnic segregation existing in Corpus Christi schools was unconstitutional. In 1975, a new school system was established upon court order, but only in 1997 was the decision fully implemented.

Change was apparent in the African American community in other ways in these critical years. The size of the black population grew from 7,164 in 1950 to 10,605 in 1970. The first black debutantes were presented in 1957. In 1960, the primarily black Solomon M. Coles School football team won its second state championship. Churches continued to provide social and spiritual comfort, while over 100 social clubs offered companionship and a sense of community. In the late 1960s, the Cotton Club opened in the Harlem Theater building, thus enabling both black and white audiences to watch black performers. The Reverend Harold T. Branch, benefiting from the renewed assertion of civil and political rights, won election to the city council in 1971.

White supporters aided the community as well. Elected in 1961, Mayor Ben McDonald worked with and for the black community to eliminate segregation in public accommodations, including restaurants, bowling alleys, and swimming pools. He established a human rights commission in 1963. Democratic politician and educator Frances Tarlton "Sissy" Farenthold supported black efforts, as did the national government, which enacted the Civil Rights Act of 1964 and the Voting Rights Act of 1965. In 1968, the *Corpus Christi Caller-Times* carried a 20-page report on the African American community.

By 1974, black leader W. Boyd Hall had died, and on the national scene, Barbara Jordan, a black congresswoman from Texas, served on the House committee that recommended impeachment for Pres. Richard Nixon. Members of the black community of Corpus Christi moved forward to clarify their roles during the ensuing years.

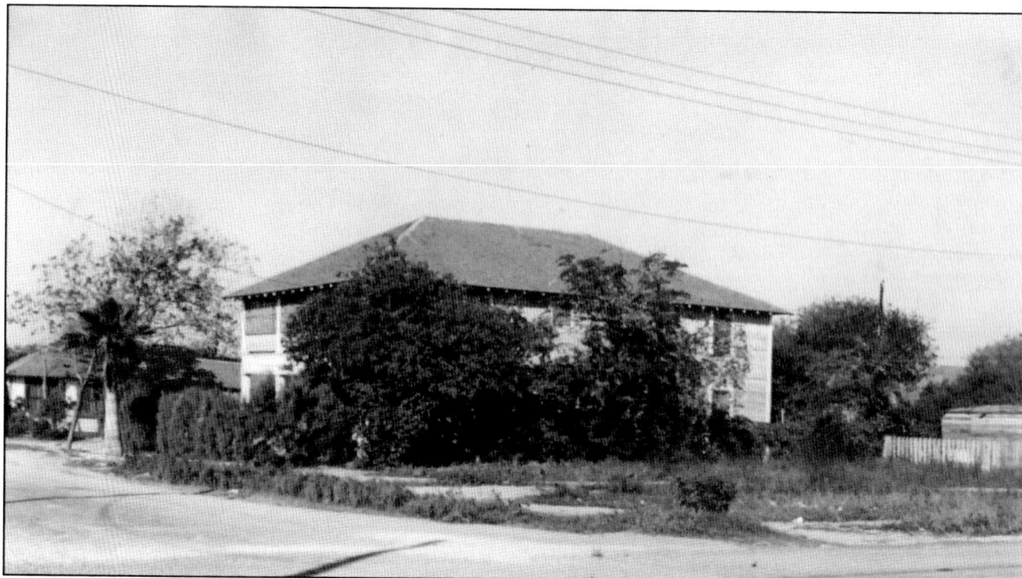

As late as the mid-1950s in Corpus Christi, black youths too often were neglected. In 1956, local NAACP leader Dr. H. Boyd Hall attended a meeting of the city council to appeal the closing of the Howard Street Home for Negro Girls. Hall was successful, and young black women continued to have a place to stay in an emergency. (Courtesy of the *Corpus Christi Caller-Times*.)

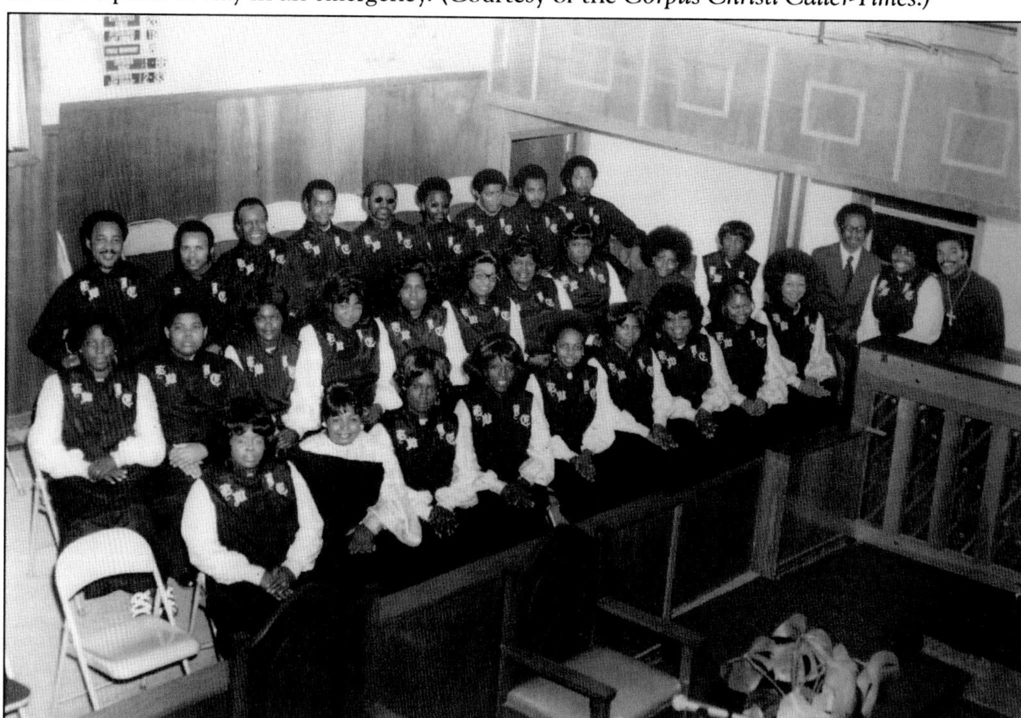

The Rising Star Baptist choir poses in the church for this photograph. Rising Star began in the home of Rev. Edward Russell in 1948. After the congregation moved to several other homes, a church was built on Barrera Street. Rising Star eventually moved to this building on Holly Street. (Courtesy of Robert Russell.)

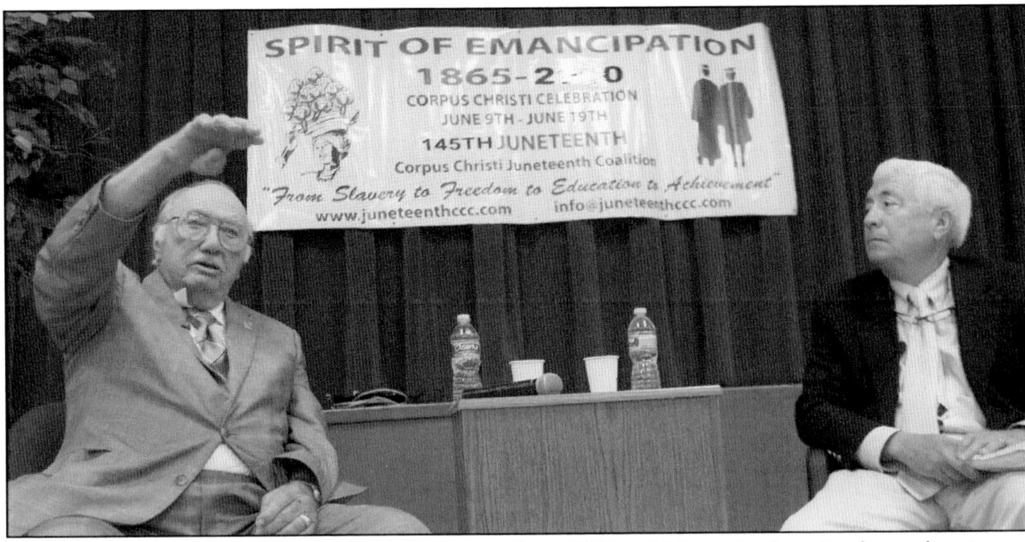

As part of the opening celebration of Juneteenth in 2011, which took place in the auditorium at Solomon M. Coles School, Ben McDonald (left) discusses his activities as mayor during the early 1960s. Listening intently is Joe Adame, mayor of Corpus Christi in 2011. (Courtesy of *Corpus Christi Caller-Times.*)

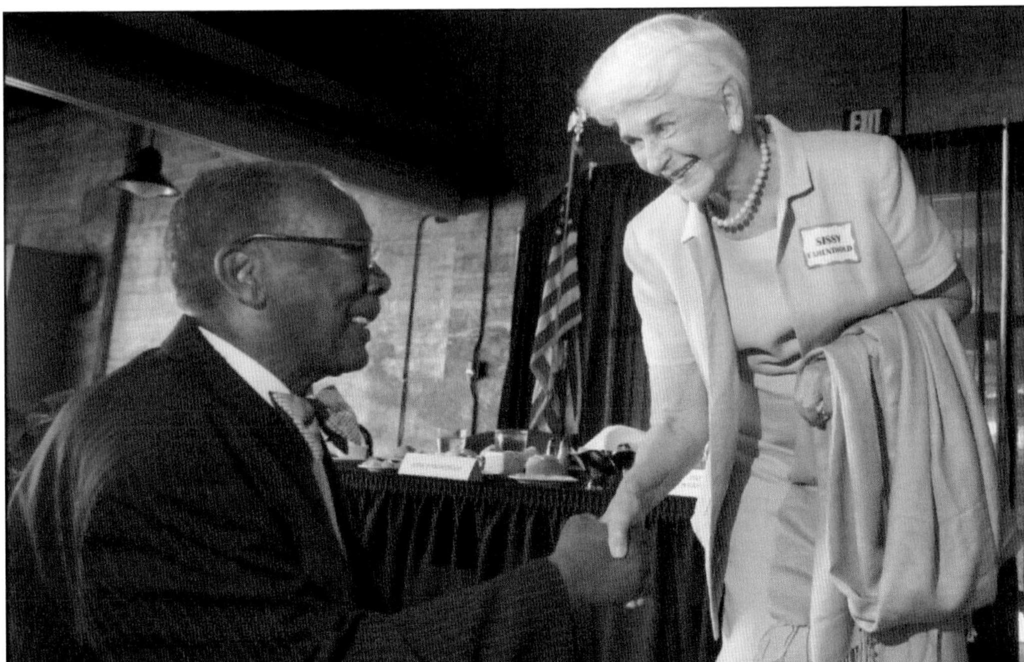

Frances "Sissy" Farenthold shakes hands with Reverend Bennett. Farenthold actively worked with Ben McDonald during his term as mayor to improve conditions for blacks within the city. She served on Corpus Christi's Human Relations Commission and the Texas Advisory Committee to the US Commission on Civil Rights. In 1972, she was a Democratic nominee for US vice president. (Courtesy of *Corpus Christi Caller-Times.*)

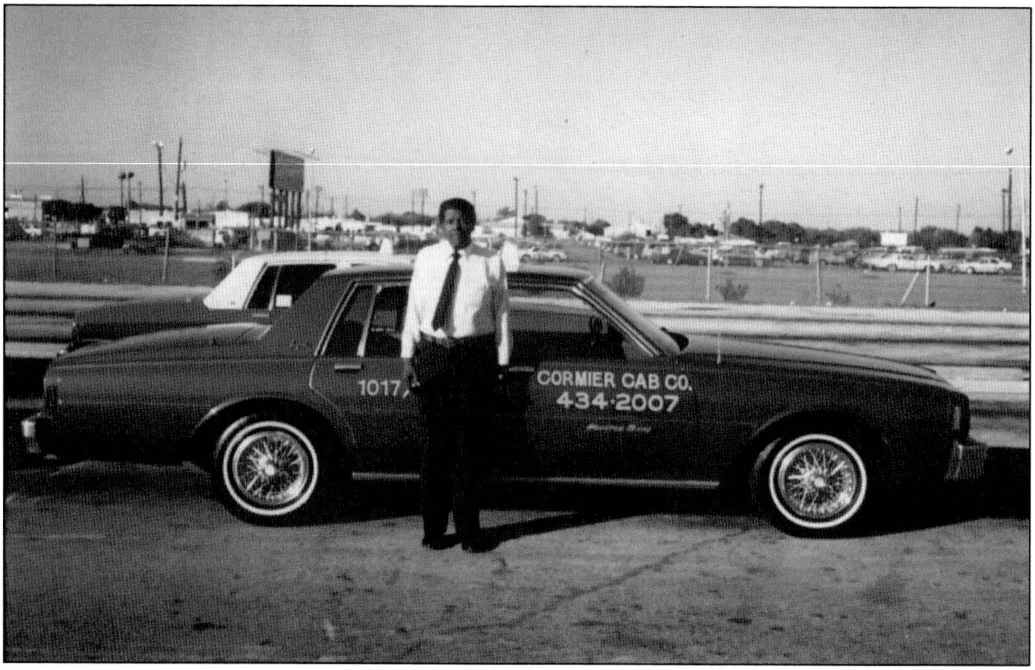

Getting around in Corpus Christi was not always easy. A means of leaving the Northside African American community, or being transported within it, was to use a cab. Ben McCullough, a graduate of the Solomon M. Coles class of 1942, drove a car for Cormier Cab Company; he is shown standing next to his cab. (Courtesy of Solomon M. Coles School.)

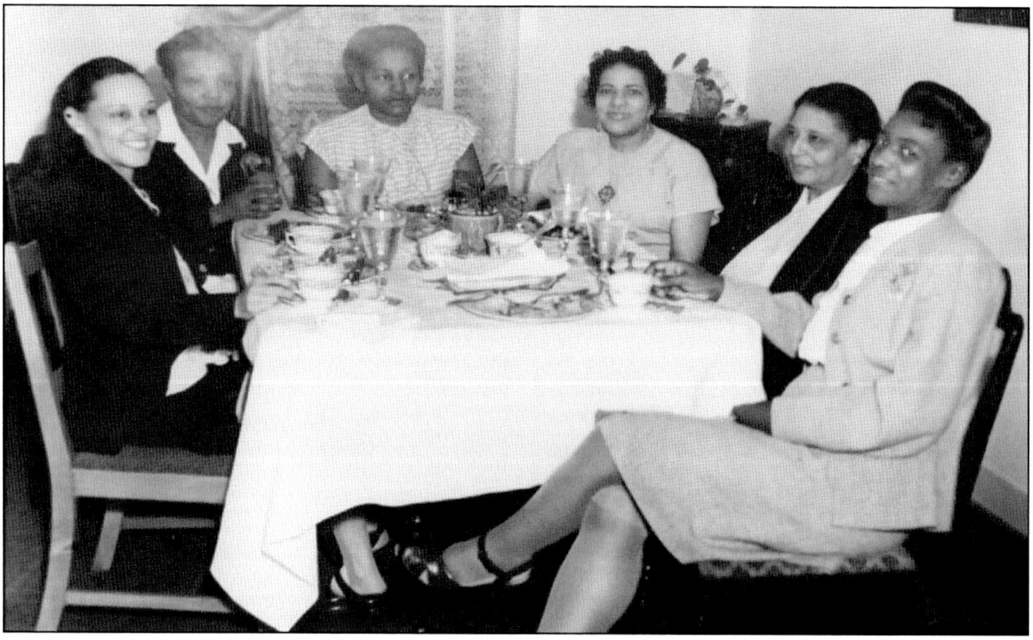

Activism blended with effectiveness, the Progressive Women's Club was a major influence in the Northside during the mid-20th century. Among those pictured at a conference are Alclair Pleasant (left), Nina Reed Hill, Annie Bohmann (second from right), and Jane Ramsoure. (Courtesy of the Corpus Christi Museum of Science and History, Alclair Pleasant Collection.)

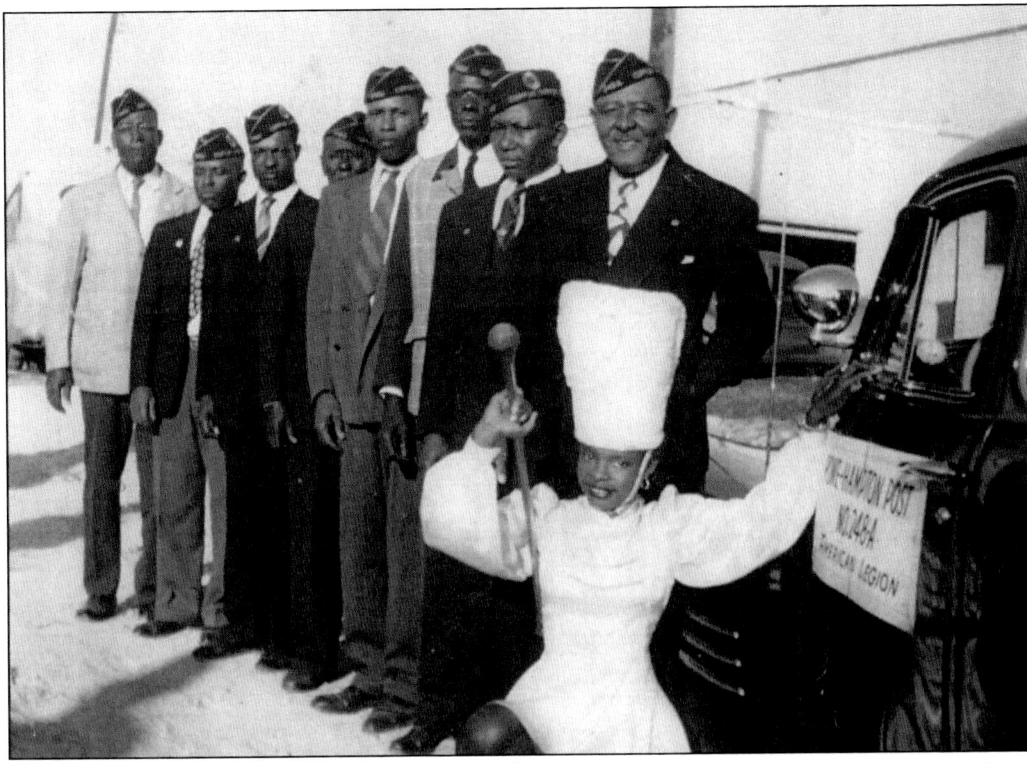

African Americans in Corpus Christi, as in other national and state urban centers, gladly served in the US armed forces when war came. In this photograph, unidentified black veteran members of the American Legion and an attractive drum majorette pose for a picture. (Courtesy of Solomon M. Coles School.)

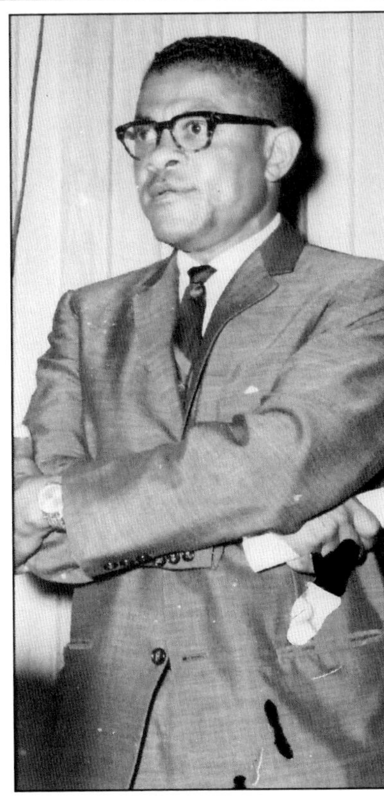

A medical doctor and local civil rights activist, Dr. H.J. Williams strove within his profession and his community to ensure equitable treatment and rights. In the mid-1960s, he was at the forefront of efforts to eliminate segregation in public accommodations. He presided over the local NAACP and argued that blacks should be represented on the city council. (Courtesy of the *Corpus Christi Caller-Times*.)

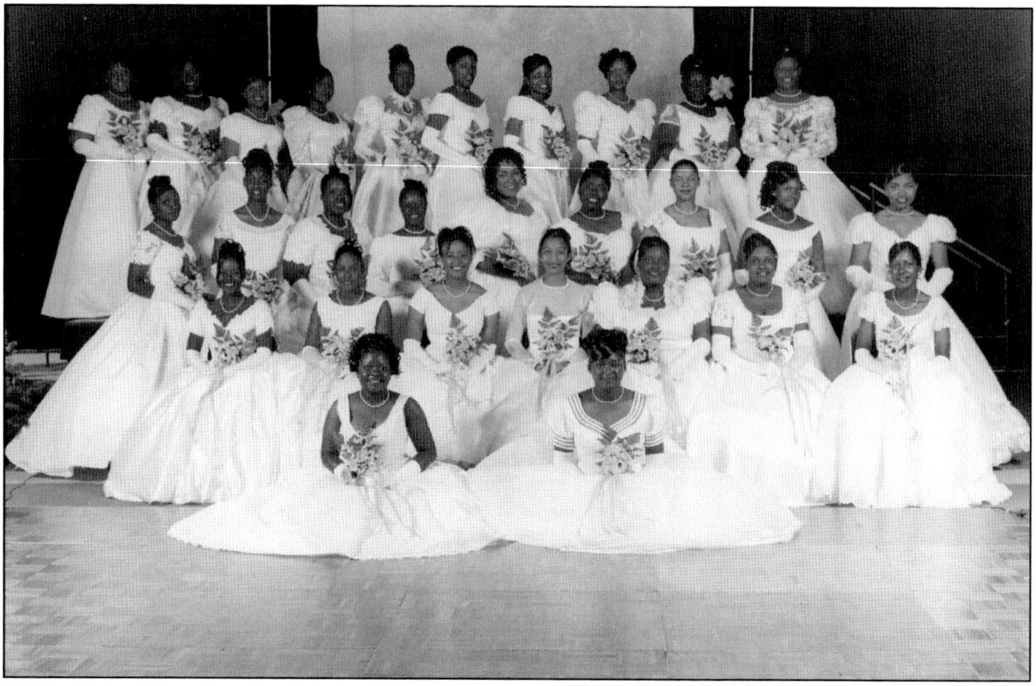

This group of unidentified black Corpus Christi women, each dressed in white and holding a bouquet of flowers, relaxes and smiles for the photographer. They are debutantes, first organized and presented in 1957 by Eddie Bolden. (Courtesy of the *Corpus Christi Caller-Times*.)

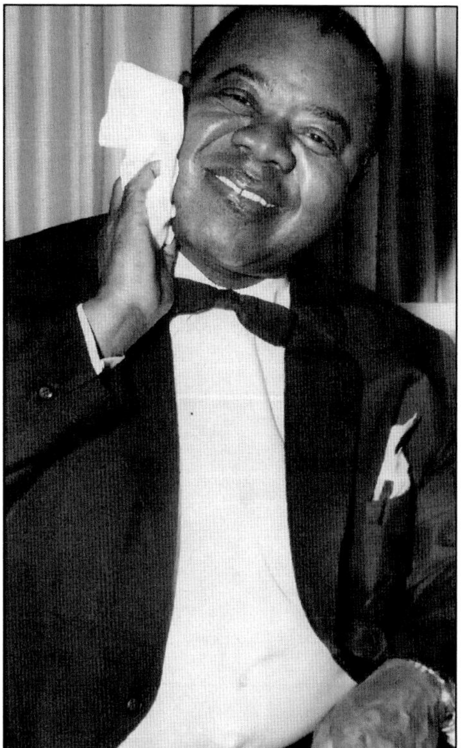

Nationally known black musicians came to Corpus Christi to perform. Louis Armstrong, with his classic handkerchief and smile, was among them. Armstrong performed near the end of 1964 for the debutante ball at the Driscoll Hotel. Raised in New Orleans, Armstrong learned early to play the cornet and then the trumpet, and he acquired fame with the Louis Armstrong Five while in Chicago. (Courtesy of the *Corpus Christi Caller-Times*.)

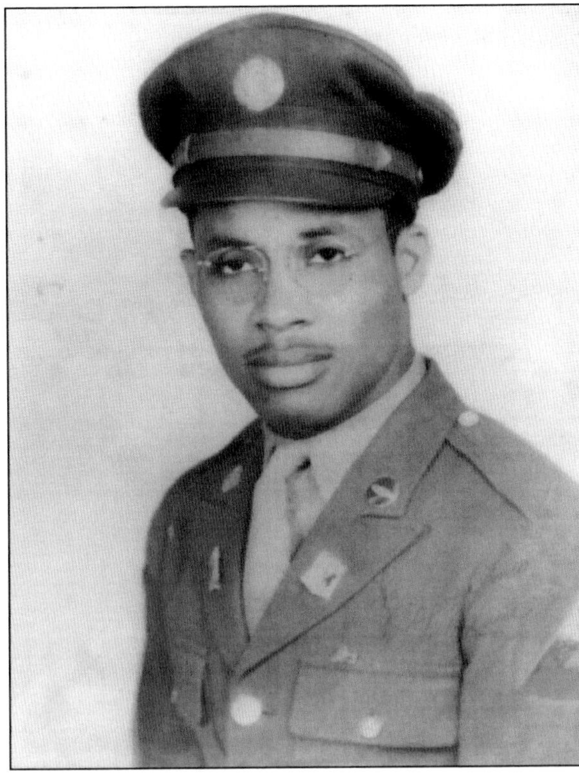

Warren G.H. Crecy was known as "the baddest man" in World War II black units. In 1998, a Corpus Christi street was named for him. Crecy earned a battlefield commission, a Silver Star, a Bronze Star, and four Purple Hearts in military service during World War II and the Korean War. (Courtesy of Bernice Crecy.)

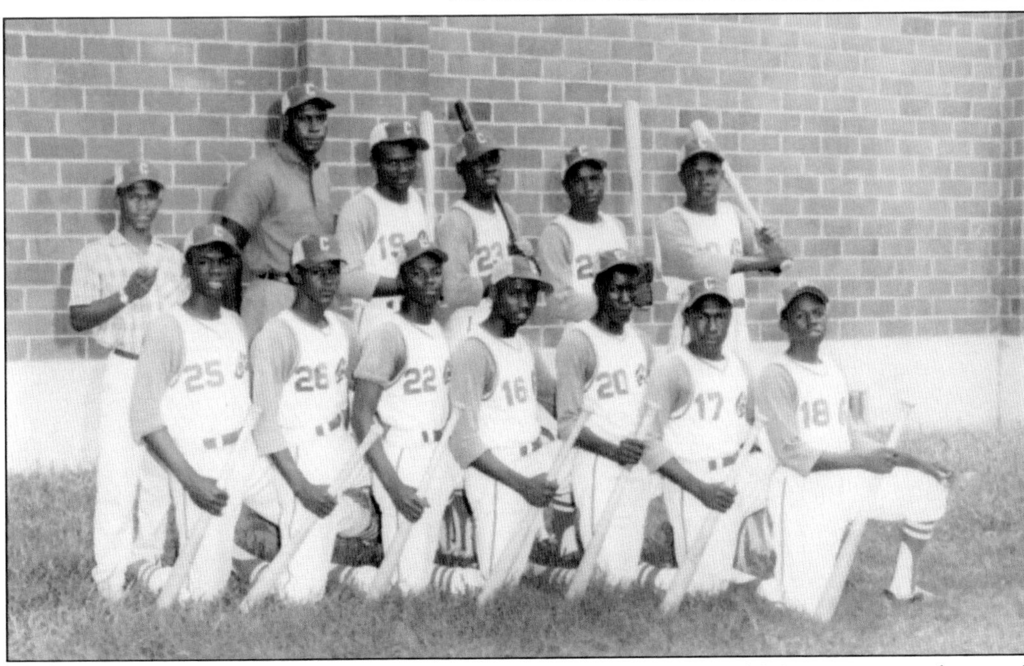

Athletes at Solomon M. Coles School earned a championship in 1965. Many team members took this winning spirit and sharpened their skills in other areas. Thomas Walker (No. 22) went on to Dartmouth College, became an architect, and later was named the executive director of the Public Building Commission in Chicago. (Courtesy of Solomon M. Coles School.)

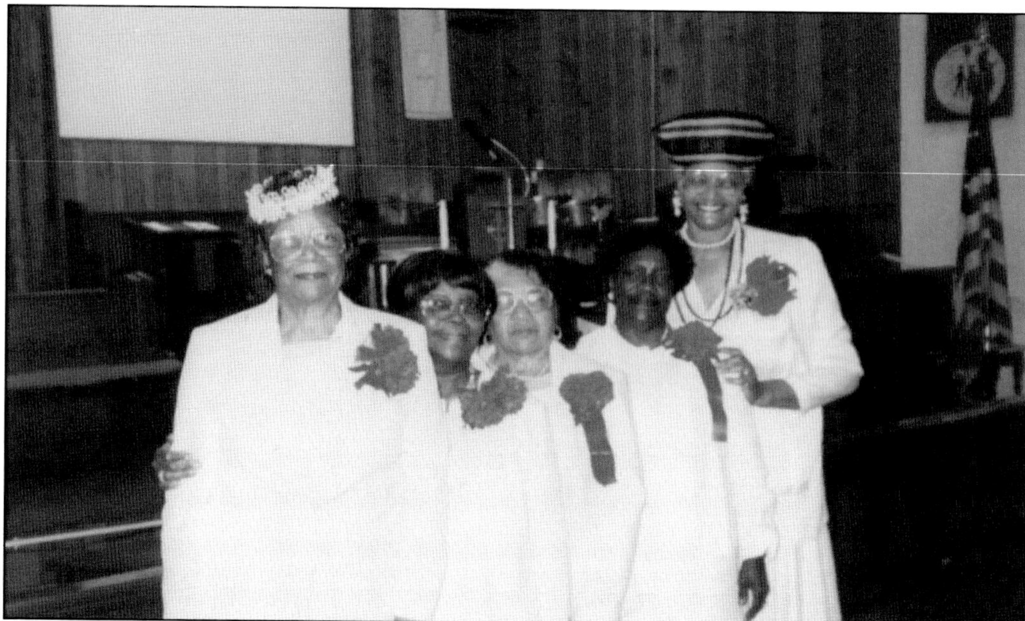

Members of St. Paul United Methodist Church, each adorned with a corsage, pose in the 1960s for this picture inside their attractive church. St. Paul's dates back to the early 20th century and was one of the first black churches in the Corpus Christi community. (Courtesy of St. Paul United Methodist Church.)

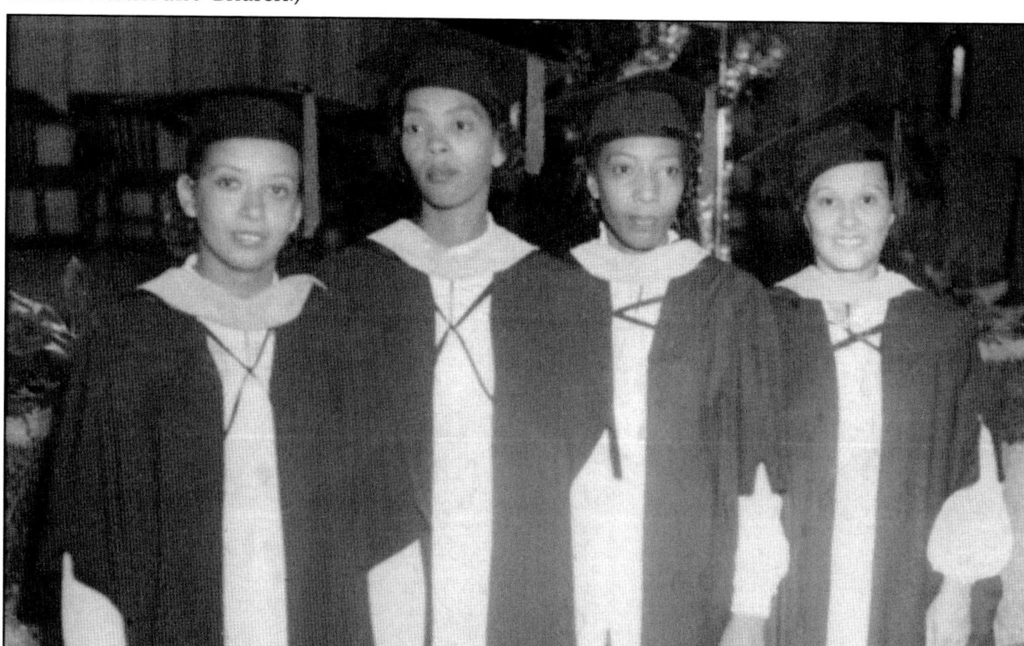

There can be no greater joy for a teacher than to see her student graduate—unless they can graduate together. Alclair Mays Pleasant (far right) taught first grade to Oneal Harris Crawford. In August 1953, they (pictured with two others) receive the master of arts degree in the same ceremony at Prairie View University. (Courtesy of the Corpus Christi Museum of Science and History, Alclair Pleasant Collection.)

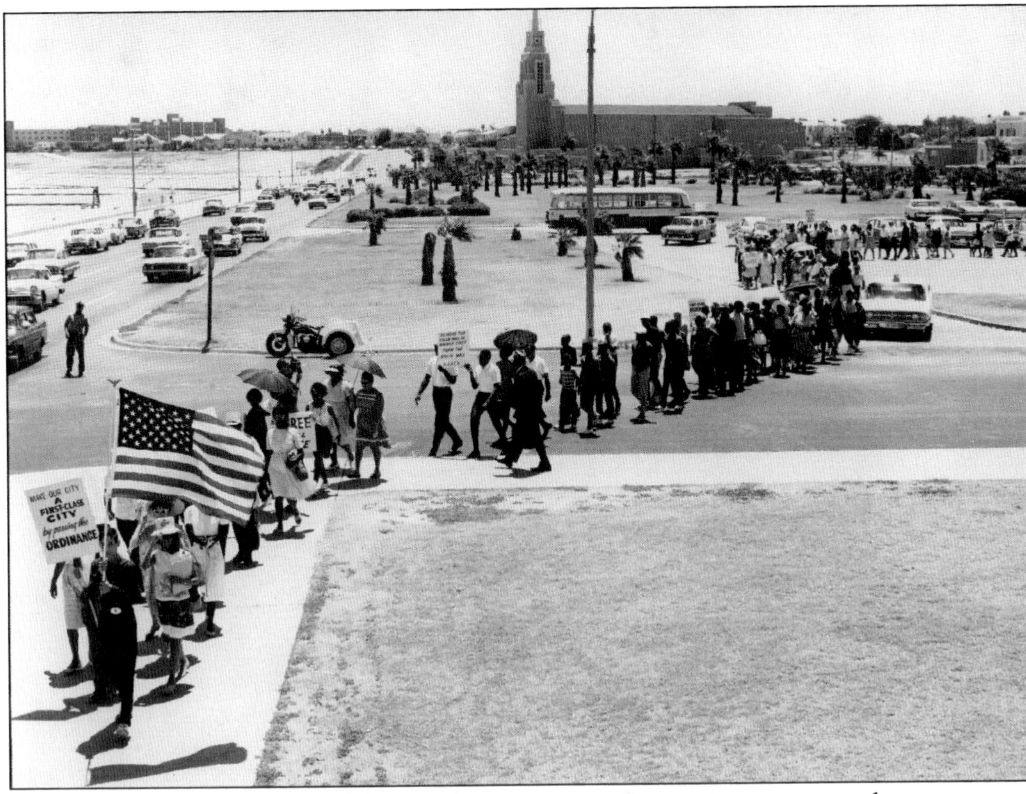

As in other cities in Texas and the South, one means of garnering support and awareness was through marches. In this 1965 Corpus Christi civil rights march, black and white community members have joined to bring about changes, especially in housing and public accommodations. They are also urging passage of a city ordinance for integration in public accommodations. (Courtesy of *Corpus Christi Caller-Times*.)

The black community of Corpus Christi came together for various reasons. In this photograph taken outside during the 1960s, three community members pose—Mrs. E. Whitley (left), Harry B. Davis (center), and Mrs. D.N. Leathers. (Courtesy of Thurma Hilton.)

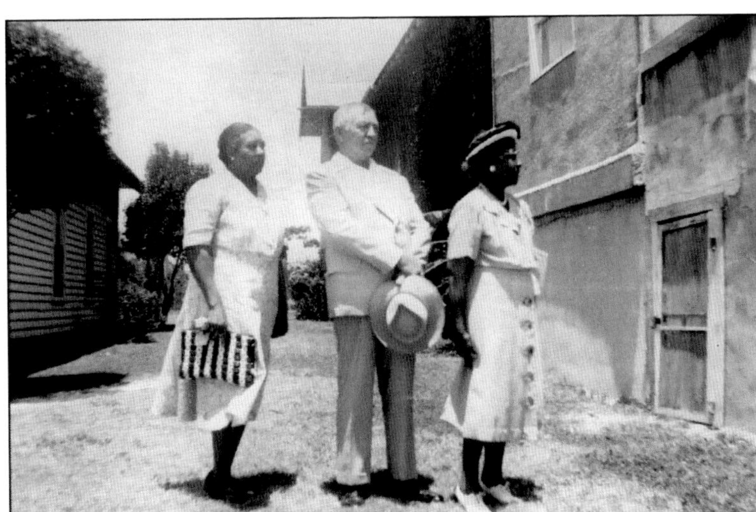

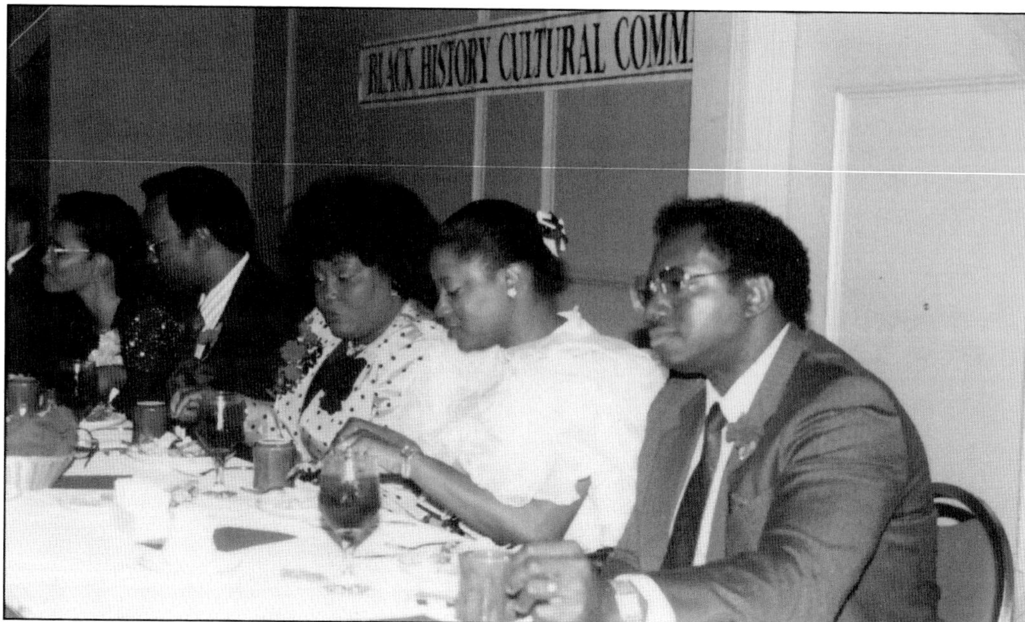

The Black History Cultural Committee holds an annual banquet to present scholarship awards. This organization started in 1976 with Jennifer Butler Wimbish as the first chairperson. It has conducted many fundraisers and given several hundred scholarships to deserving students. The committee sponsors concerts, attracts national speakers, and has television specials concentrating on black history and culture. (Courtesy of Robert Russell.)

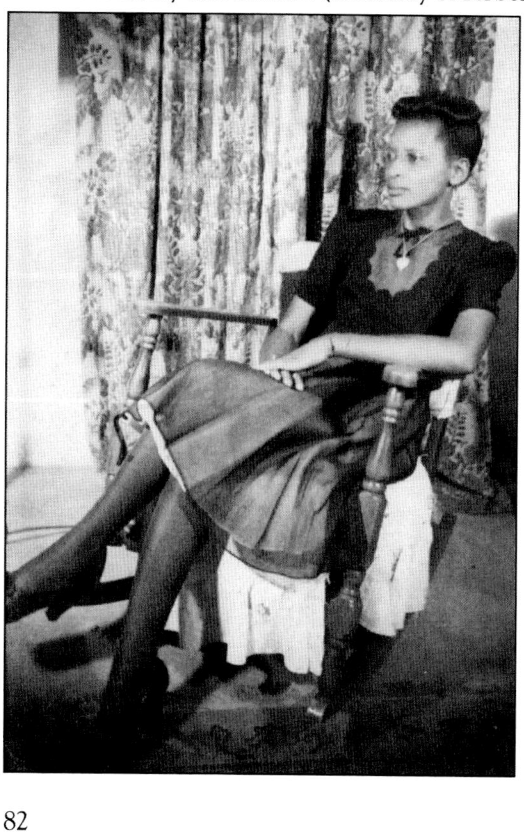

Relaxing in a rocking chair in her early life is Mary Ella Middleton Fucuals. An active member of St. Matthew Missionary Baptist Church and the NAACP, Fucuals passed away in March 2000 at the age of 88. In 2004, the former church parsonage was named in her honor: the Mary Ella Fucuals Christian Learning Center. (Courtesy of Ronald H. Fucuals, grandson of Mary Fucuals.)

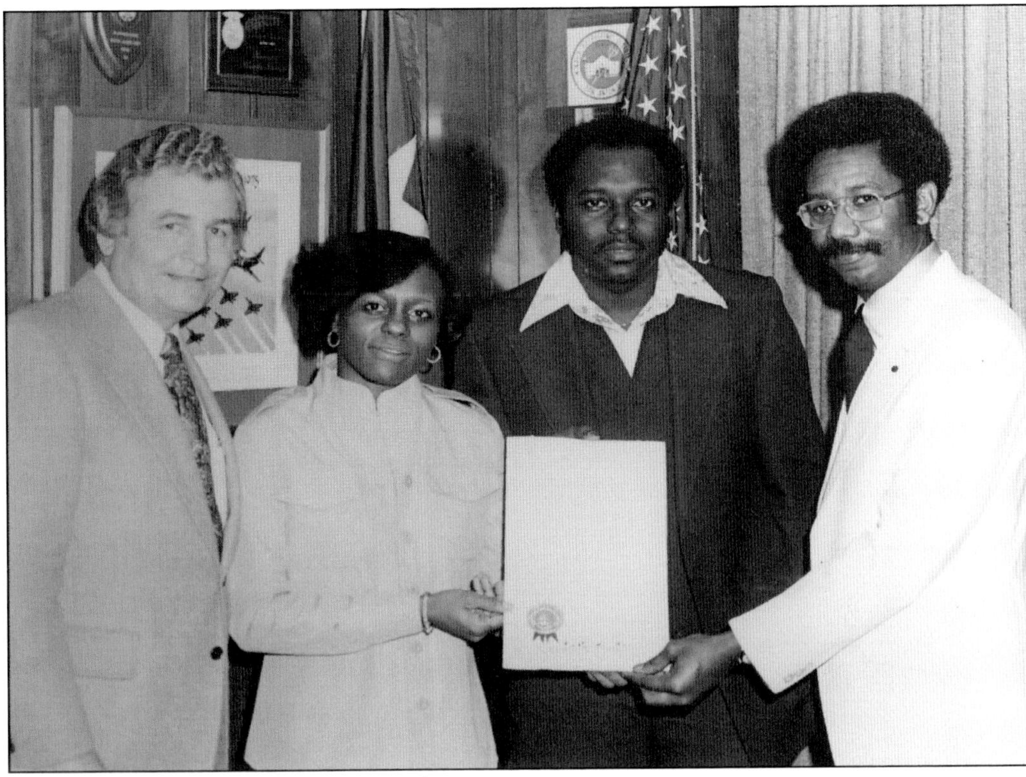

To encourage young students to attend or continue in college, several black groups provided scholarships. In this picture, the Black History Cultural Committee Scholarship is being presented to a welcoming recipient. In the photograph are, from left to right, J.P. Luby, Claudia Booker, Lavernis Royal, and Edward Sample. (Courtesy of Robert Russell.)

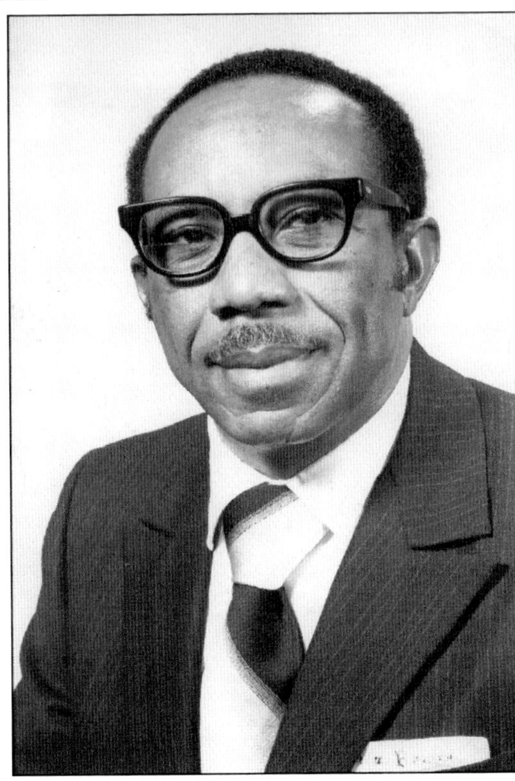

Corpus Christi black leadership included the Reverend Harold Branch, who was pastor of St. John Baptist Church, a school board member, NAACP leader, and civil rights activist. Branch aided the community spirit of black Corpus Christi. He also gained support from and worked with the white community. (Courtesy of the *Corpus Christi Caller-Times*.)

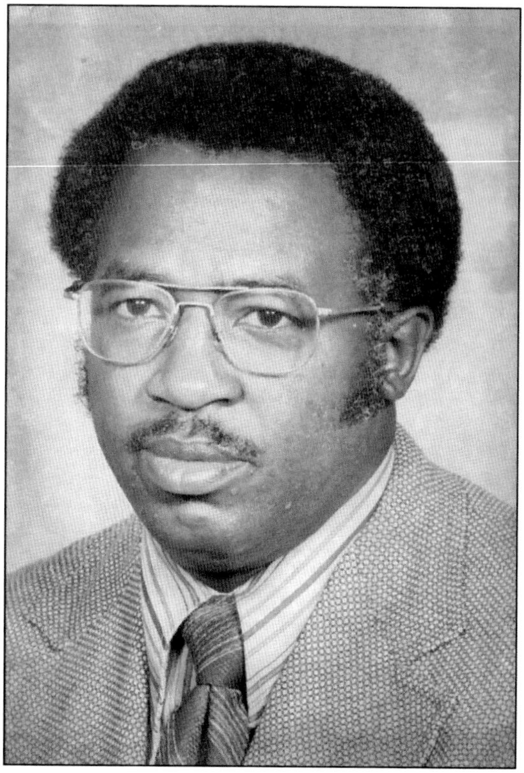

Curtis Williams was a Mobil Oil employee and a widower who had four children in West Oso School when he ran for reelection in the West Oso District. Williams, an active Mason and civic leader, served on the West Oso board for more than six years. He hailed from Luling and attended Texas Southern University and Texas A&M University-Kingsville. (Courtesy of the *Corpus Christi Caller-Times*.)

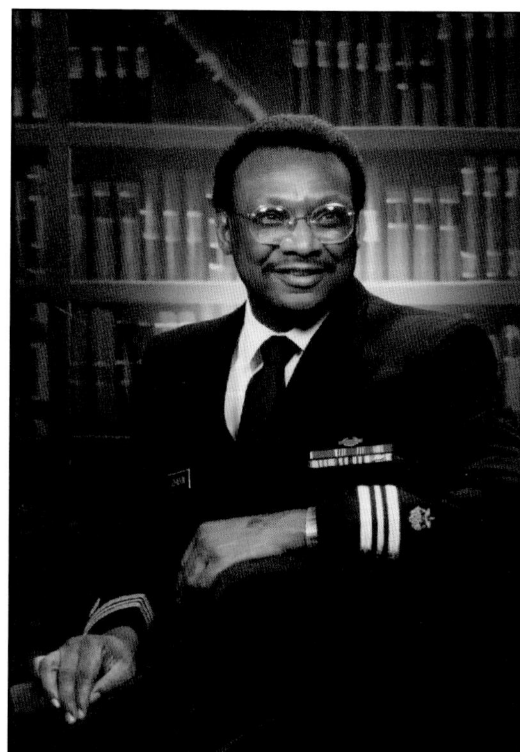

Corpus Christi physician Dr. Tone Johnson Jr. learned in 1996 that he earned a high honor for bravery—the Bronze Star—while engaged in battle during the Vietnam War in 1965. Johnson later continued his military service, not as a private first class, but as a lieutenant colonel in the US Army Reserve. (Courtesy of Tone Johnson.)

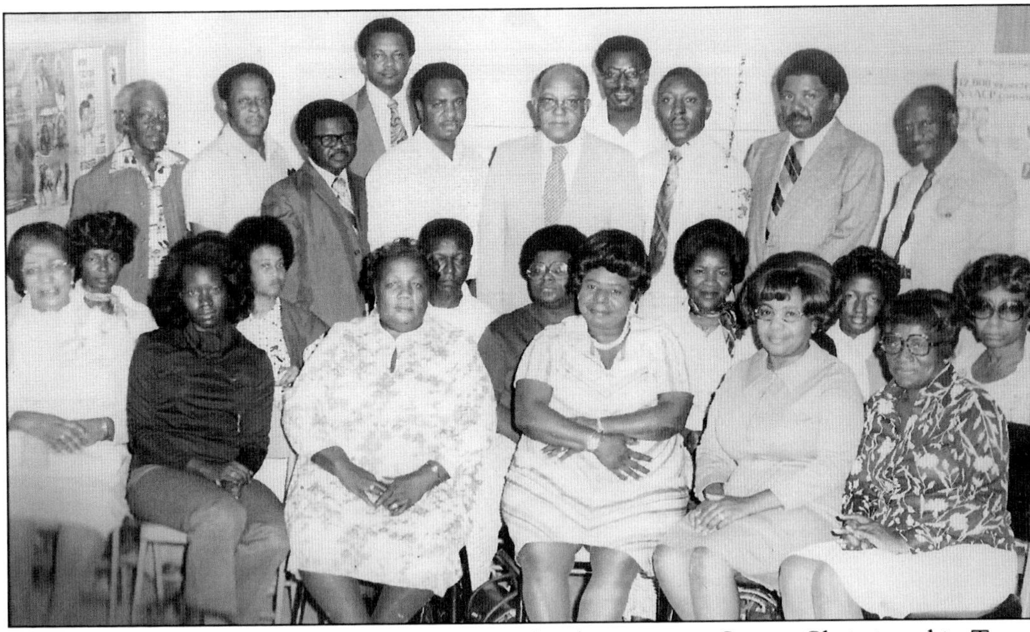

Certainly the most prominent and effective civil rights group in Corpus Christi, and in Texas, has been the National Association for the Advancement of Colored People (NAACP). It has welcomed young and old, both men and women. This photograph of unidentified NAACP leaders and members is indicative of its widespread appeal in Corpus Christi. (Courtesy of the Corpus Christi NAACP.)

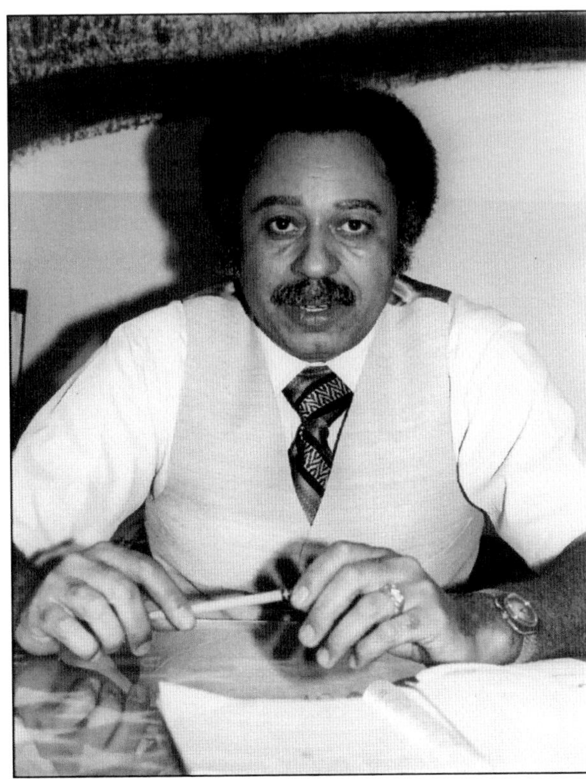

Shown in this 1978 photograph, Claude Lee Melton began his administrative career in 1971 when he became principal of Fisher School. Melton later became president of the Texas Jazz Festival, which drew 25,000 music enthusiasts to the Bayfront Arts and Sciences Park by 1989. The jazz festival began in 1960. (Courtesy of the *Corpus Christi Caller-Times*.)

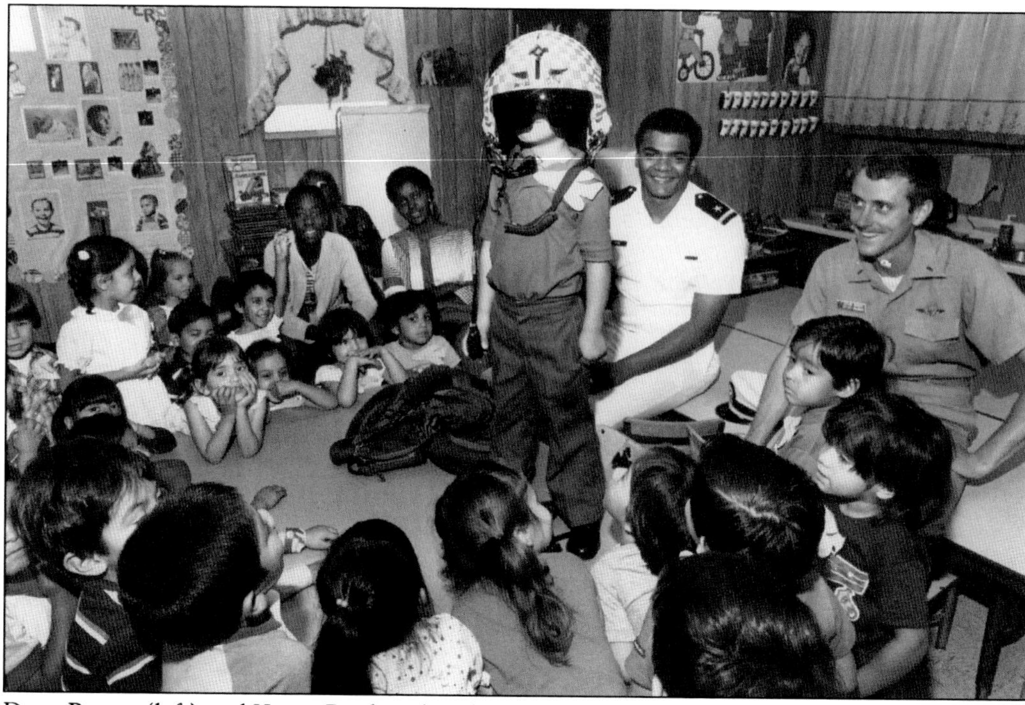

Drew Brown (left) and Kevin Brady, pilots from Naval Air Station Corpus Christi, encouraged students to don helmets as part of Black History Week at the Tuloso Midway Clarkwood School. (Courtesy of the *Corpus Christi Caller-Times.*)

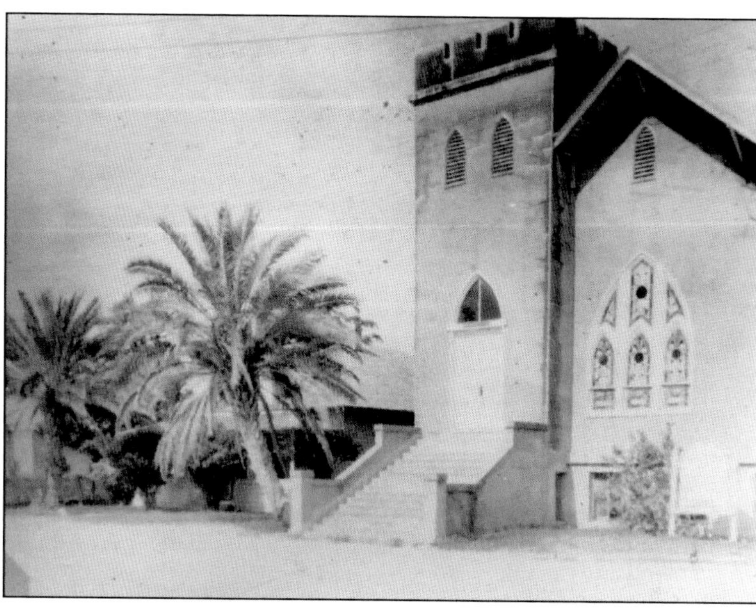

The history of the First Congregational Church in Corpus Christi goes back to the close of the Civil War era. It was the church that Solomon Coles pastored, and it has played an important role in Corpus Christi since its beginning. This photograph is of the newly built church. The original church was torn down after years of serving the community. (Courtesy of Thelmaline Hilton.)

Community activist and successful businesswoman Bernice Crecy, née Bernice Crawford, worked as a buyer for Lichtenstein and the Godwyn Shop for more than a decade. She later opened the first black-oriented clothing store, the Boutique Shoppe, in Padres Staples Mall. The successful business was sold a few years later to allow Bernice to care for a sick relative. She later went back into retail and assisted her husband, Robert Crecy, with his catering business. (Courtesy of Bernice Crecy.)

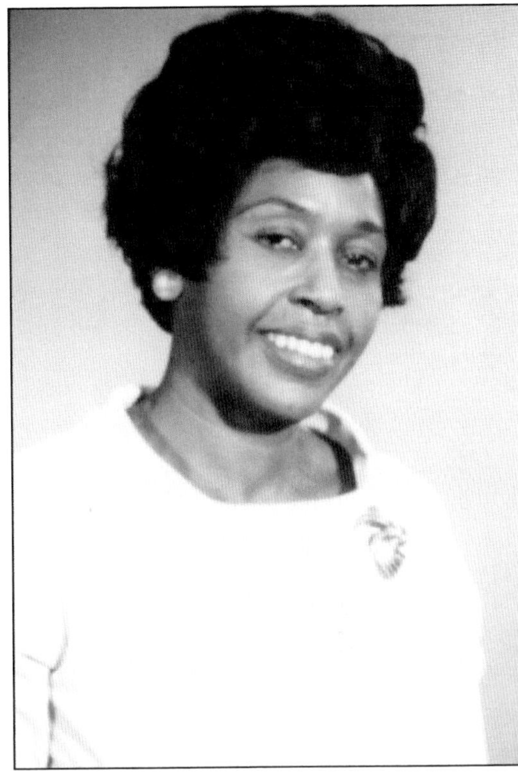

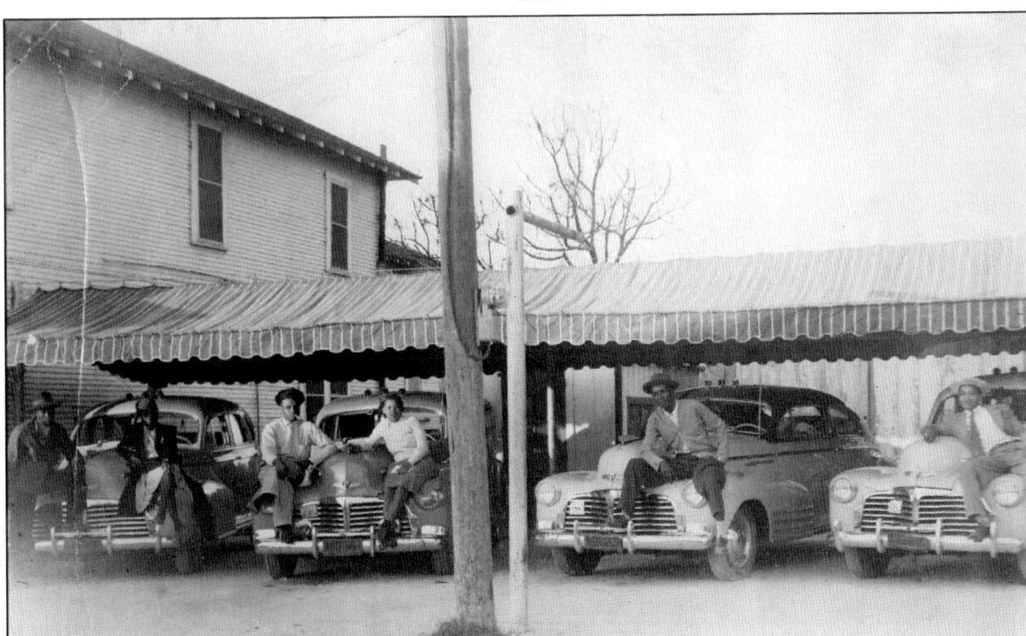

This is a photograph of the Crecy Cab Barn. These cabs and cab drivers were concentrated in the black community of Corpus Christi. The site was later enclosed and became the basis for the Down Beat Club, a popular eating and dancing establishment for African Americans in Corpus Christi. (Courtesy of Bernice Crecy.)

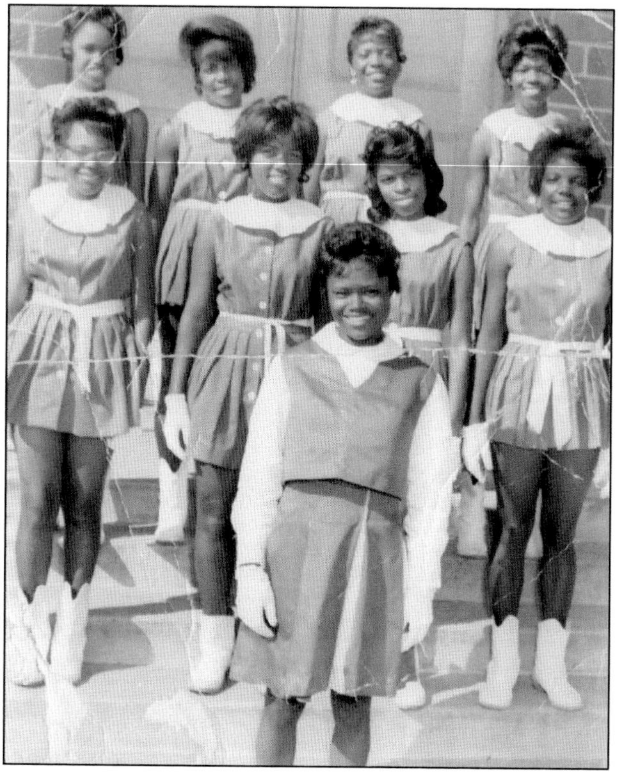

Cheerleaders from Solomon M. Coles School stand in front of the building in 1964. Included in this photograph, in no particular order, are Rose Dickson, Janice Lattimer, Irma Hodge, Christine Wade, Beverly Jones, Gloria Dickson, Lula Jones, and Gloria Green. (Courtesy of Gloria and Rose Green.)

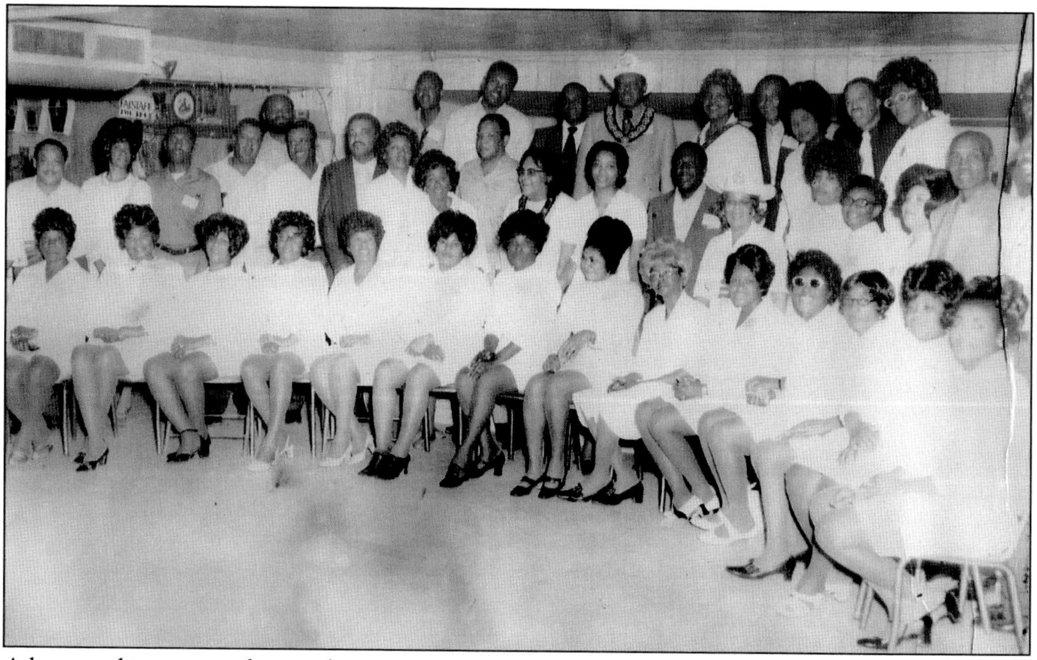

A large and important fraternal group in Corpus Christi among members of the black community was the Elks. Taken at the Down Beat Club in the late 1950s or early 1960s, this photograph of unidentified men and women of the Elks Club includes a dashing man in a western hat at the center of the third row. (Courtesy of Bernice Crecy.)

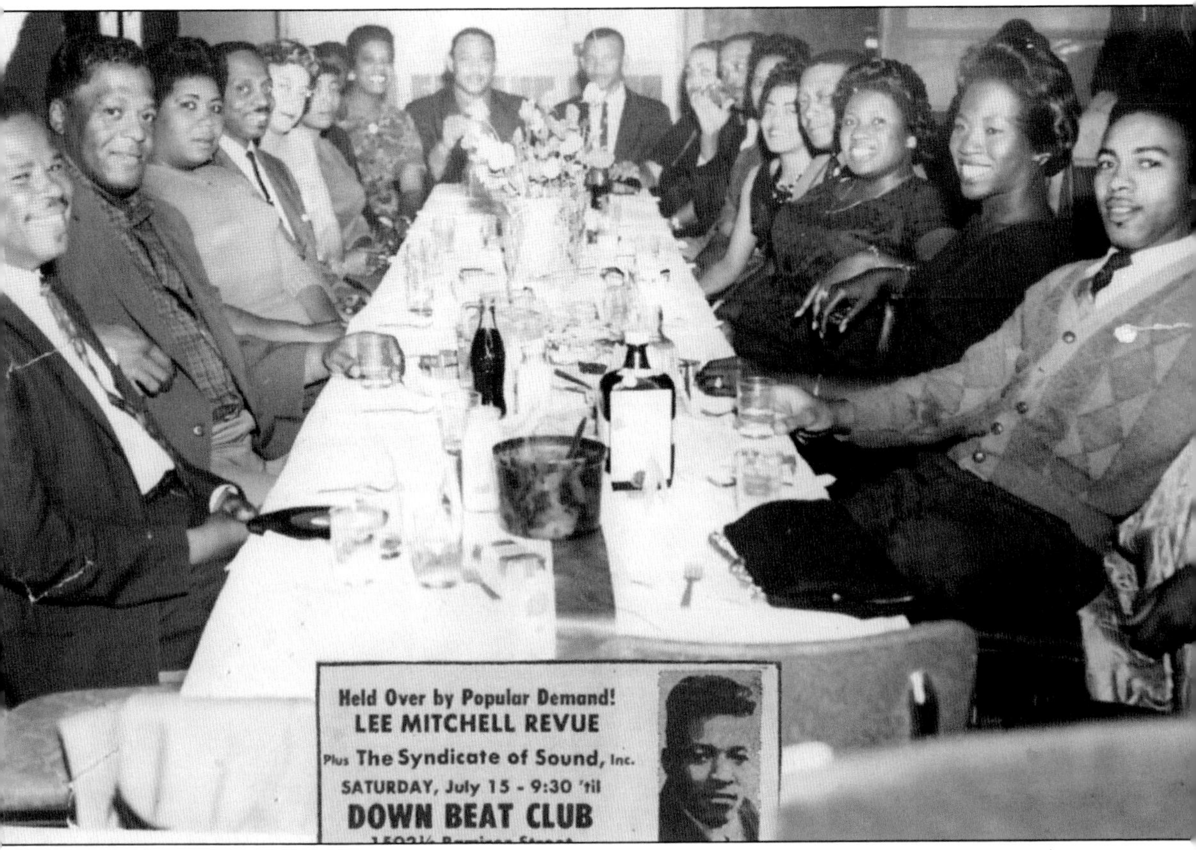

Attending a function at the Down Beat Club are men and women from the Corpus Christi black community. Whether they played that evening is not known, but the club featured the Lee Mitchell Revue and the Syndicate of Sound. A big draw was the singer known as Mr. Soul. No one in the photograph is identified. (Courtesy of Bernice Crecy.)

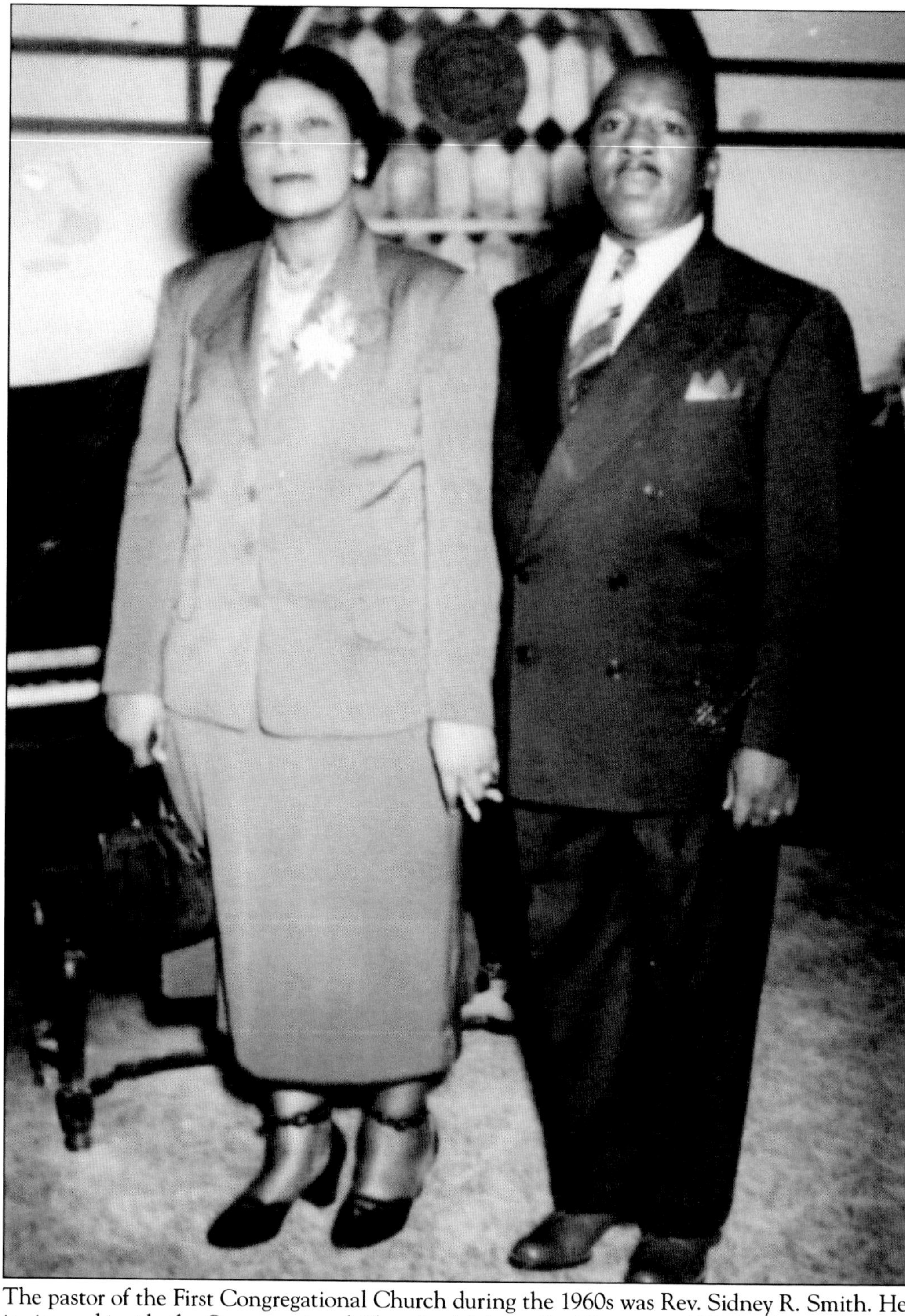

The pastor of the First Congregational Church during the 1960s was Rev. Sidney R. Smith. He is pictured inside the Congregational Church with his wife. (Courtesy of Thelmaline Hilton.)

Five

Generating Pride
1975–1990

This 15-year period in black Corpus Christi history began with an auspicious start when former city councilman Rev. Harold T. Branch ran for mayor. Even though he lost, he generated enthusiasm and pride in the local African American community. In 1977, Capt. Richard E. Williams assumed command of Naval Air Station Corpus Christi. Other measures further enhanced community pride, such as the 1979 placement of a historical marker at the Solomon M. Coles School. In 1987, prominent black leader Jesse Jackson returned to Corpus Christi to assist the League of United Latin American Citizens (LULAC) while at the same time seeking support for his presidential campaign.

By 1990, the 12,347 African Americans in Corpus Christi resided in a supportive and active community. Since the black portion of the city's population was only about 4.5 percent, its strength and commonality depended on each community member. Both churches and educational institutions enhanced community togetherness and spirit. Activist organizations, such as the National Association for the Advancement of Colored People (NAACP) and the Black Chamber of Commerce, also worked on behalf of the interests of the black community.

A number of black leaders stepped forward. Rheba Jones represented the city's teachers while serving as president of the Corpus Christi Classroom Teachers Association. Other educators enhanced schools in Corpus Christi. Ora Ruth Williams served as assistant principal at Cunningham Junior High. The Solomon M. Coles School continued to be a gathering place and a source of pride. The contribution and success of Lena D. Coleman and the HIALCO-NIOC organization (Hillcrest, Ayers, Leathers, Coles Neighborhood Industrial Opportunity Center), which provided funds for scholarships and classes in the black community, cannot be overlooked.

In 1985, the Corpus Christi Fire Department hired Deborah Johnson as its first black female firefighter. Other leaders and community activists during these years included Harry Williams, Welder Brown, Beaulah Williams, and Rufus Avery. Eddie Bolden, the founder of the Moore Community Center, died in 1980. Ernest Carter spurred the development of 40 low-income housing units for the black community. Civil rights activist the Reverend Elliott Grant retired in 1987. Grant had been the first African American to serve on the Corpus Christi School District's board of trustees.

The import of the Corpus Christi black community can be noted in the talented national musicians who performed in the city by the sea. They included stalwart jazz musician B.B. King, country-western singer Charley Pride, and vocalist Natalie Cole, who sang for an art museum benefit.

Other aspects of entertainment and relaxation included fraternal group gatherings, Martin Luther King's birthday, Juneteenth, Black History Month activities, debutante presentations, dancing contests, and a Miss Teen Pageant, as well as informal get-togethers among members of the community.

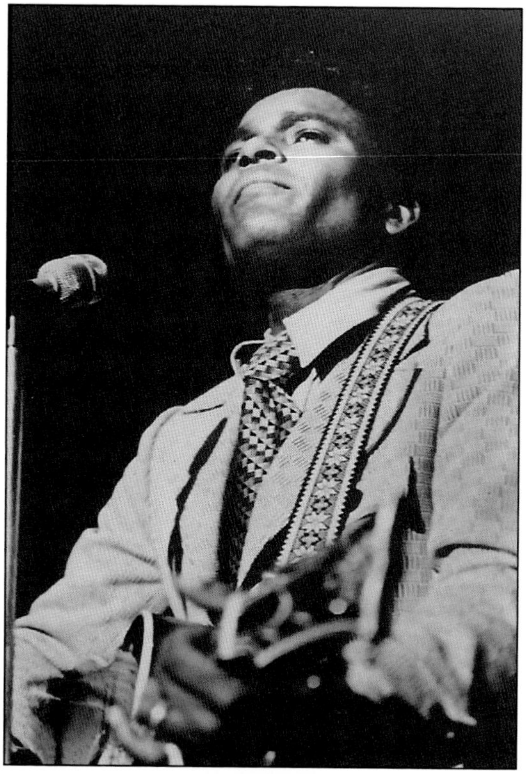

Country and western singer Charley Pride performs in 1976 for a Corpus Christi telethon for cerebral palsy; pledges totaled nearly $50,000. Earlier in his career, Pride, from Montana, had performed locally at least five years in a row between 1969 and 1973. He earned numerous national singing awards and was honored by the mayors of Corpus Christi and Robstown during his 1973 performance. (Courtesy of the *Corpus Christi Caller-Times.*)

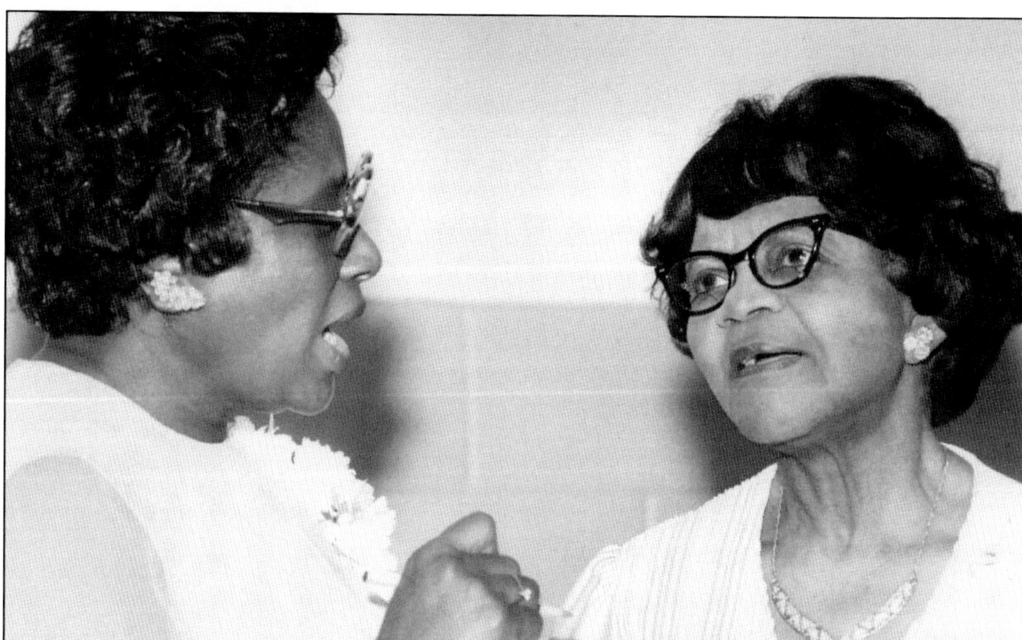

At the 1982 NAACP Martin Luther King dinner, the speaker was Beulah M. Williams, the first black principal in Memphis, Tennessee, following integration. The dinner meeting was chaired by the Corpus Christi NAACP (chartered in 1938) president Vanilla Polk. The theme of the meeting was based on King's "I Have a Dream" speech. (Courtesy of the *Corpus Christi Caller-Times.*)

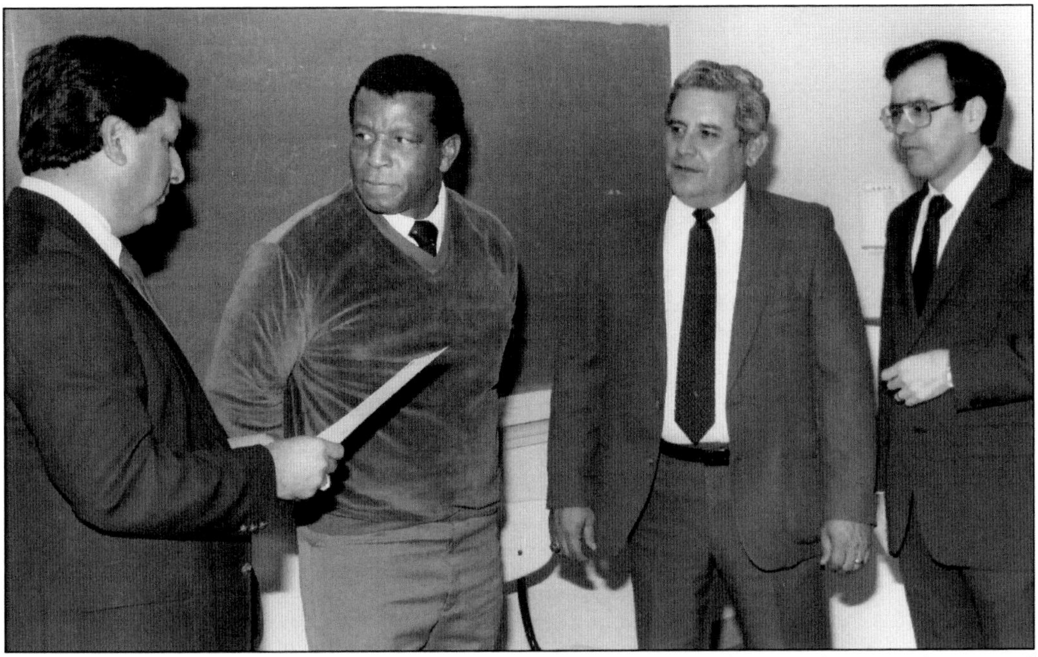

Outstanding Educator of the Year Vance Heard, of Roy Miller High School, received an award from LULAC. Heard, a history teacher and coach, always stressed studies to his team but admitted that both sports and academics fostered success. From left to right are Elbert Ocanas, Vance Heard, Ernest Barrera, and Ruben Bonilla. (Courtesy of *Corpus Christi Caller-Times.*)

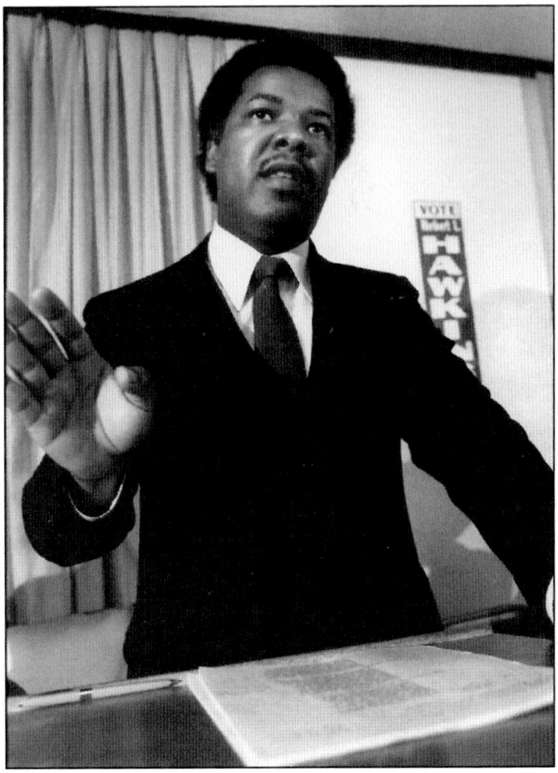

Herbert Hawkins Jr. served on the city council for two terms. His campaign marked a strong effort among city minority leaders to work together to gain a voice in the city process. An accomplished legal representative, Hawkins ran unsuccessfully for county attorney in 1984. (Courtesy of the *Corpus Christi Caller-Times.*)

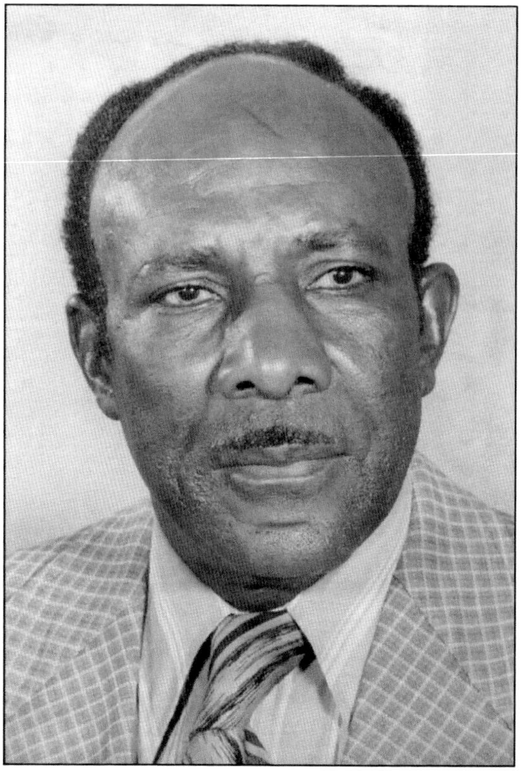

Likely the first African American to serve on a school board in South Texas, Welder Brown joined the West Oso Independent School District Board in 1964. Brown served for 19 years and as president for 6 years. In 1984, he filled a position on the Corpus Christi City Council. Brown, born in Smithdale, moved to Corpus Christi in 1939. (Courtesy of the *Corpus Christi Caller-Times.*)

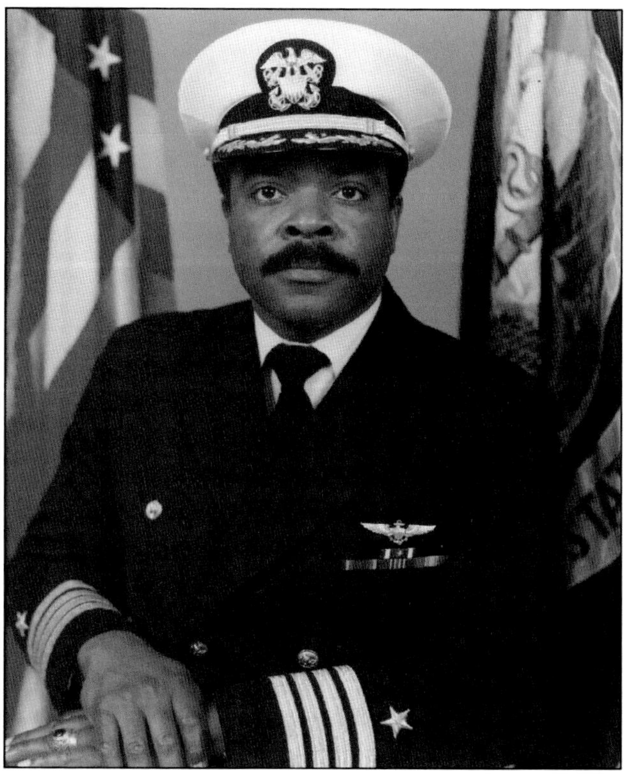

In 1977, Capt. Richard E. Williams, USN, assumed command of Naval Air Station Corpus Christi. Born in Jacksonville, Florida, Williams earned a bachelor's degree from Kentucky State University and entered the Navy in 1956. He subsequently earned a master's degree and nearly completed his doctorate degree. He performed his duties with effectiveness, receiving numerous awards and commendations along the way. (Courtesy of the *Corpus Christi Caller-Times.*)

In 1980, Corpus Christi residents honored one of their own when Mayor Luther Jones proclaimed Eddie Bolden Day. Her life and slogan were dedicated to "doing for others." By 1980, she completed 31 years as executive director of the Robert L. Moore Community Center; its vital component was a day care center. Eddie Bolden arrived in Corpus Christi in 1941 and immediately became active in the black community. (Courtesy of the *Corpus Christi Caller-Times.*)

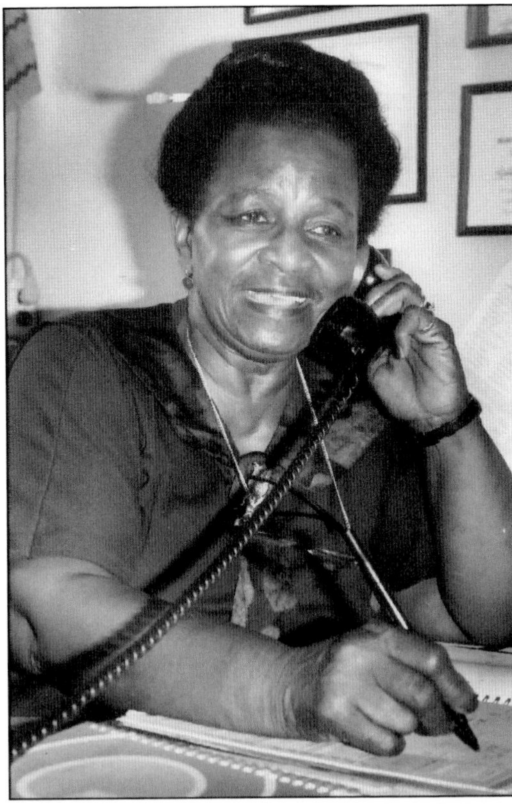

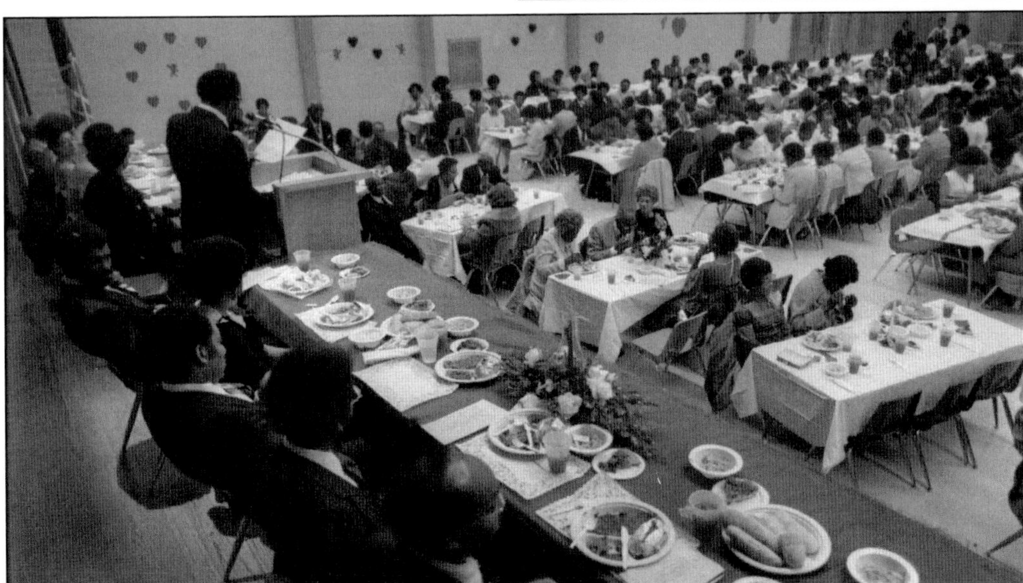

For Corpus Christi, as for other cities in both the state and nation, Black History Month was a time for special remembrances and celebration of African American history. At the 1979 Corpus Christi dinner banquet, the black history gathering honored its senior citizens, whose compelling stories reminded others of how and why they survived slavery and segregation and developed community awareness. (Courtesy of the *Corpus Christi Caller-Times.*)

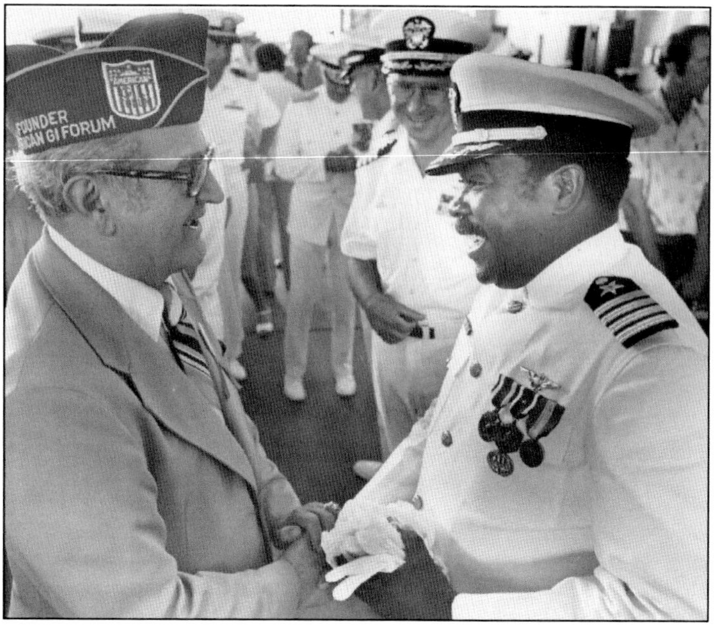

In 1978, almost a year after his appointment as commander of the Naval Air Station Corpus Christi, Capt. Richard E. Williams (right) is reacquainted with legendary Corpus Christi civil rights activist Dr. Hector P. Garcia. As founder of the American GI Forum, which aided many former veterans and others in their struggle for equality, Garcia befriended Williams almost immediately after he assumed command. (Courtesy of the *Corpus Christi Caller-Times*.)

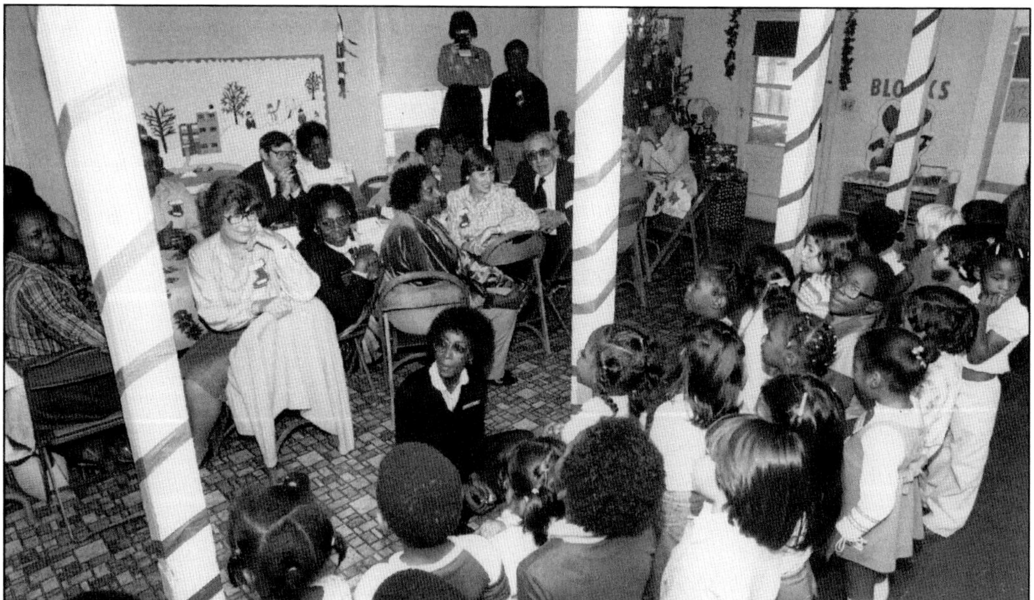

Children at the Bethune Day Nursery in Corpus Christi sing Christmas carols for the board of directors in 1982. The nursery was started in 1942, after one child was killed and another injured in a fire while left at home. Many black women had no alternative but to leave their children alone while they worked. Bethune, a nonprofit organization, provides low-income families and single-parent homes a place to bring their children while they work. (Courtesy of the *Corpus Christi Caller-Times*.)

Corpus Christi's music scene received an exciting turn when blues great B.B. King gave a concert in 1983 at the Bayfront Plaza Auditorium. Born in Mississippi, King learned the blues and brought them to a national audience. King set high standards; his attire, his eagerness, and his ability made him into possibly the best-known blues guitarist. (Courtesy of the *Corpus Christi Caller-Times*.)

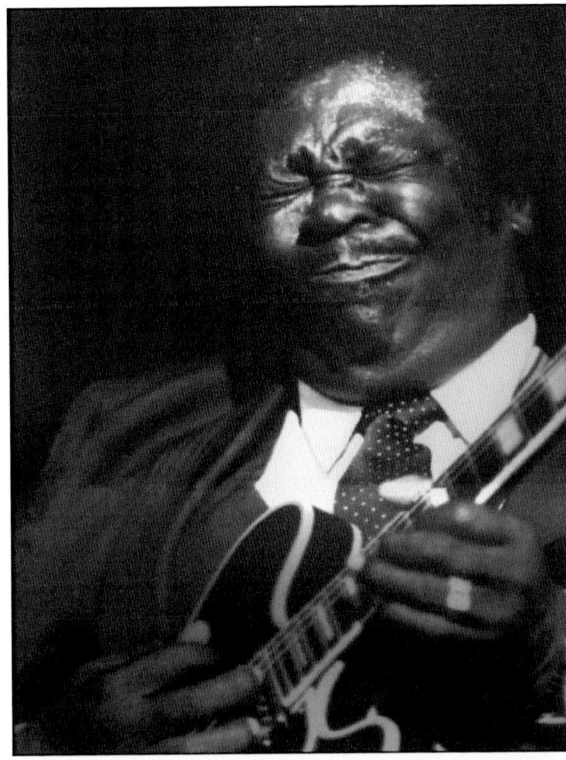

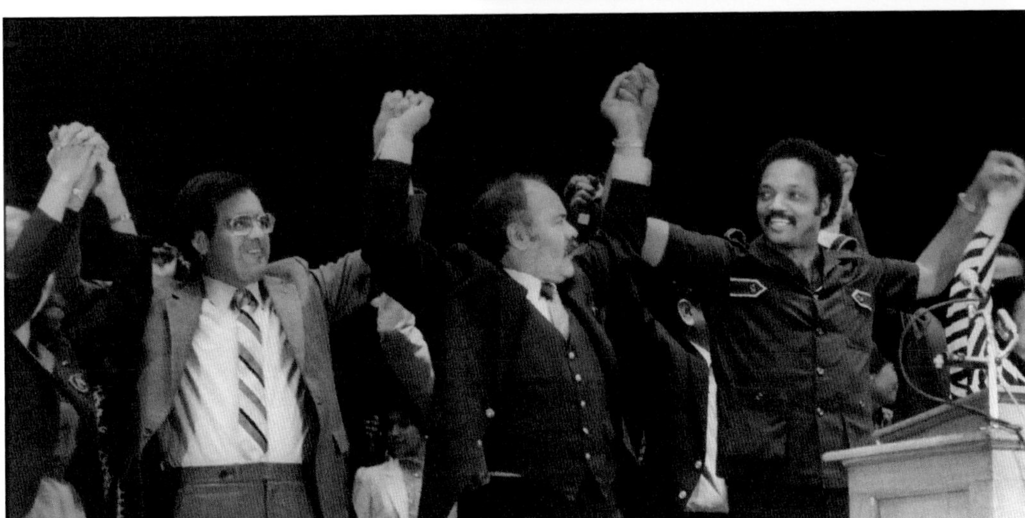

During the fall of 1983, the Reverend Jesse Jackson (far right) arrived in Corpus Christi to inspire blacks and Mexican Americans to register to vote, as well as to encourage support for his Rainbow Coalition. He also lined up backing for his presidential bid in 1984; three prominent supporters are pictured—Ruben Bonilla (left), Tony Bonilla (center), and the Reverend Elliott Grant. Jackson spoke to an enthusiastic crowd of 1,200 at Del Mar College. (Courtesy of the *Corpus Christi Caller-Times*.)

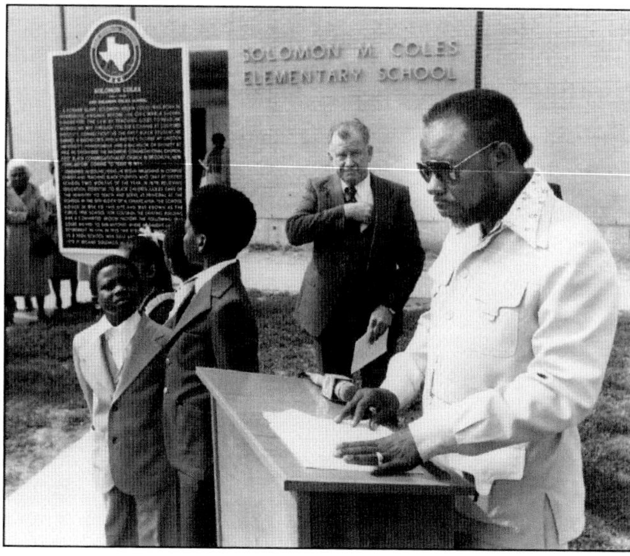

Solomon M. Coles, the man and the school, received their due in February 1979, when a historical marker was placed in front of the Solomon M. Coles Elementary School. Presiding at the ceremony, with proud students nearby, is Rufus Avery, chairman of the Solomon M. Coles School Alumni Association. Avery, a community activist who taught children an appreciation for their heritage, was also instrumental in preventing the destruction of the Solomon M. Coles School in 2003. (Courtesy of the *Corpus Christi Caller-Times.*)

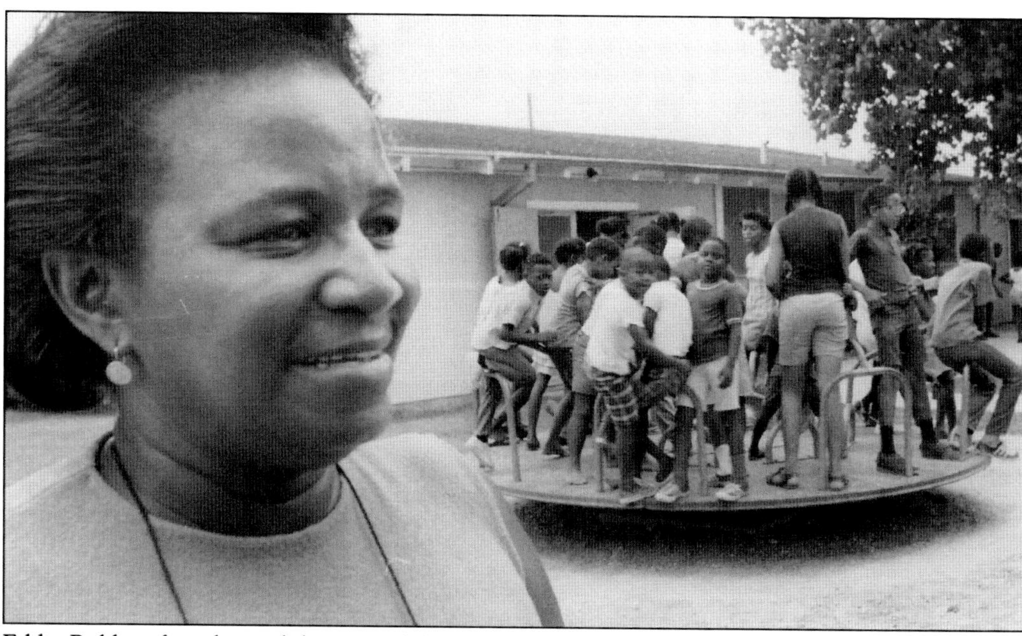

Eddie Bolden, founder and director of the Robert L. Moore Community Center, died in 1980 at the age of 85. Bolden and the center performed many functions for the Corpus Christi community. The center ran a day care facility, prepared youths to enter first grade, and held dances for black youths who had no other place to go. Bolden also organized and presented black debutantes in Corpus Christi. (Courtesy of the *Corpus Christi Caller-Times.*)

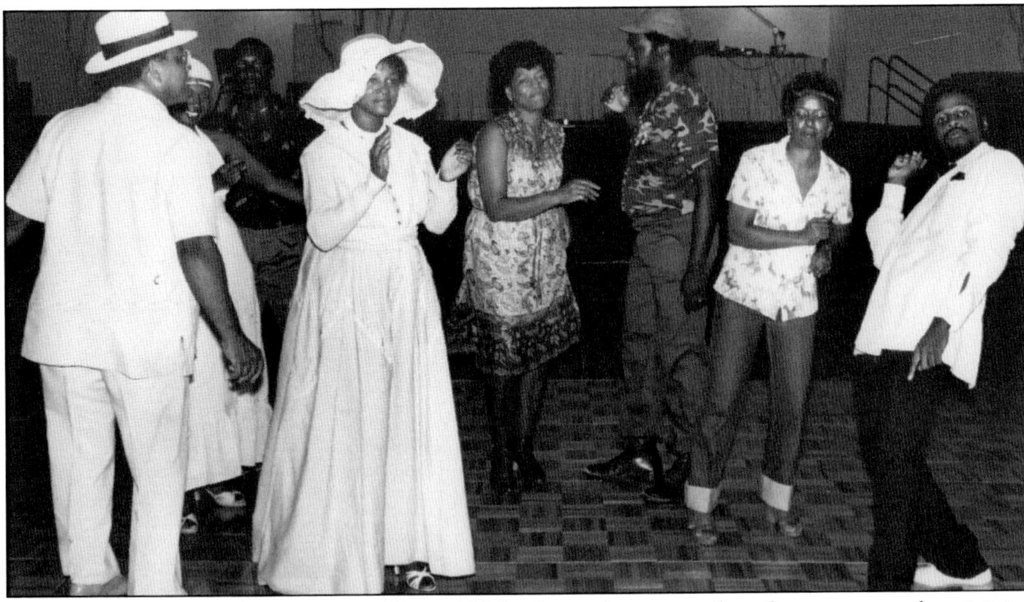

Corpus Christi's Black Awareness Day 1983 had a wide range of performances and activities, including dancing. Here, some dancers perform at the Bayfront Plaza Banquet Hall. Among the organizers for the extensive 1983 events were Preston Smith, Waunell Madison, Lena Coleman, and Curtis Williams. (Courtesy of the *Corpus Christi Caller-Times.*)

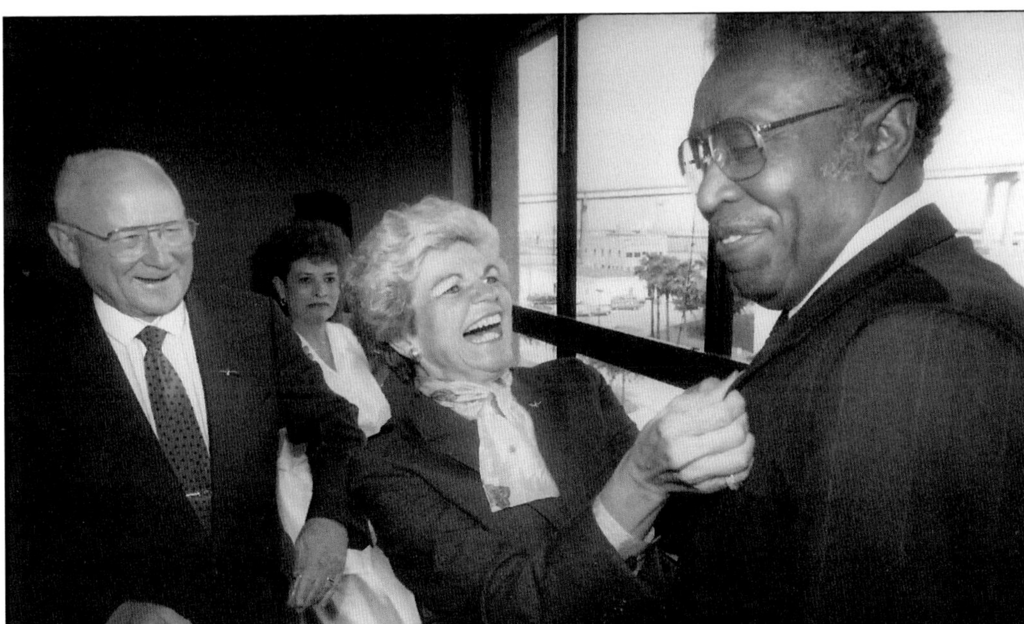

Mayor Betty Turner pins Rev. Elliott Grant. Grant, a political force and compelling leader and civil rights activist, worked with both black and white communities. He arrived in Corpus Christi in 1962, and retired as pastor of St. Matthew Missionary Baptist Church in 1987. Grant was the first black elected to the CCISD Board of Directors. Also pictured is former mayor Luther Jones (left). (Courtesy of the *Corpus Christi Caller-Times.*)

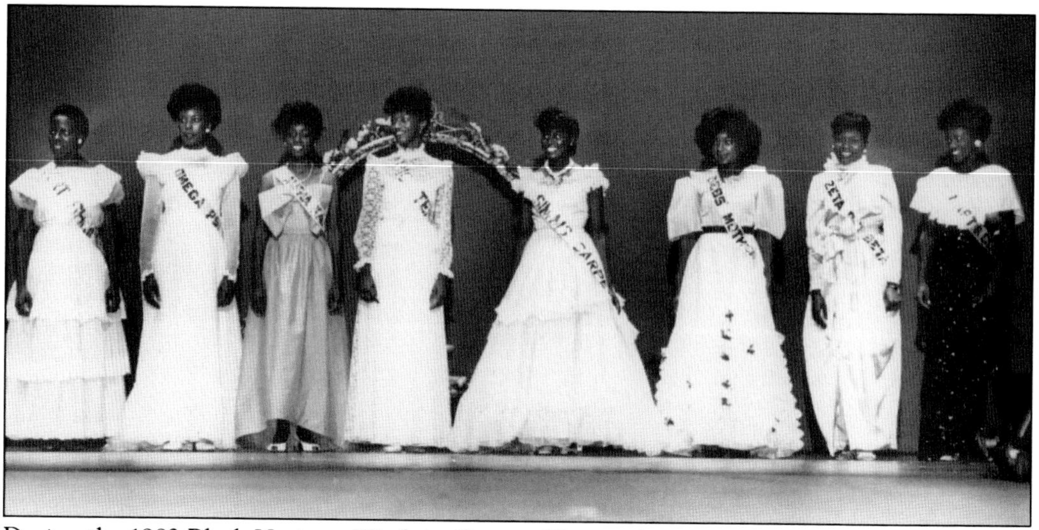

During the 1983 Black Heritage Week in Corpus Christi, there was also a beauty pageant. The contestants for the Miss Teen Pageant provided viewers with grace and ability. In the gown exhibition, each is adorned with the name of the sponsoring organization or business. (Courtesy of the *Corpus Christi Caller-Times.*)

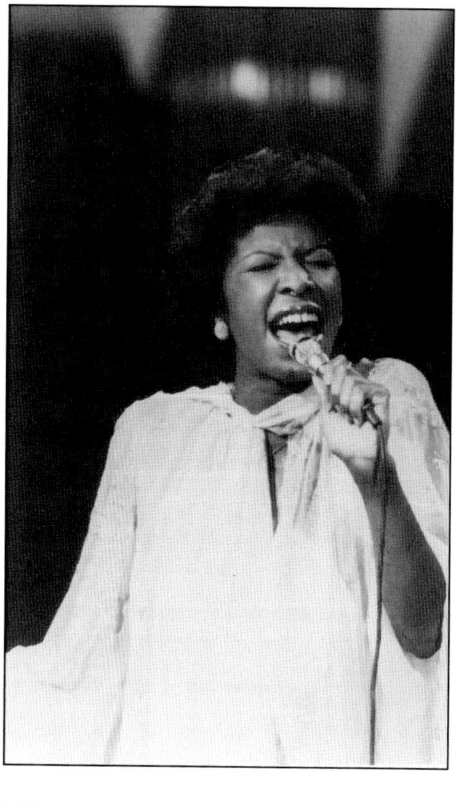

Prominent award-winning vocalist Natalie Cole performed at the Black and White Ball at the Bayfront Plaza Banquet Hall in October 1987. The performance benefitted the Art Museum of South Texas. Cole's songs included the popular "Pink Cadillac," "When I Fall in Love," and "Split Decision." Cole, the daughter of singer Nat King Cole, has won nine Grammy Awards. (Courtesy of the *Corpus Christi Caller-Times.*)

Among Corpus Christi African American firsts is that of Deborah Johnson. In 1985, Johnson became the first black female firefighter hired in Corpus Christi. Now retired, Johnson remains the only black woman firefighter in Corpus Christi history. When she was hired, three black men were firefighters, and around 15 eventually worked in the department. (Courtesy of the *Corpus Christi Caller-Times*.)

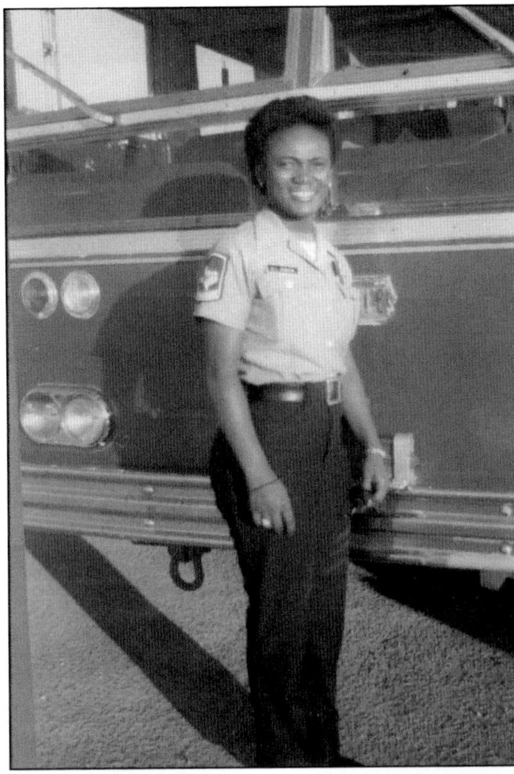

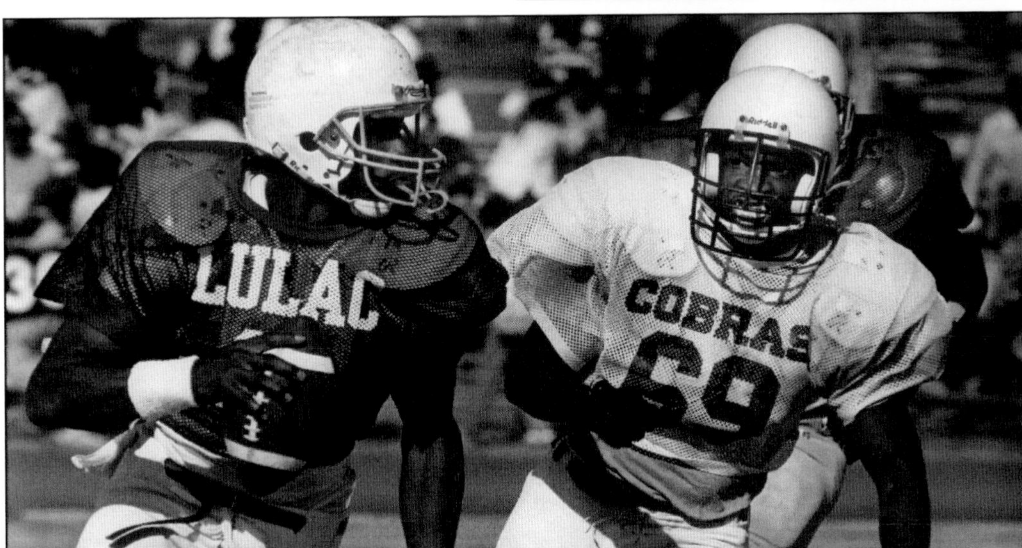

Sports, especially football, have played an important role for numerous young men. The LULAC quarterback Clyde Coleman is chased by an Army Depot Cobra in this 1988 game. Teams from across town, and varying entities, played each other. (Courtesy of the *Corpus Christi Caller-Times*.)

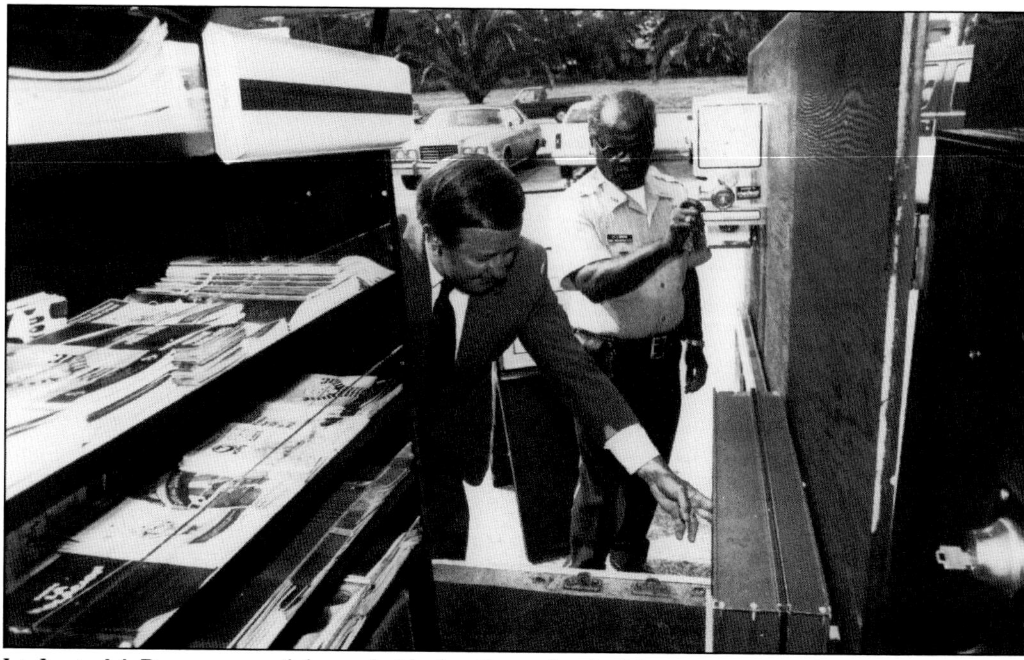

Lt. Irwin M. Brown, one of the early black officers for the Nueces County Sheriff's Department, shows a new crime-prevention van to the regional manager of Southwestern Bell. Tragically, Brown died of a heart attack while driving a Drug Abuse Resistance Education (DARE) vehicle in 1995. Brown had been in charge of the DARE program since 1987. (Courtesy of the *Corpus Christi Caller-Times*.)

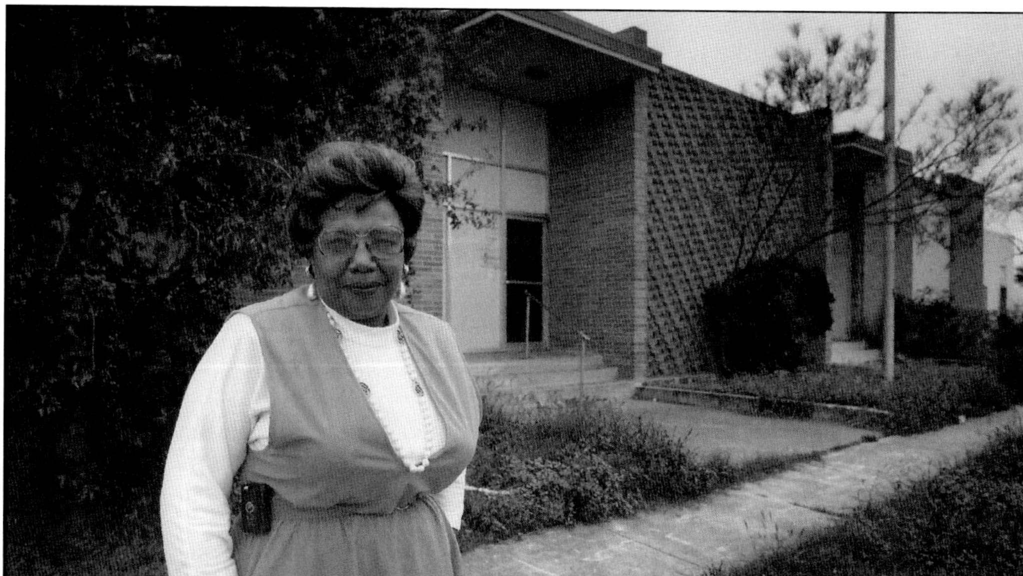

Among African American leaders and champions in Corpus Christi is Lena Coleman. In her position as director of mental retardation vocational services of the Nueces County Mental Health and Mental Retardation (MHMR) Community Center, Coleman, formerly executive director of HIALCO, successfully wrote a proposal for a project to make an old veterans hospital into a center for the developmentally disabled. (Courtesy of the *Corpus Christi Caller-Times*.)

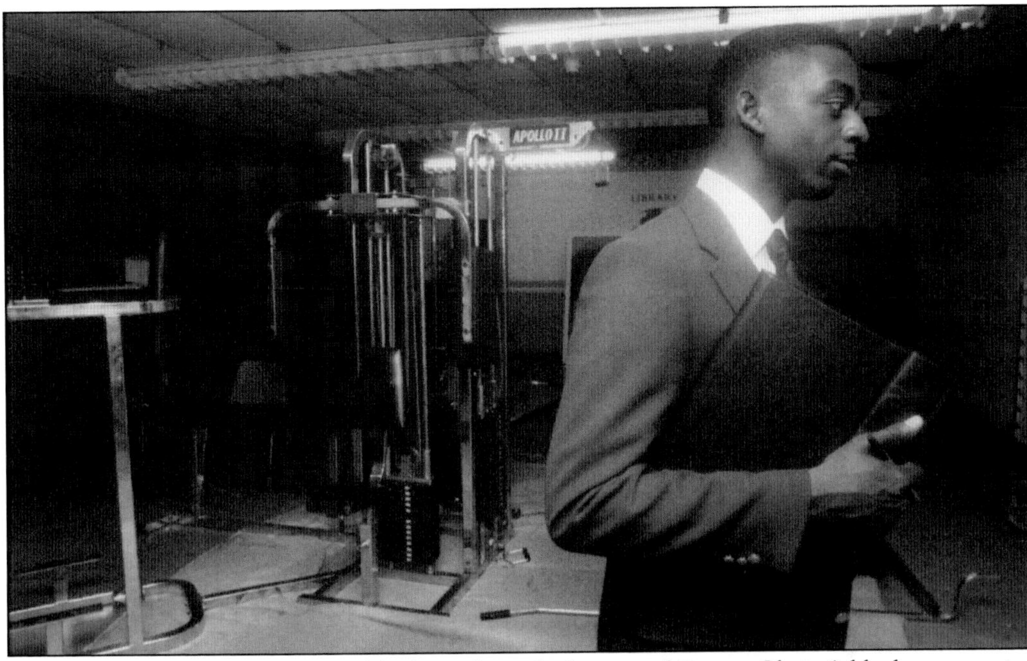

Not everything has worked smoothly throughout the history of Corpus Christi's black community. In 1989, troubleshooter Julius Lott arrived from Atlanta, Georgia, to help the Boys Club of America solve problems occurring at the Boys Club on Greenwood Drive. (Courtesy of the *Corpus Christi Caller-Times*.)

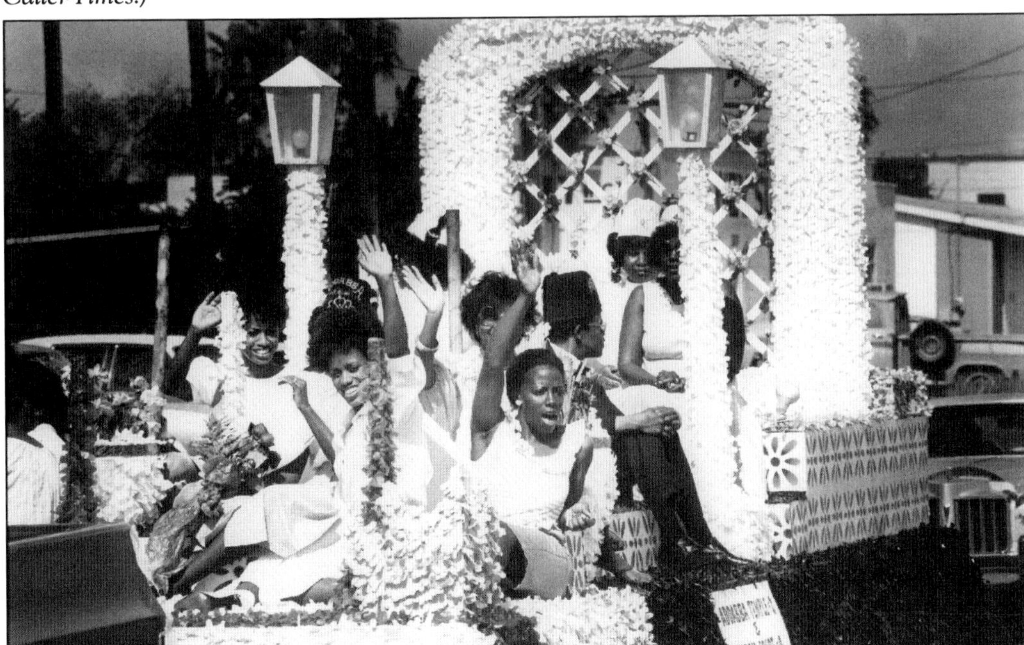

An attractive feature of any holiday or celebration is a parade. Black History parades were no exception. In this photograph, black women ride on the Addabba Shrine float in a parade near Buc Stadium. The float and the women are elaborately dressed and elegant. (Courtesy of the *Corpus Christi Caller-Times*.)

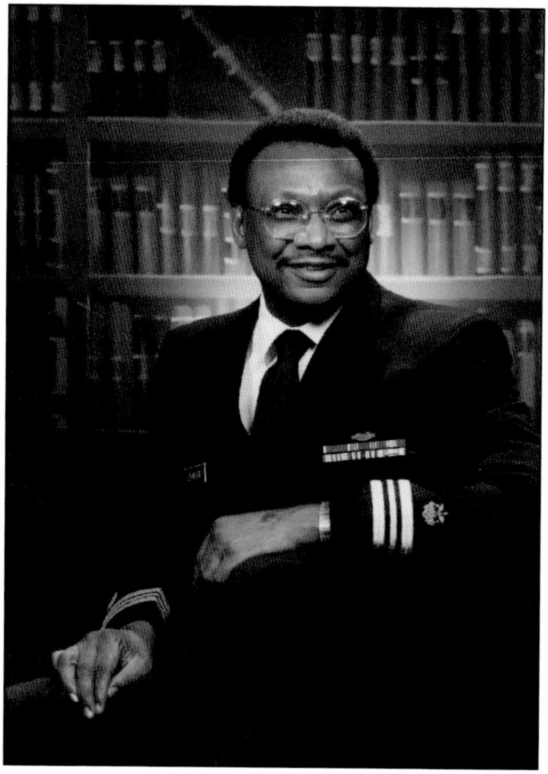

After serving in the military during the Vietnam War, for which he later received the Bronze Star, Tone Johnson Jr. left the service and enrolled in Grambling State University. From Grambling, he went to the University of Buffalo School of Medicine, where he earned his medical degree. Johnson then moved to Corpus Christi, where he continues to engage in family practice. (Courtesy of Geraldine and Tone Johnson.)

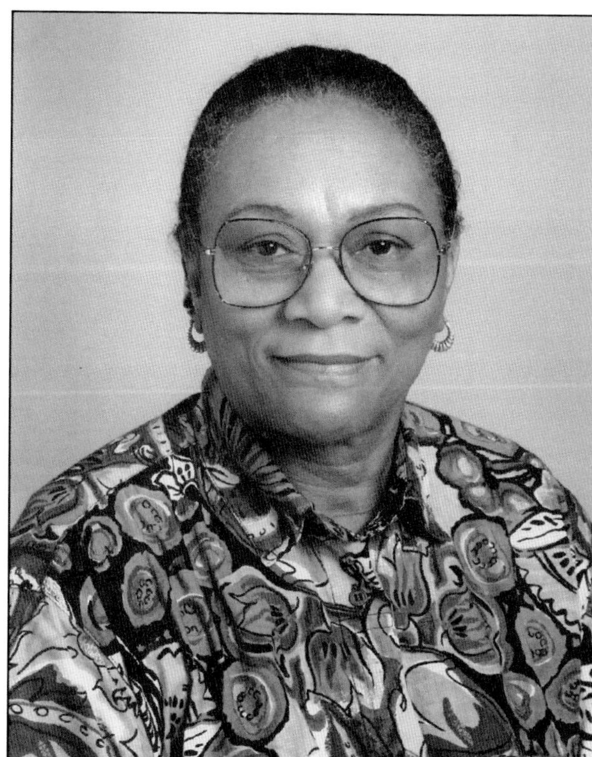

An educator, a teacher, and an administrator, Ora Ruth Williams assumed office as an assistant principal at Cunningham Junior High. Williams then moved her skills and interests to the Corpus Christi Student and Guidance Center, where she served as administrator beginning in 1986. (Courtesy of the *Corpus Christi Caller-Times*.)

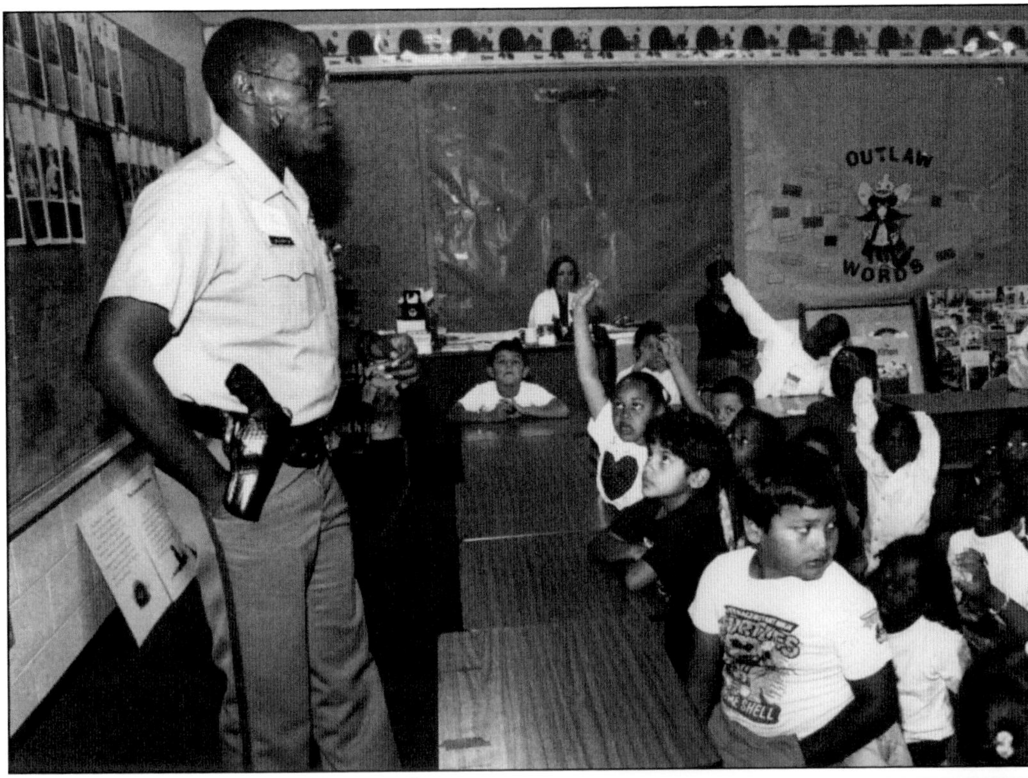

An important means of enabling students to appreciate and to understand—perhaps even aspire to—the jobs of others is to have professionals visit a classroom. Sgt. C. Williams, of the Corpus Christi Police Department, speaks to a classroom at Crossley Elementary in 1990 as part of Black History Week. The students appear intent and interested; so does the teacher, Catherine Pellegrino. (Courtesy of the *Corpus Christi Caller-Times*.)

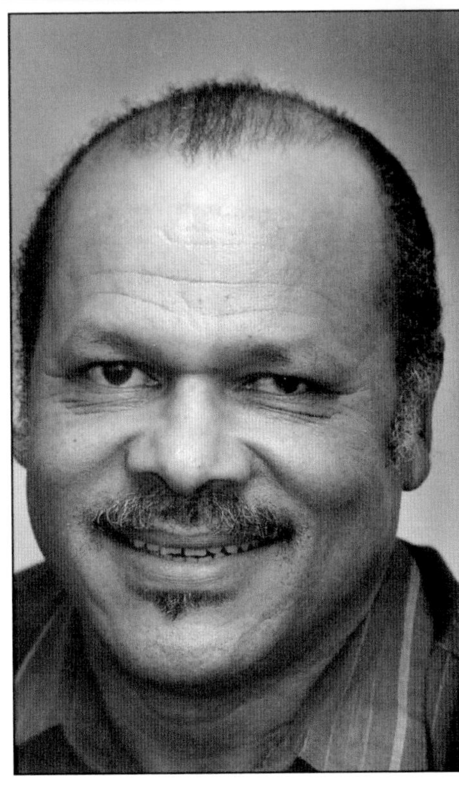

Ernest Carter, HIALCO director and prime mover behind construction of 40 units of housing for low-income elderly people, saw the project completed in 1987. Born in Huntsville, Texas, he moved to Corpus Christi in 1961 after serving in the US military. Carter graduated from St. Peter Claver Academy in San Antonio and was one of the first three black graduates of St. Mary's University in San Antonio in 1953. (Courtesy of the *Corpus Christi Caller-Times*.)

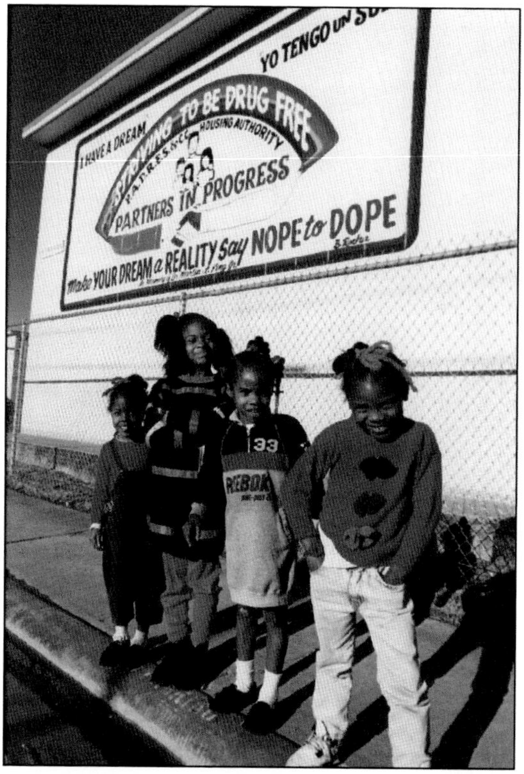

A problem associated with urban communities in Texas as well as the rest of the nation is drug use. The youths posing in front of a mural painted on an apartment in the Leathers housing complex are, from left to right, Latara Jackson, Fallon Lewis, Candice Lewis, and Tenasha Jackson. The mural *Say Nope to Dope* symbolizes a partnership between PADRES and the Corpus Christi Housing Authority to provide drug and alcohol prevention on the Northside. (Courtesy of the *Corpus Christi Caller-Times*.)

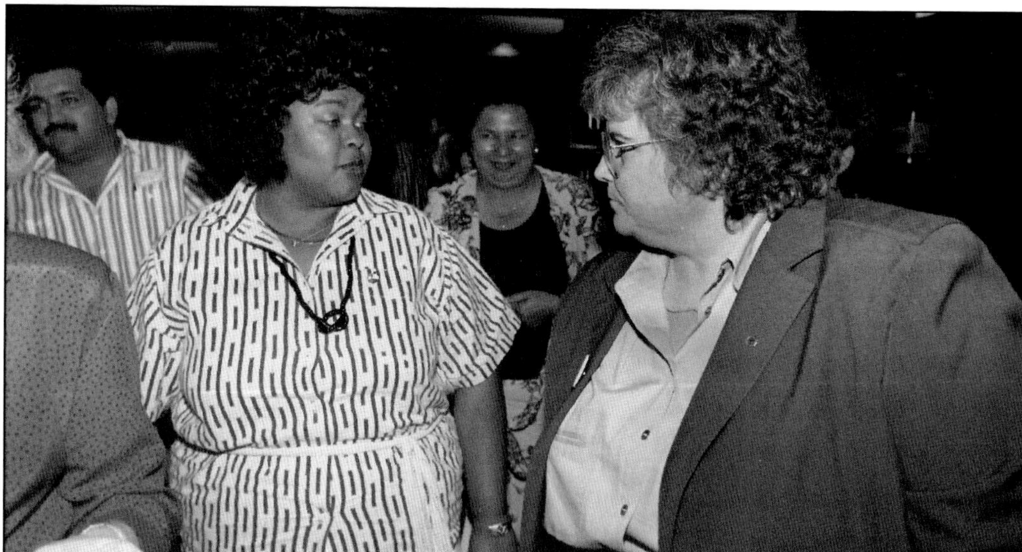

"Teachers should be the number-one priority," argued Rheba Jones, president of the Corpus Christi Classroom Teachers Association (CCCTA) in 1987. She sought to increase salaries for teachers. A former classroom teacher, Jones works full-time at her current position as head of the union that consults with the Corpus Christi Independent School District (CCISD). However, in the fall of 1988, the CCCTA was defeated by the American Federation of Teachers (AFT) for the right of consultation. Here, Jones (center) congratulates winning AFT president Linda Bridges. (Courtesy of the *Corpus Christi Caller-Times*.)

Activities at Juneteenth Day celebrations were varied. In 1988, youths competed in sack races. In this image, Tina Walker (left) and Gloria Strait make the effort. This particular race took place at the naval air station. (Courtesy of the *Corpus Christi Caller-Times.*)

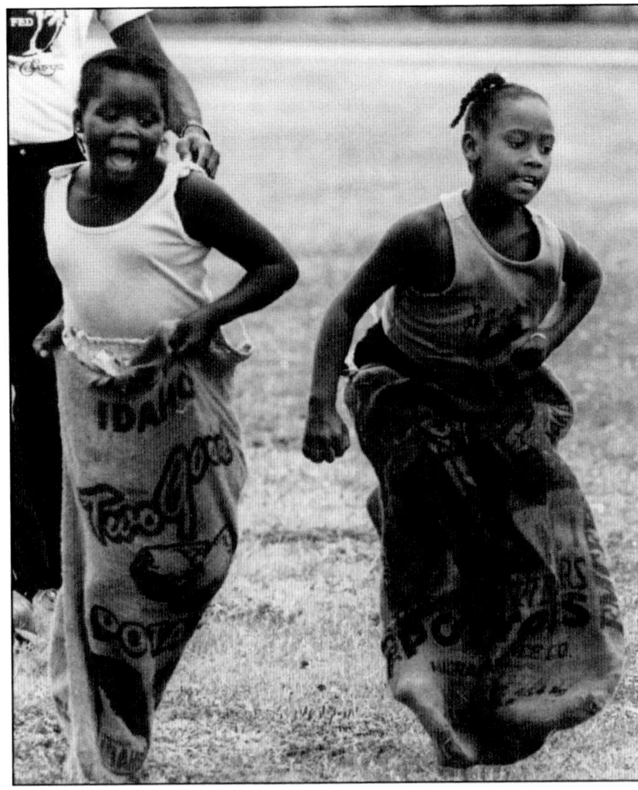

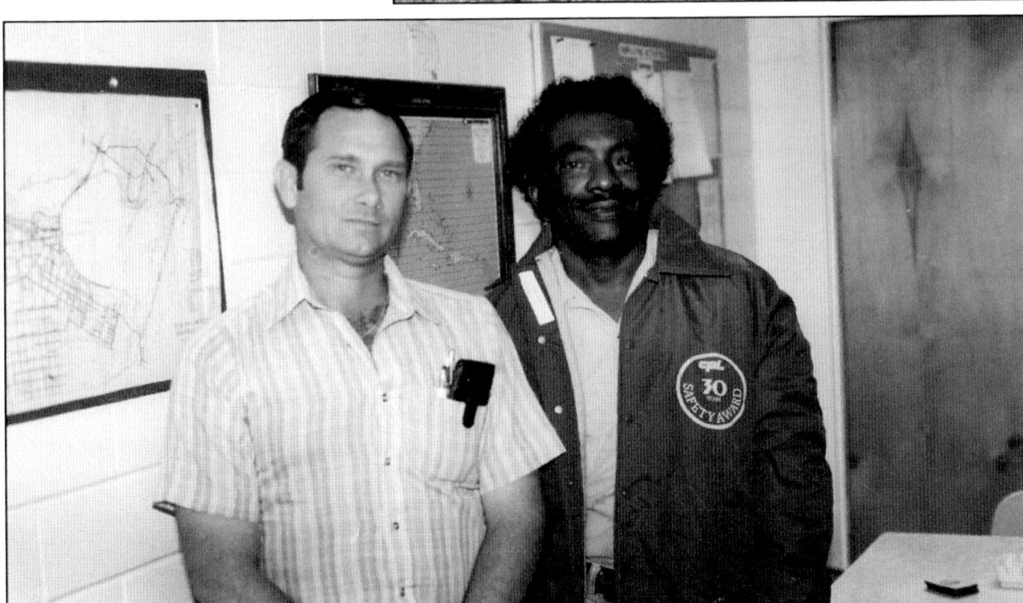

Thedford Bowers (right) received a jacket for 30 years of safety and service from Central Power and Light (CPL). He retired from CPL when American Electric Power (AEP) bought the company. Bowers then made his part-time job his full-time occupation. An active member in the community, Bowers still provides excellent customer service for James Mathis Exxon. The man at left is unidentified.

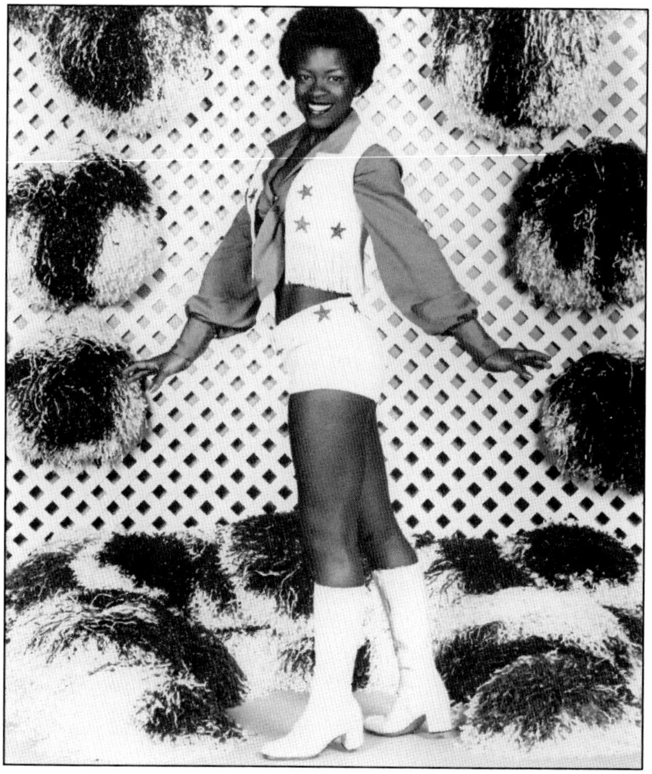

A cheerleader since junior high school, Angel Bland Hazley received the ultimate position in 1978 as the first black Dallas Cowboys cheerleader chosen from South Texas. She also won the title of Miss Black Dallas. Hazley moved back to Corpus Christi, received the key to the city, and became the first black local stenographer/court reporter. She also worked in the Corpus Christi school system for several years. (Courtesy of Angel Bland Hazley.)

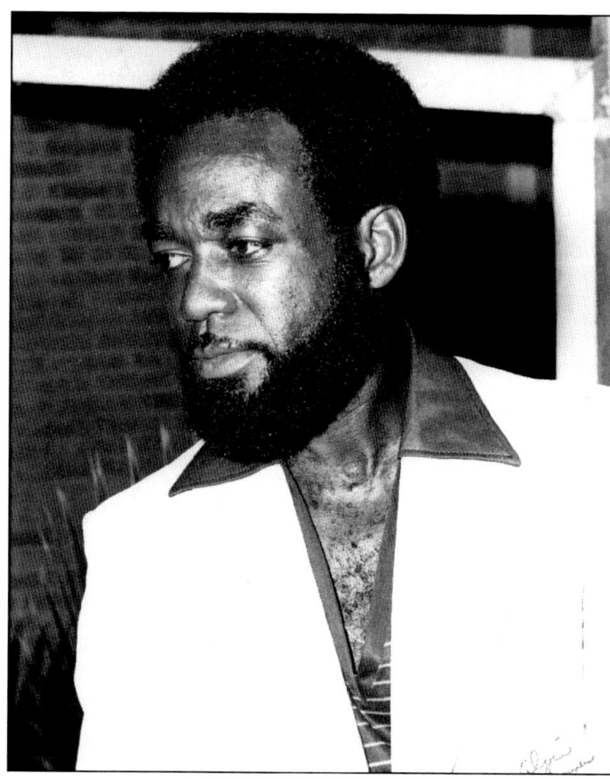

Alvin Bonner, the first black to be awarded the Harbor Playhouse acting award for his role in *Driving Miss Daisy* in 1978, enjoyed acting. A local Army depot electrician by profession, Bonner found acting a natural element of his personality and relished the hard work and practice that took up most of his spare time. (Courtesy of Jewel Wilson.)

Six

Clarifying Roles 1991–2011

For the past two decades prior to this book's publication, the African American community of Corpus Christi, although a small proportion of the total population, found itself in a strong and enduring position. It fought for rights, gained some, and is still in need of others. Its members have opportunities for building on their previous strengths, and they are clarifying their roles as participants in the broader community. However, not all is rosy. The black population declined by a little over 200 between 2000 and 2010. The number of black teachers is declining, and black college graduates tend to leave town after graduation.

At the same time, there are considerable reasons for excitement. After serving as president of the Girl Scouts of America, vice president at Clark University in Atlanta, and president of Bennett College for Women in North Carolina, well-known black leader Gloria Randle Scott retired to Corpus Christi. Rev. E.F. Bennett, pastor of Mount Pilgrim Baptist Church and referred to as "a voice for unity," published his book *Character Counts: Do You Agree?* Community activist Dr. Geraldine Johnson and her husband, Bronze Star recipient Dr. Tone Johnson Jr., also settled in Corpus Christi. In 1993, Carl Lewis, the first black Nueces County Attorney, assumed office.

Organizations also bolstered the community. The Juneteenth Coalition effectively broadened the sweep of Corpus Christi's celebration to 10 days. Pastor Don Leavell's megachurch, the Corpus Christi Christian Fellowship Church, brings attention to religious activity in and around the city. Led by Geraldine Johnson, the Corpus Christi Black Chamber of Commerce supports and publicizes efforts of the black business community. The NAACP became involved in the community under the leadership of Harold Moore and continues its work with the two-term presidency of Terry Mills. The vitally important Corpus Christi Black History Cultural Committee assures an interest in and activities for blacks in Corpus Christi.

A book that says much about Corpus Christi attractions for African Americans is Brenda Mazone Glasgow's *Why She Stayed*. Del Mar College named a classroom building after black leader Solomon M. Coles, and two other black community activists had buildings named after them: Mary Ella Fucuals (children's center) and Oveal Williams (senior center). At the time of his 25th birthday, Corpus Christi native Billy Smith Jr. was a talented, up-and-coming screenwriter in Hollywood.

The community continues to celebrate and to relax; such occasions include New Year's Eve galas, Rosa Parks Day, the MLK March, a Soul Food Festival, Kwanzaa, Juneteenth, and Black History Month. The black community of Corpus Christi, its leaders, its organizations, and its residents have continued the strong tradition of emphasizing the importance of community and clarifying its role in the city by the sea.

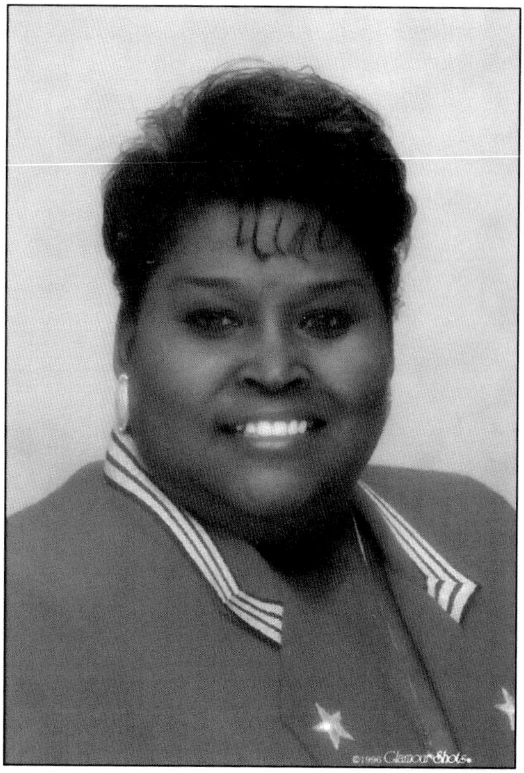

Dynamic and personable, Beverly Sue Winters seemed to create opportunity everywhere she went. Born in Corpus Christi, she lived for a time in San Antonio and then returned to the Northside where she founded the South Texas Educational Foundation Inc. A member of the West Side Corpus Christi Rotary Club, she also headed the Corpus Christi Black Chamber of Commerce and was president of the Coalition of Black Democrats. (Courtesy of *Corpus Christi Caller-Times*.)

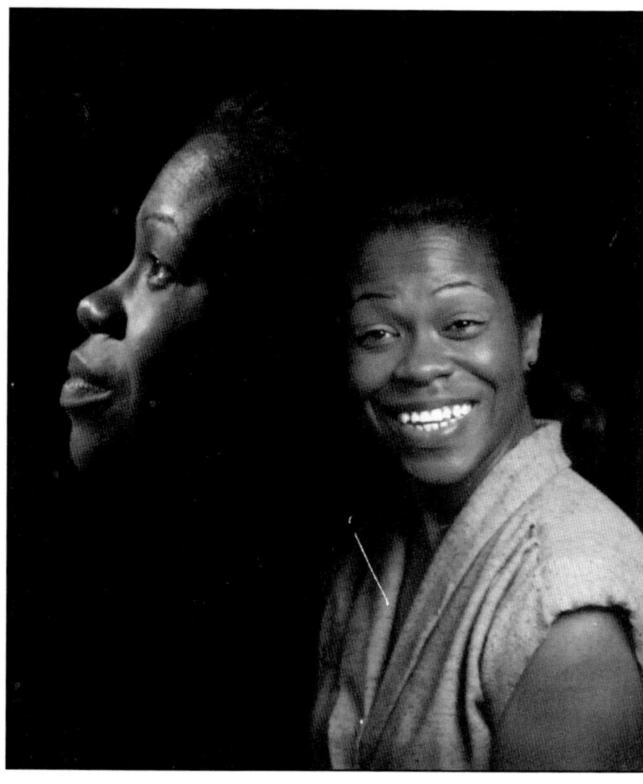

A successful Texas A&M University-Corpus Christi nursing graduate, Jewel E. (Bland) Wilson became the first black head nurse/supervisor at Spohn Hospital. She was instrumental in forming HIALCO and served as its president for two terms. Wilson went to Austin and testified for the expansion of Texas A&M University-Corpus Christi. She is also a longtime member of the NAACP and serves as local vice president for this organization. (Courtesy of Jewel Wilson.)

Dr. Geraldine Johnson, chairman of the board for the Corpus Christi Black Chamber of Commerce and a successful entrepreneur, poses for the camera during a banquet. Johnson owned and operated Coastal Bend Day Care Centers. She also has belonged to several other organizations, including the Juneteenth Coalition, and is a strong member of Zeta Phi Beta sorority, Gamma Alpha Zeta chapter. (Courtesy of Geraldine Johnson.)

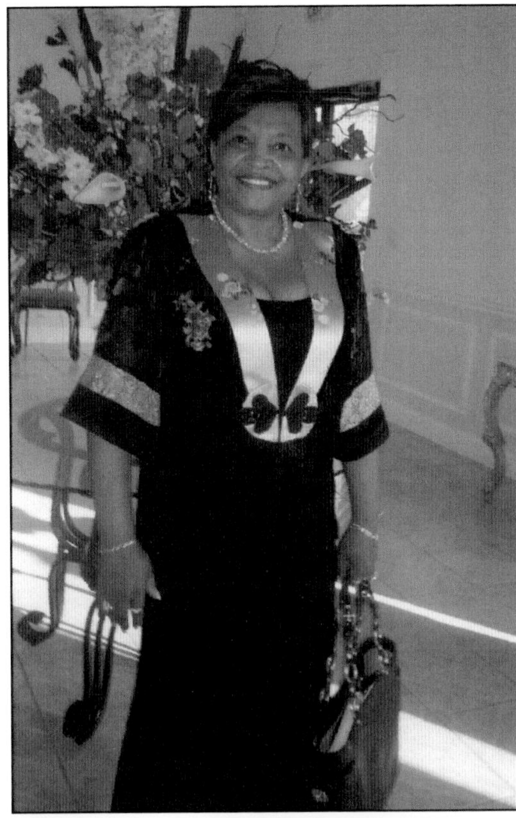

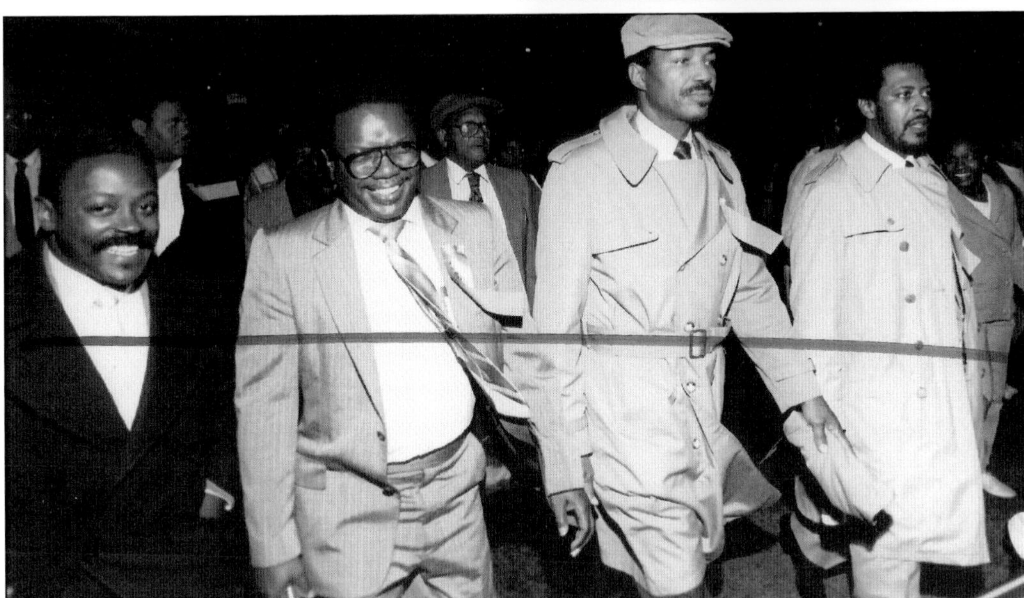

From left to right, the Reverends Roy Malreau, Claude Axel, Harry Williams, and Gary Roberts—four greats honoring a giant—lead a Martin Luther King Commemorative March in 1992. Starting at H.J. Williams Park near Port Avenue, they guided the procession down to Solomon M. Coles School. (Courtesy of *Corpus Christi Caller-Times*.)

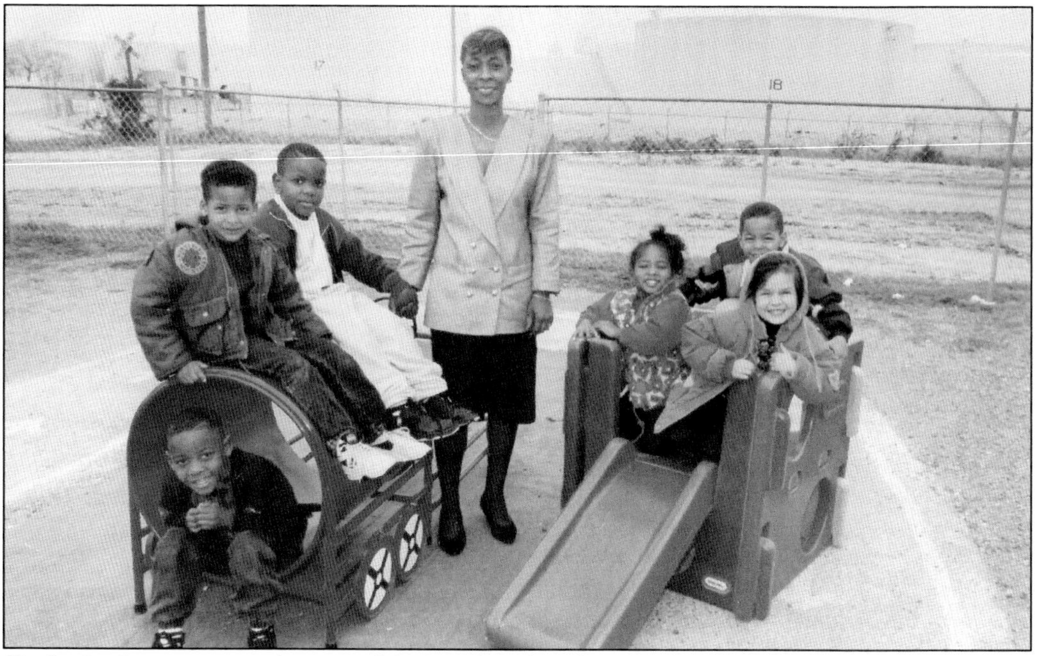

Shirley Jordan, executive director of the Brooks Chapel Early Childhood Development Center on Port Avenue, poses with some of her charges in February 1993. Pictured with her are, from left to right, O'Quatis "CQ" Toliver, Michael Gut, Evarista Coleman, Bobbie Brown, Nina Garza, and Justin Rodriquez. (Courtesy of *Corpus Christi Caller-Times.*)

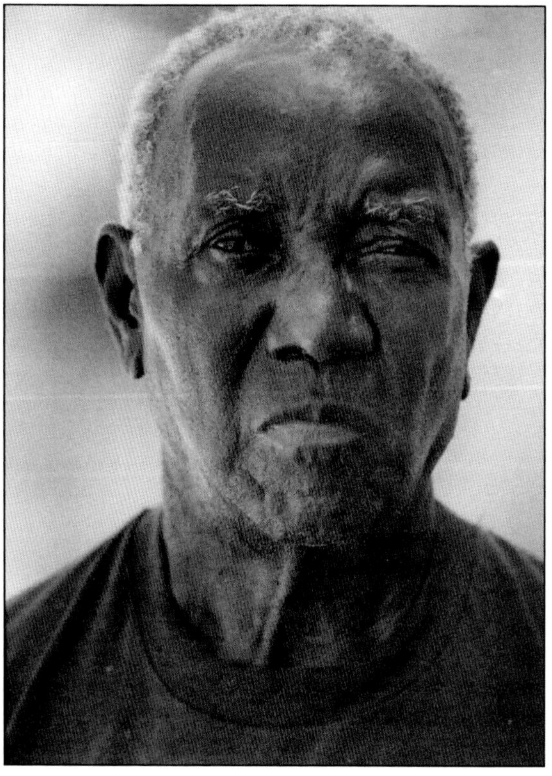

Surrogate father and staunch friend to many Northside youngsters, Oveal Williams was a longtime leader in St. John Baptist Church. Honored by the church in 1991 with an "Oveal Williams: This is Your Life" event, he also was facility chairman for that year's national meeting of ushers in the American Baptist Church in Los Angeles. (Courtesy of *Corpus Christi Caller-Times.*)

A strong civic leader with an interest in community history, Rev. Henry Williams ministered at the Corpus Christi Christian Fellowship for over a decade. He has been involved with many community projects and has long tried to aid those in need. (Courtesy of Rev. Henry Williams.)

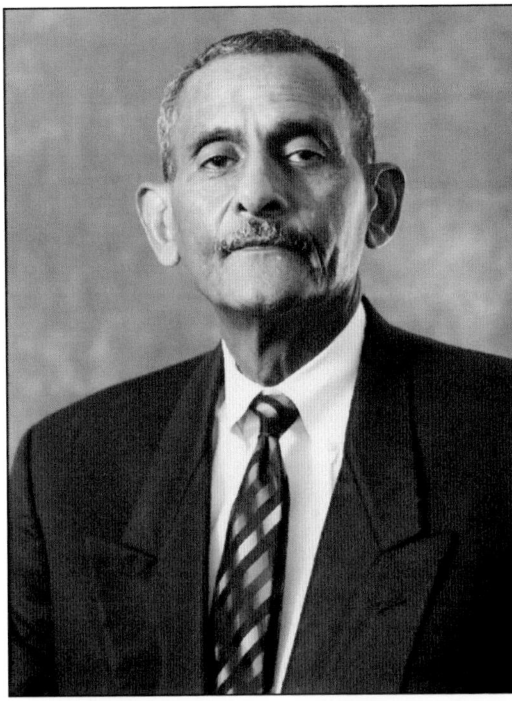

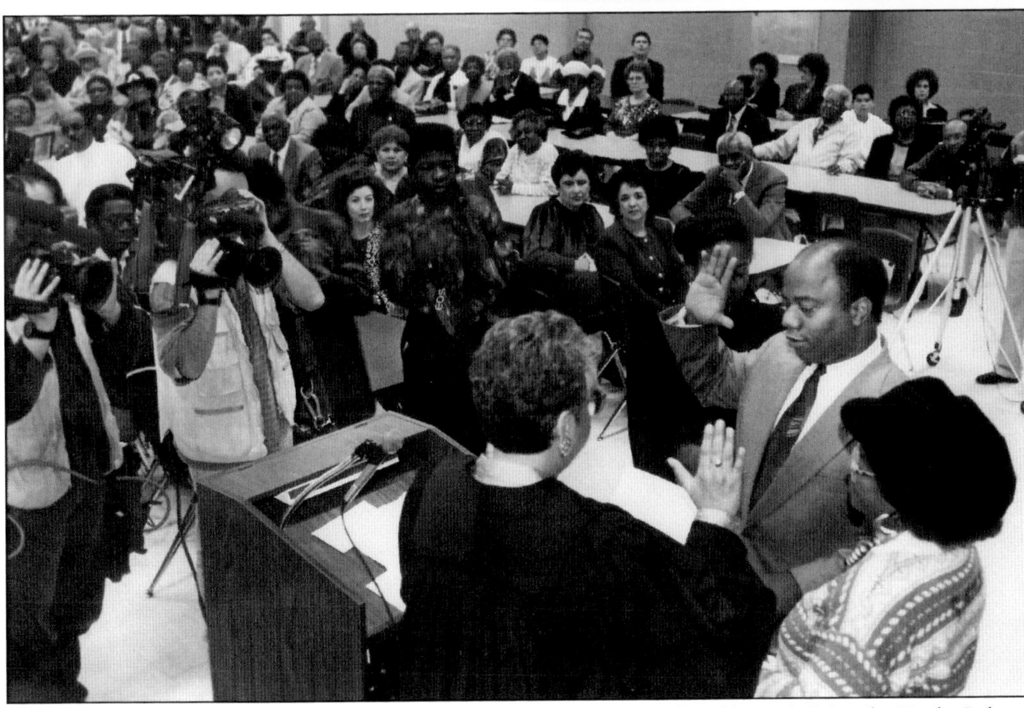

Carl Lewis was the first black elected in Texas to a statewide office. A Moody High School graduate, he attended Yale and received a degree in English. Lewis returned to Corpus Christi but soon left for the University of Texas Law School. After graduation, he practiced as a criminal defense attorney for 10 years before running for the office of Nueces County Attorney. At his suggestion, he was sworn into office at the Moody High School cafeteria.

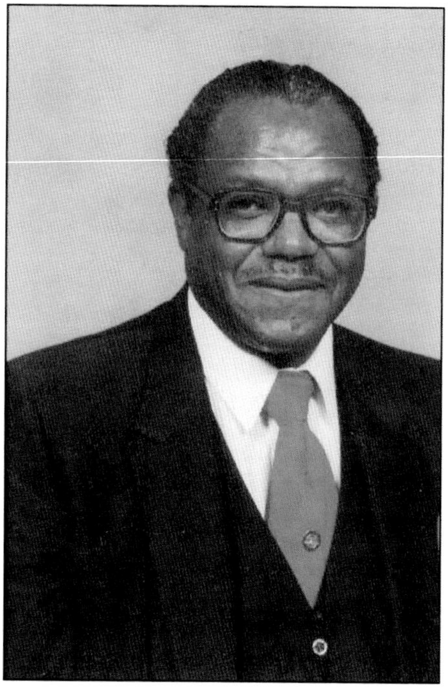

Earl Coleman served in the US Army for 20 years, earned a master's degree, and became the first African American director of vocational education and director of maintenance/transportation at West Oso Independent School District in 1975. In 1988, Coleman cofounded and became chairman and president of Brooks Chapel AME Early Childhood Development Center, and in 2004, he received the Presidential Honor Award from the NAACP. (Courtesy of Jeremy Coleman.)

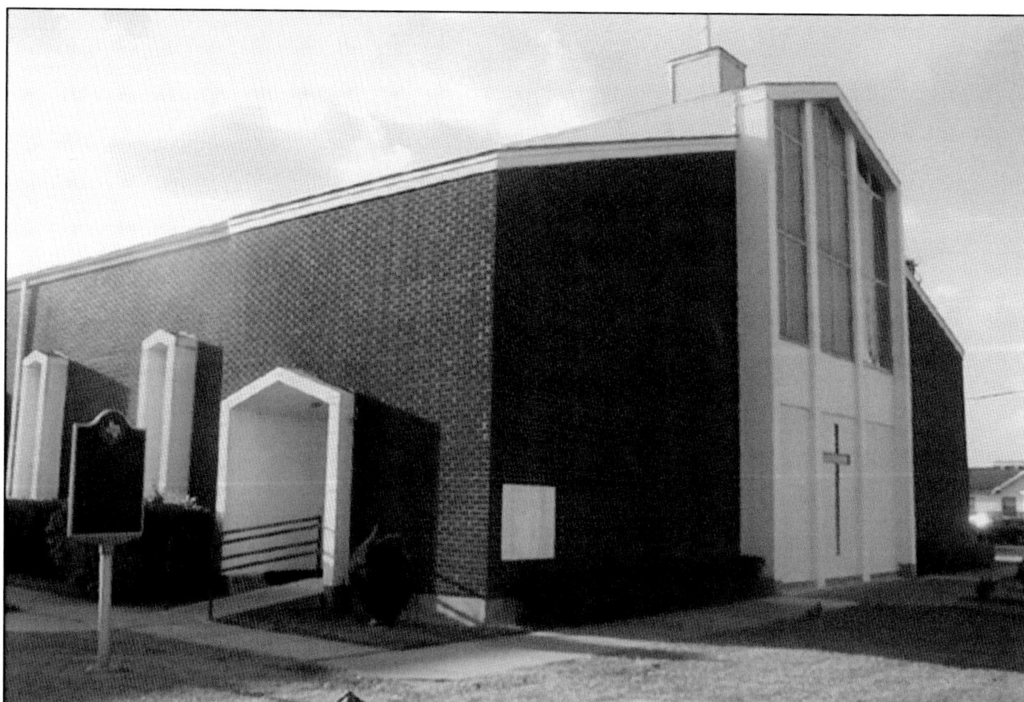

St. John Baptist Church dedicated this building in 1969. It is one of the founding churches in this community, which evolved from survivors of the 1875 Indianola storm who moved to Corpus Christi. Originally named the St. John Free Mission Baptist Church, the congregation met in a barn until a small building was erected on North Broadway and Twigg Streets. In 1910, the church moved to Ramirez Street. (Courtesy of Jeremy Coleman and St. John Baptist Church.)

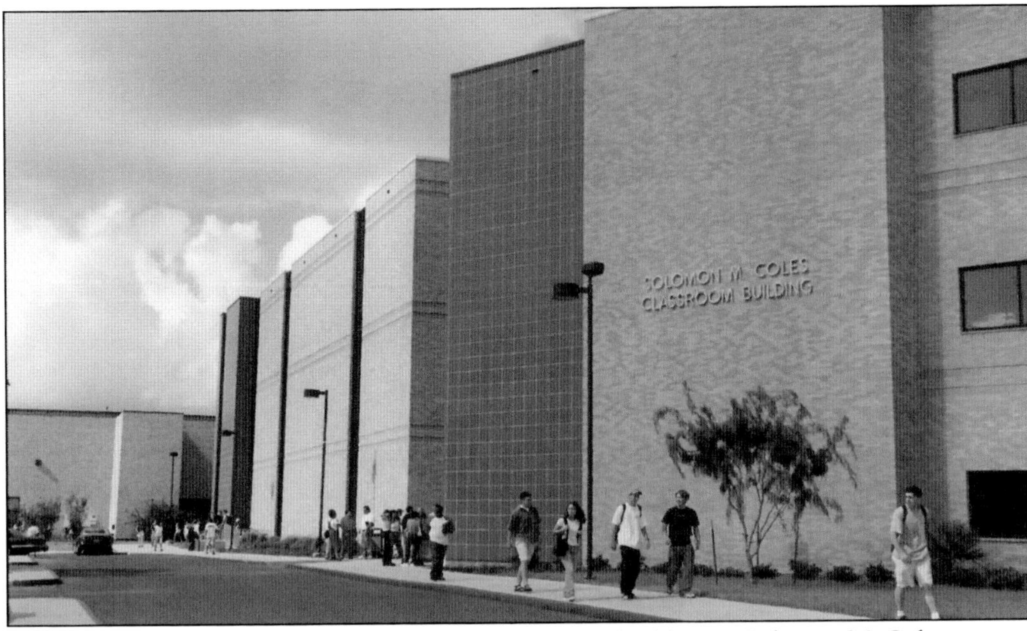

Del Mar College's dedication of its new educational arts building to Solomon M. Coles was one of the greatest acknowledgments granted to Coles by an institution. Opened in 2000, it has since benefited thousands of young students just as Coles himself did a century earlier. (Courtesy of Del Mar College Campus Relations Office.)

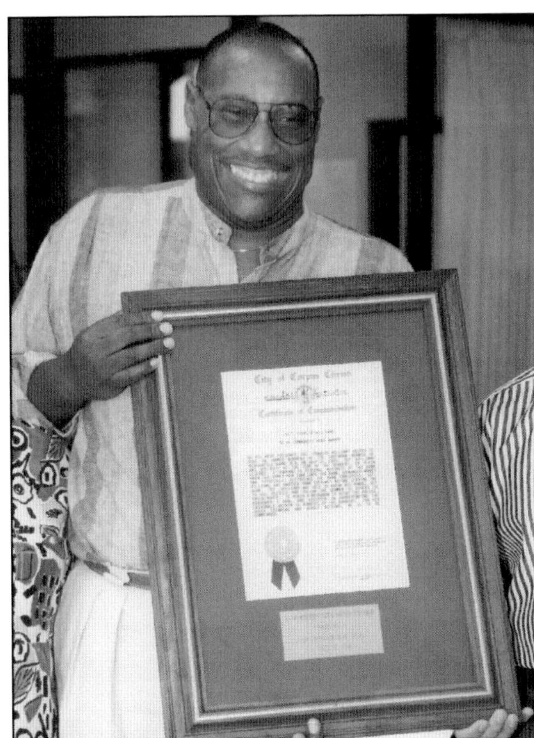

Acclaimed both by the public and by local radio station K-99, Sgt. Charlie Williams, of the Corpus Christi Police Department, receives the K-99 Community Hero Award in 1994. A longtime officer in the force, Sergeant Williams helped foil an armed robbery at Mercantile Bank a year earlier. (Courtesy of *Corpus Christi Caller-Times*.)

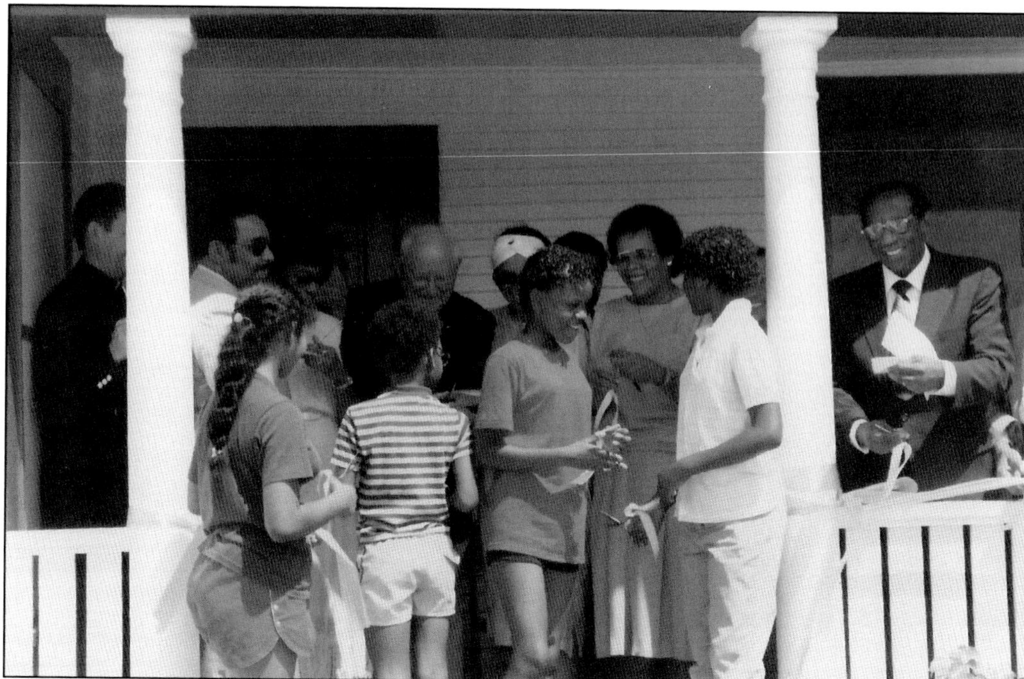

The Littles-Martin House was finally moved, renovated, and joyfully opened its doors to the community in September 1986. Mayor Luther Jones cut the opening ribbon with several other area dignitaries. (Courtesy of the Corpus Christi NAACP.)

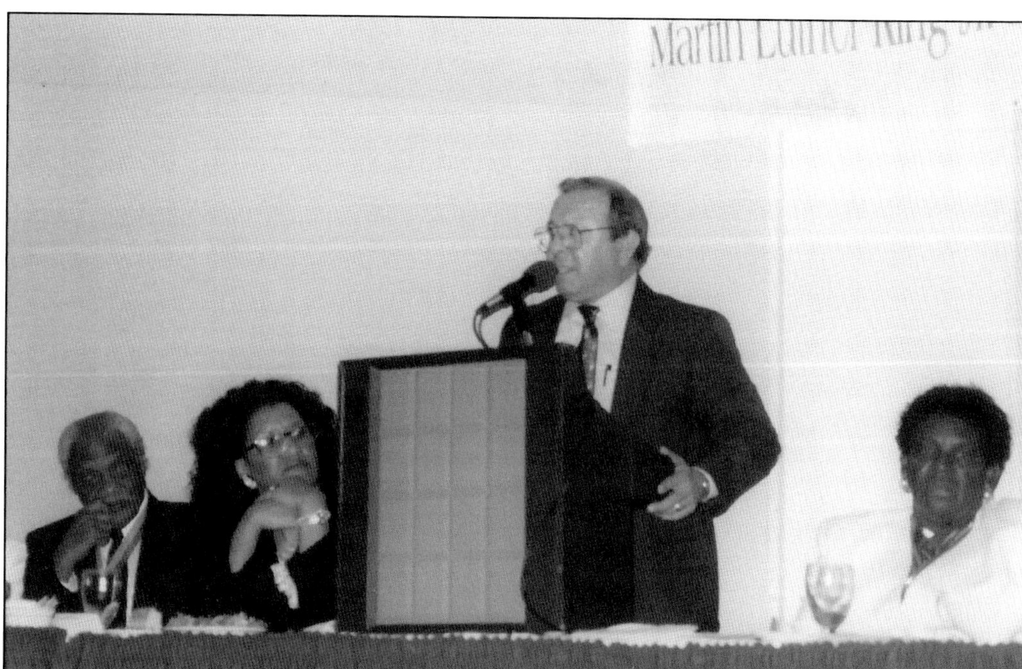

State Representative Carlos Truan speaks at the Martin Luther King Commemorative Banquet in 1992. (Courtesy of the Corpus Christi NAACP.)

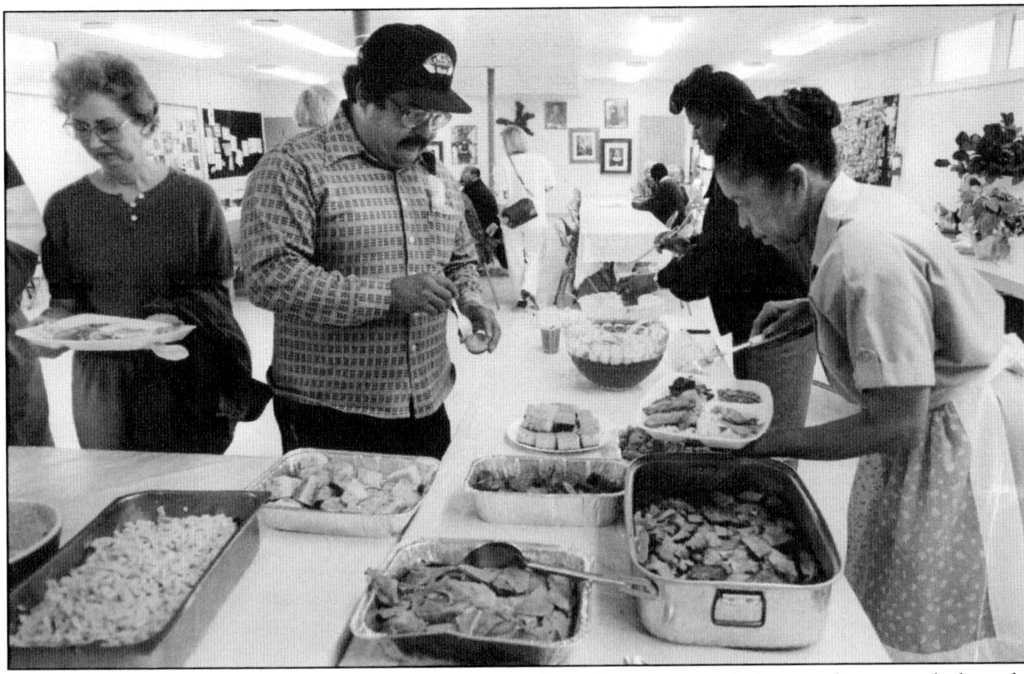

Macaroni and cheese, sweet potatoes, and corn bread are some of the staples provided at the Soul Food Festival in 1993. Participating as part of Black History Month in Corpus Christi are Annie Wilson and other members of the Holy Cross Catholic Church on North Staples Street. (Courtesy of *Corpus Christi Caller-Times.*)

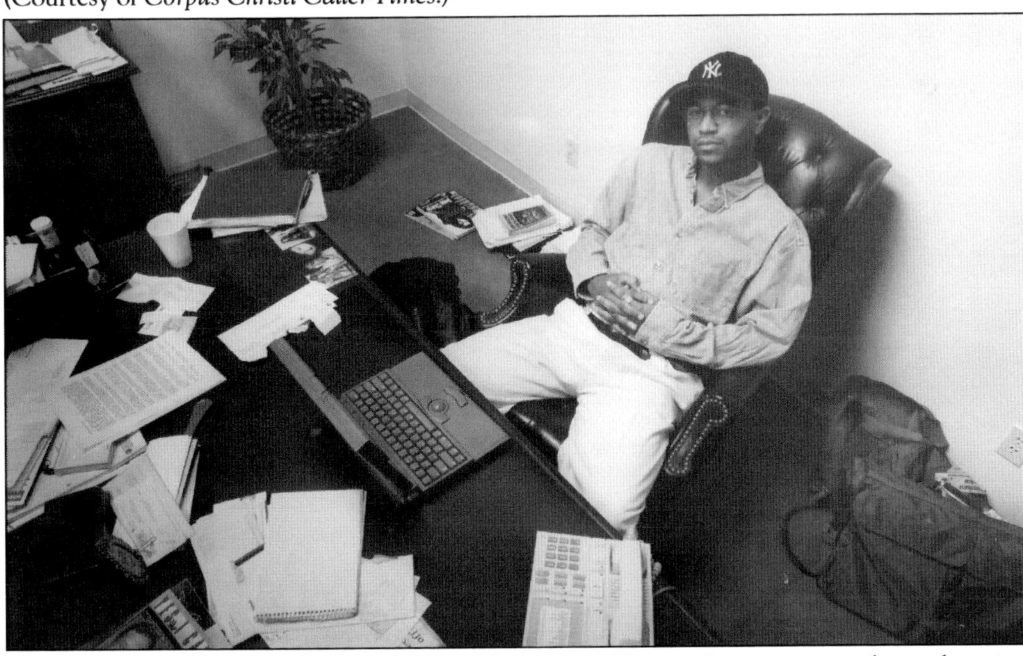

Some talented African American youths left Corpus Christi after acquiring their education. Bobby Smith Jr. graduated from Ray High School and headed west. At the age of 25, he became one of Hollywood's gifted young screenwriters. His films include *Jason's Lyric* and the television adaptation of *Their Eyes Were Watching God.* (Courtesy of *Corpus Christi Caller-Times.*)

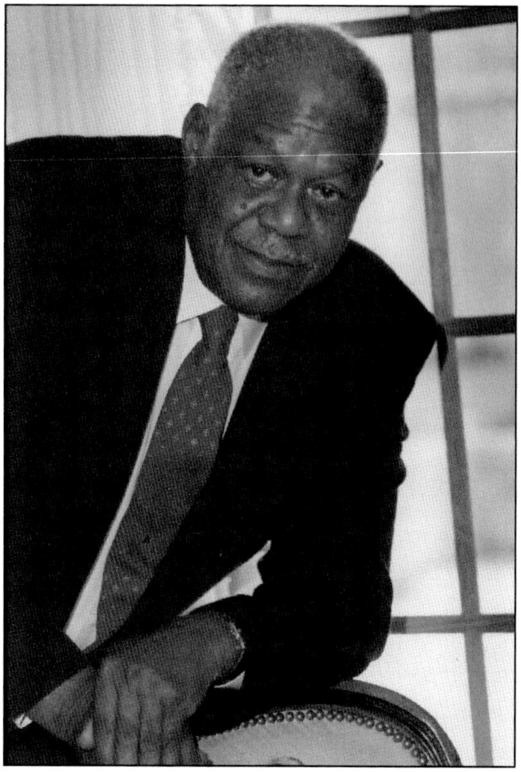

Harold Moore assumed the presidency of the local branch of the NAACP in 1993. His goal was to go back to the grassroots of the organization, help increase membership, and work for the impoverished. Moore sought to unite the community and address the concerns of the population. (Courtesy of *Corpus Christi Caller-Times*.)

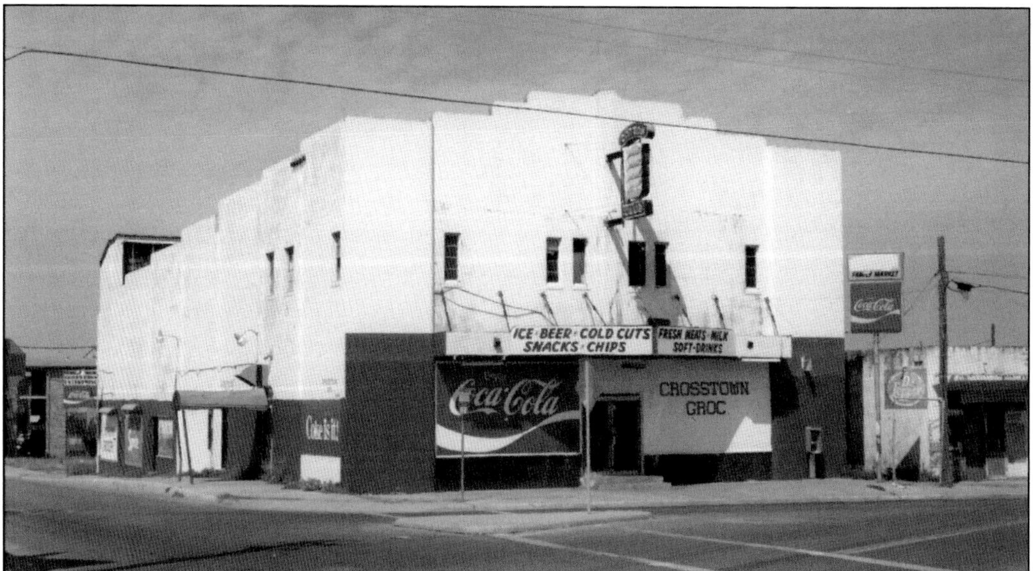

Benjamin's Family Supermarket was in the 1941 building that originally housed the Harlem Theater, one of the first theaters in the city for African Americans. In 1968, after over 15 years as a theater and a period of sitting empty, the structure became home to the Cotton Club, which operated for the next 14 years before the space was converted to Nickey's Family Supermarket and, a year later, to Benjamin's. The building was demolished by 2010. (Courtesy of the Texas A&M University-Corpus Christi Archives.)

Community leader and black activist the Reverend Elliott Grant eloquently calls for a school holiday for Dr. Martin Luther King's birthday. A peacemaker as well, Reverend Grant died in San Antonio in 1991. (Courtesy of *Corpus Christi Caller-Times*.)

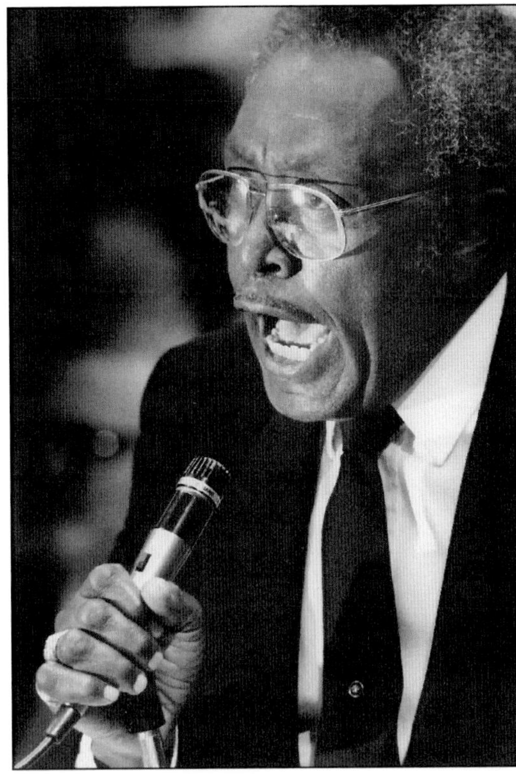

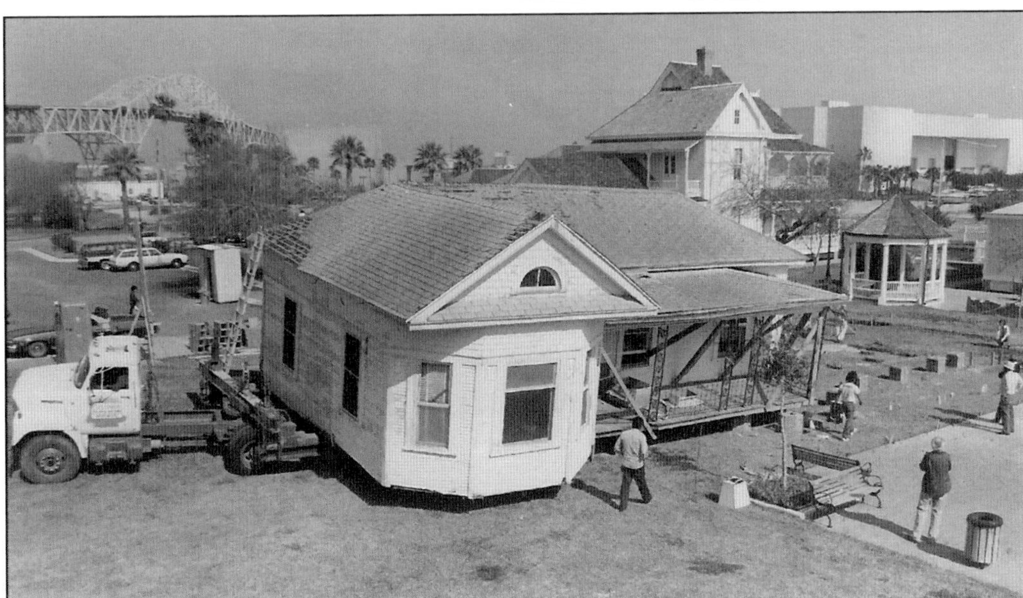

January 20 saw the moving of the historic Littles-Martin House from its original location on North Staples Street to its present site in Corpus Christi's Heritage Park. Renovated by the Boyd Hall Branch of the NAACP, it now houses the administration offices of the chapter, an artifacts room, and a research library. (Courtesy of the Corpus Christi NAACP.)

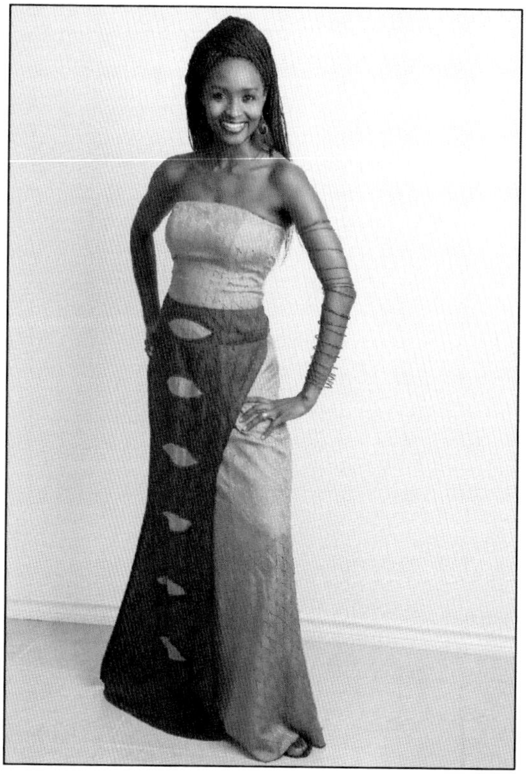

Liza Mucheru-Wisner received numerous awards for her contributions to Corpus Christi and its broader community. She was one of three finalists on Season 10 of Donald Trump's *The Apprentice*. With both bachelor's and master's degrees, Wisner started a program that educates children about technology and participates in alumni, church, and city events. (Photograph by Eddie Seal, courtesy of Liza Mucheru-Wisner.)

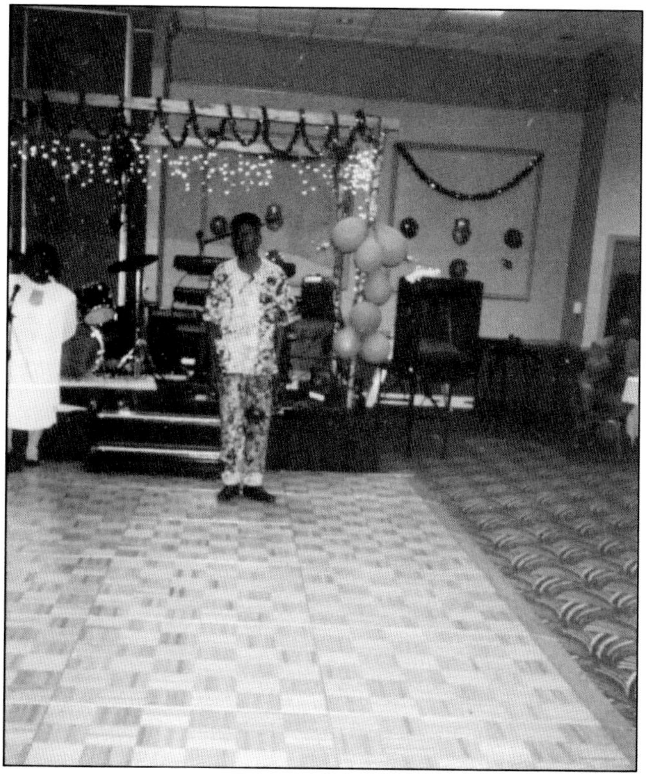

Willie B. Scott and Pinky Hillman (a former teacher at Coles) speak at a Solomon M. Coles School reunion. (Courtesy of Dr. Gloria Randle Scott.)

Willie Hardeman worked at the naval air station on the fire-control system for the Apache gun helicopters. He later received a position as first personnel specialist intern at the Pentagon. After several years, he worked for the US Department of Transportation as an equal opportunity investigator until his retirement in 1997. Hardeman returned to Corpus Christi and served as president of the Corpus Christi NAACP. (Courtesy of the Corpus Christi NAACP.)

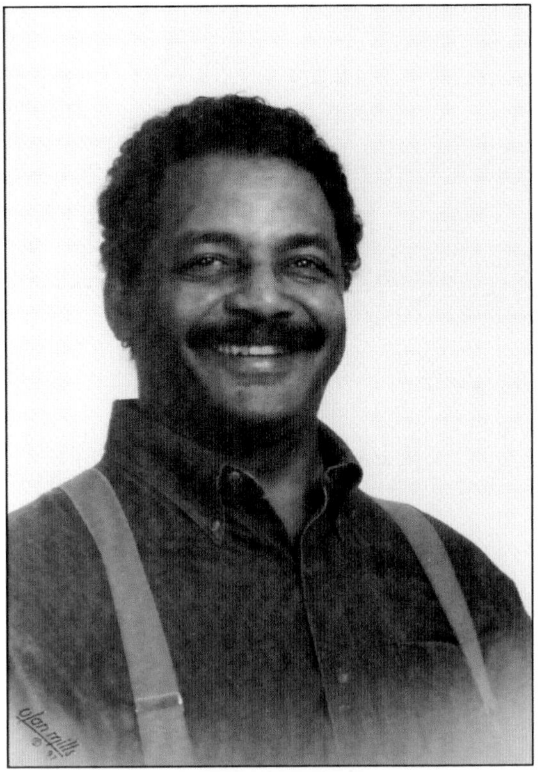

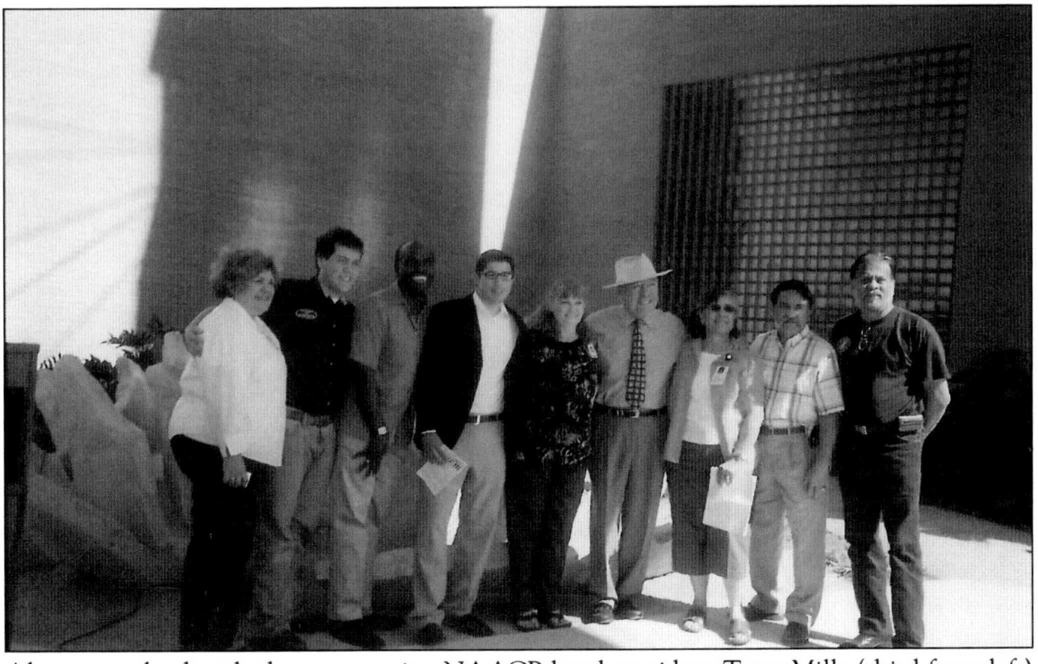

Always involved with the community, NAACP local president Terry Mills (third from left) often joined local activists, including state representative Chuy Hinojosa (sixth from left) and Judge Manual Bañuales (second from right) at the annual health fair. (Courtesy of the Corpus Christi NAACP.)

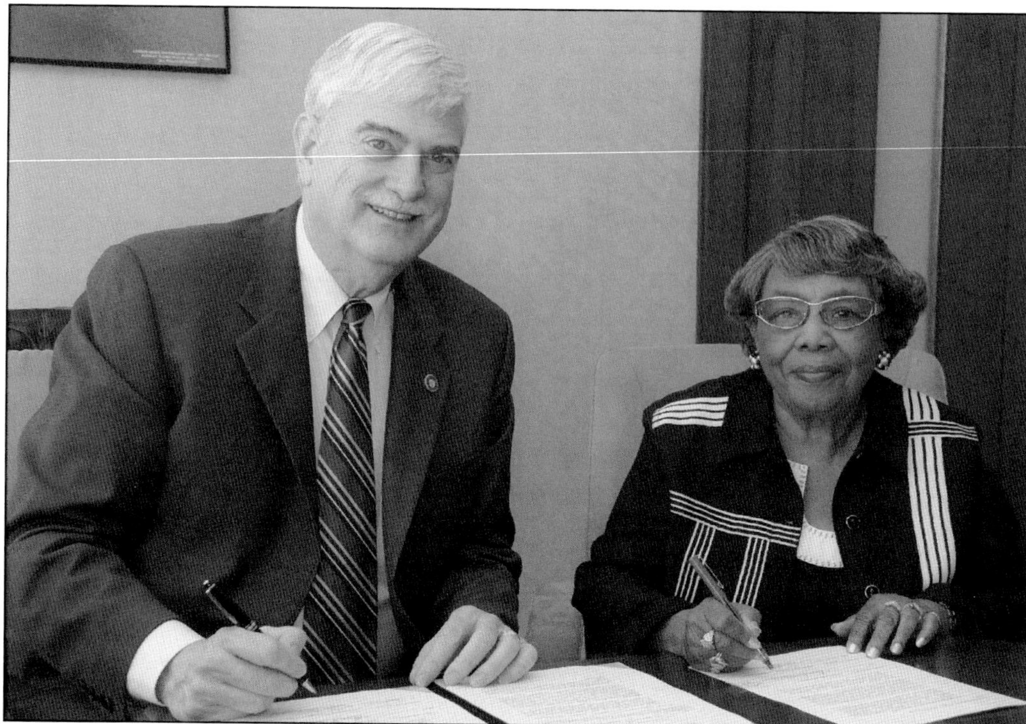

Entrepreneur and civic leader Lena Coleman-Wilson signs papers for a scholarship bearing her name, the Lena Coleman-Wilson Hope Scholarship, at Texas A&M University-Corpus Christi. Coleman-Wilson donated $200,000 to Dr. Flavius Killebrew (left) for this scholarship, which will be awarded to students in the 2012–2013 school year. She also founded the LC Foundation, which is a nonprofit organization that hires and trains people with disabilities to find gainful employment. (Courtesy of Jeff Janko, Texas A&M University-Corpus Christi.)

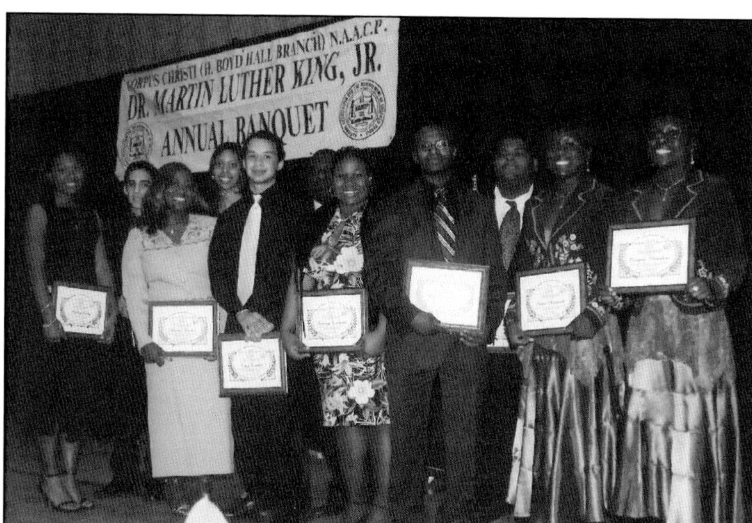

Proud members of the Corpus Christi African American community display the Community Service Awards presented to them in 2005 by the H. Boyd Hall Branch of the NAACP. Community service has been an important aspect of the NAACP since its inception. (Courtesy of the Corpus Christi NAACP.)

The Reverend E.F. Bennett, pastor of Mount Pilgrim Baptist Church, was a community servant par excellence. In addition to his community roles, including that of police chaplain, teacher, and friend, he also published a book based on his newspaper columns, titled *Character Counts: Do You Agree?* (Courtesy of the *Corpus Christi Caller-Times.*)

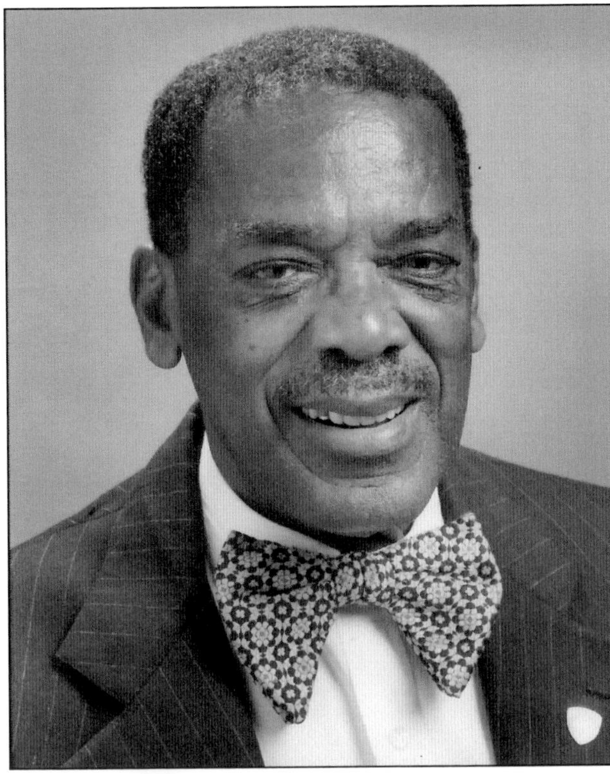

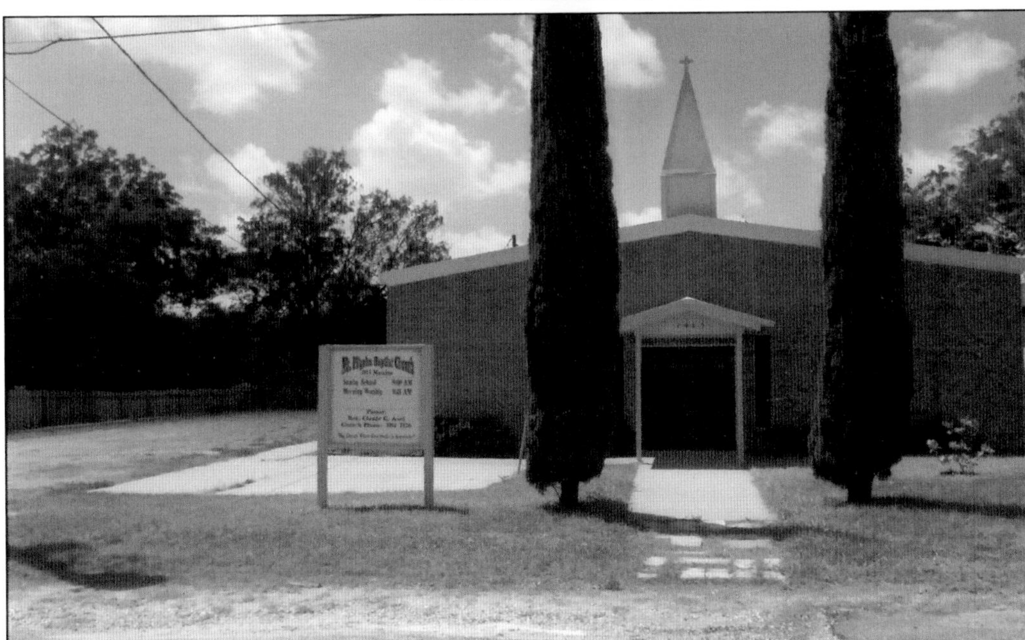

Established in 1956 by Rev. Willie N. Heard in a house on Winnebago Street, Mount Pilgrim Baptist Church moved to this building in 1992. Under the leadership of Rev. Claude C. Axel, the church has expanded and remained one of the significant churches in the community. (Courtesy of Dr. Gloria Randle Scott.)

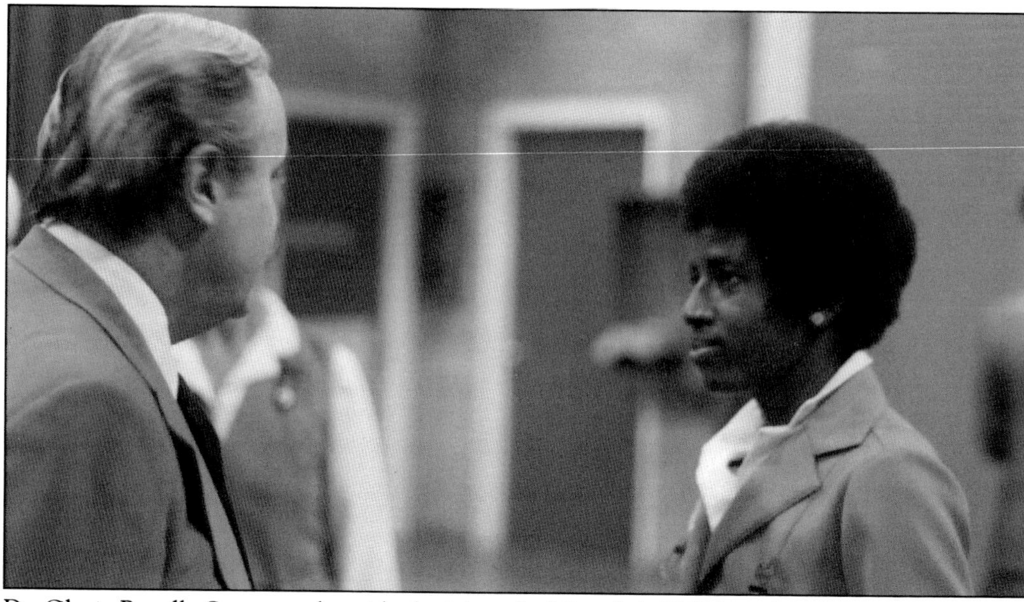

Dr. Gloria Randle Scott speaks with the *Mutual of Omaha's Wild Kingdom* director at the 1978 National Girl Scout Convention. Born and raised in Houston, Scott became the first African American president of Girl Scouts USA; she later served as a vice president at Clark University in Atlanta and as president of Bennett College for Women in Greensboro, North Carolina. Scott is an active and courageous member of the Corpus Christi black community. (Courtesy of Dr. Gloria Randle Scott.)

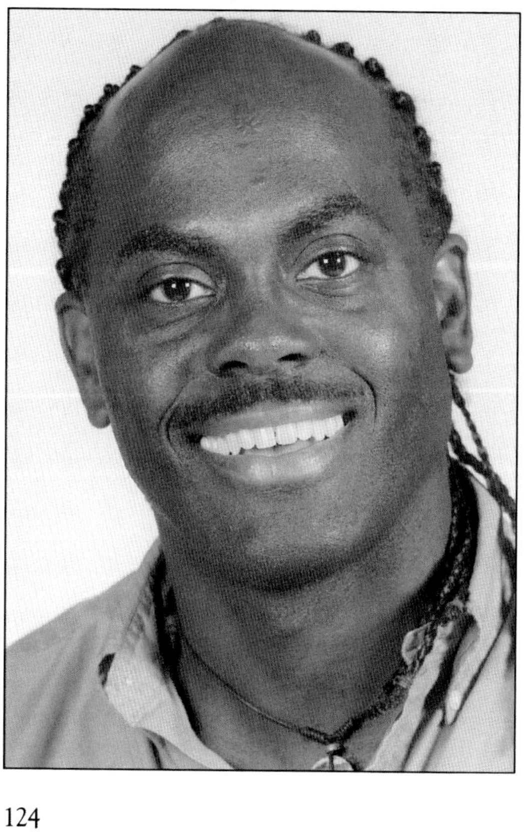

Terry Mills, a community activist and leader, was president of the Dr. H. Boyd Hall NAACP chapter for several terms. Mills, a lifelong member of this organization, grew up volunteering and working in his community. His mother, Johnnie Mills, a strong supporter of the group, encouraged his participation. During his presidency, Mills actively opened the local NAACP to all races and sought to increase membership and aid the community where he found the need. (Courtesy of the *Corpus Christi Caller-Times*.)

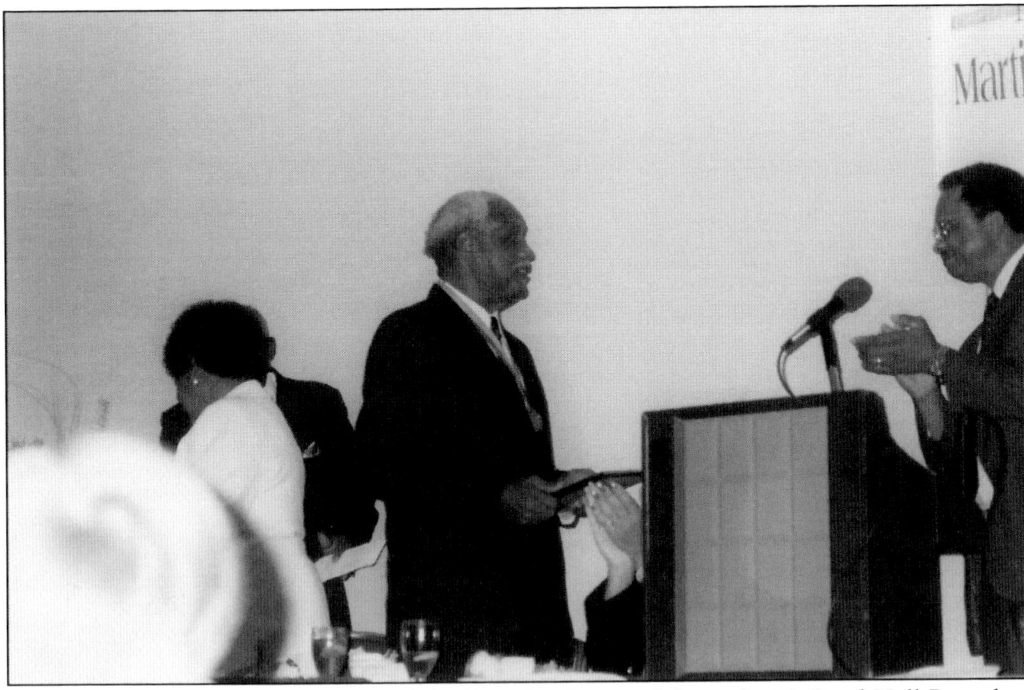

Elmer Wilson applauds a recipient of the President's Award from the H. Boyd Hall Branch of the NAACP. Beginning in 1993, after James Wagner's tenure, Harold Moore assumed duties as president of the local branch of the NAACP. During his term as president, Moore emphasized serving the needs of all the black community, especially the impoverished, unemployed, and ill-educated. (Courtesy of the *Corpus Christi Caller-Times*.)

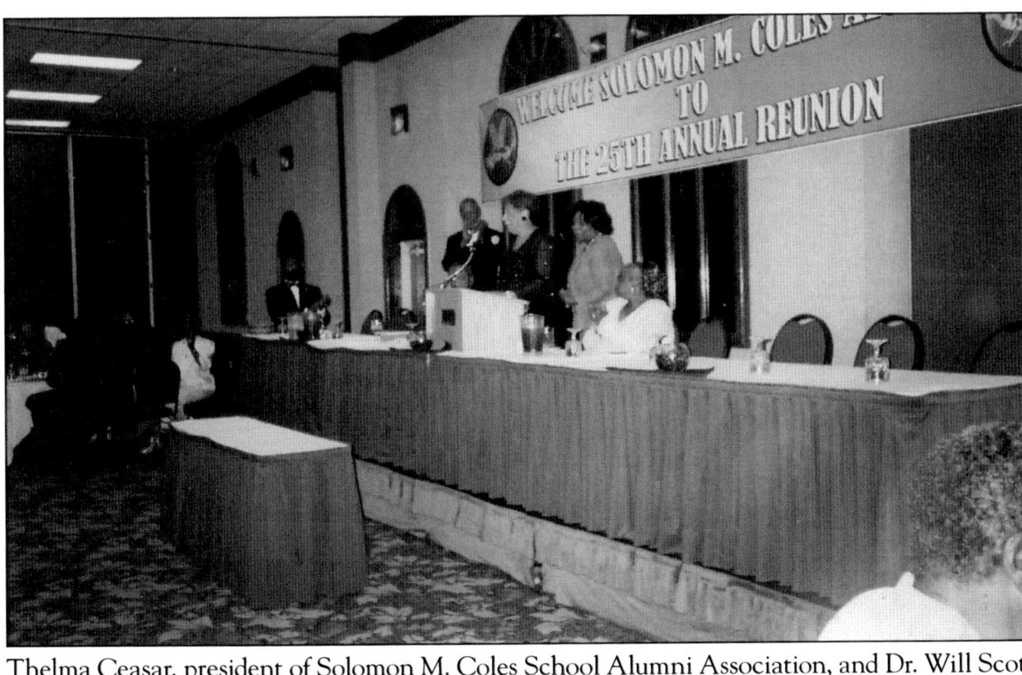

Thelma Ceasar, president of Solomon M. Coles School Alumni Association, and Dr. Will Scott welcome alumni to the 25th reunion. (Courtesy of Dr. Gloria Randle Scott.)

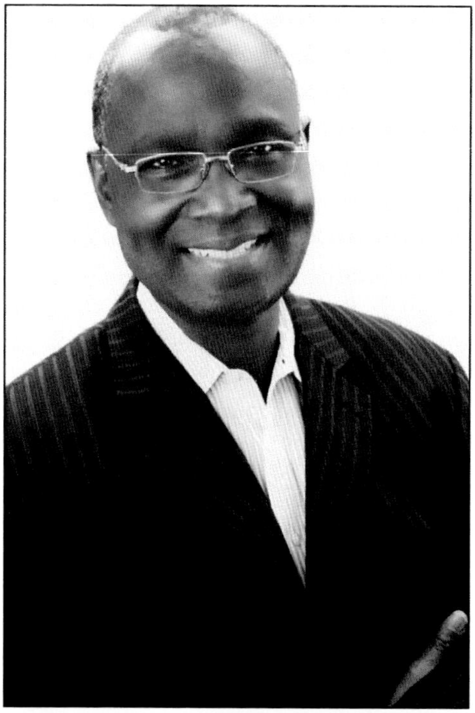

Donald G. Leavell pursued a career in the petroleum industry after graduating from Texas Arts & Industries University (now Texas A&M University-Kingsville). A religious man, Leavell continued to preach when the opportunity arose. In 1970, he started the Corpus Christi Christian Fellowship Church, a nondenominational and multicultural institution. The church has over 1,200 members as well as numerous followers via television and the Internet. Pastor Don addresses South Texas as well as the world, sharing the gospel. (Courtesy of Pastor Don Leavell.)

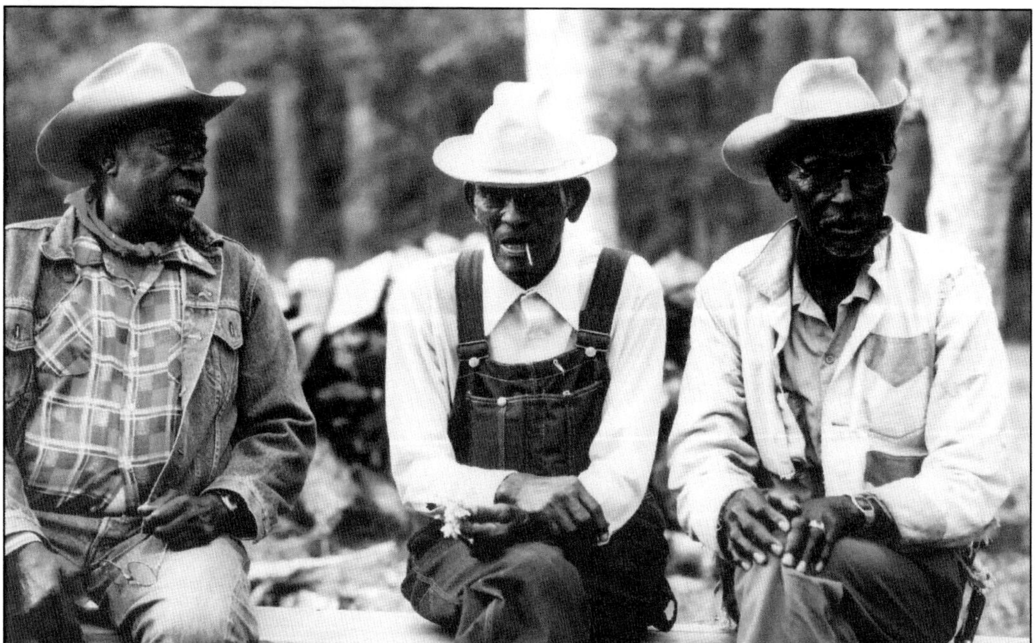

After a day of storytelling, Stephney "Tony" Lott (left), an unidentified friend (center), and Tony's brother J.Y. Lott are sitting on a fence and looking relaxed. All three longtime cowboys entertained many with their stories and escapades as area ranch workers in their youth. Tony, also an avid preacher, moved to Corpus Christi in the early 1940s and continued to minister to many residents of this city. (Courtesy of Shirley Doris [Lott] Rhodes.)

Bibliography

Bennett, Rev. E.F. *Character Counts: Do You Agree?* Corpus Christi: privately printed, 2004.

Campbell, Randolph B. "Reconstruction in Nueces County, 1865–1876." *Houston Review* 16 (Fall 1994): 3–26.

Corpus Christi Caller-Times, September 15, 1968.

Corpus Christi Caller-Times, January 26, 1998.

Eisenhauer, Anita, and GiGi Starnes. *Corpus Christi: A Picture Postcard History*. Corpus Christi: Anita's Antiques, 1987.

Givens, Murphy. *Old Corpus Christi: The Past in Photographs*. Corpus Christi: Corpus Christi Caller-Times, 2002.

Givens, Murphy, and Jim Moloney. *1919: The Storm: A Narrative and Photographic History*. Corpus Christi: Grunwald Printing, 2009.

Glasgow, Brenda Mazone. *Why She Stayed*. Knoxville, TN: Glasgow Communications, 2009.

Glasrud, Bruce A., ed. *African Americans in South Texas History*. College Station: Texas A&M University Press, 2011.

Glasrud, Bruce A., and Cecilia Gutierrez Venable. "Solomon Melvin Coles." *BlackPast Online Encyclopedia*. www.blackpast.org.

Jordan, Edna. *Black Tracks to Texas: Solomon Melvin Coles—From Slave to Educator*. Corpus Christi: Golden Banner, 1977.

Louzon, David. "Corpus Christi's Galvan Ballroom: Music and Multiculturalism in the 1950s." *Journal of South Texas* 20.2 (Fall 2007): 213–36.

O'Rear, Mary Jo. *Storm Over the Bay: The People of Corpus Christi and Their Port*. College Station: Texas A&M University Press, 2009.

Schwein, Annie Moore. "When Corpus Christi Was Young: Recollections of Annie Moore Schwein." LaRetama Public Library, Corpus Christi.

Thomas, Matt. *Hopping on the Border: The Life Story of a Bellboy*. San Antonio: Naylor, 1951.

Venable, Cecilia Gutierrez. *Historic Photos of Corpus Christi*. Nashville, TN: Turner Publishing, 2008.

Walraven, Bill. *Corpus Christi: The History of a Texas Seaport*. Sun Valley, CA: American Historical Press, 1997.

Walraven, Bill, and Marjorie K. Walraven. *Gift of the Wind, Corpus Christi Bayfront*. Corpus Christi: Javelina Press, 1997.

Wood, Rue A. "The Forging of the African American Community in Corpus Christi, Texas, 1883–1900." *Journal of South Texas* 12.1 (1999): 34–75.

———. "The Forging of the African American Community in Corpus Christi, 1865–1900." Master's thesis, Texas A&M University-Kingsville, 1998.